CW00524071

GRAIN-MILLS AND
FLOUR IN
CLASSICAL ANTIQUITY

GRAIN-MILLS AND
FLOUR IN
CLASSICAL ANTIQUITY

BY

L. A. MORITZ

OXFORD
AT THE CLARENDON PRESS

OXFORD
UNIVERSITY PRESS

Great Clarendon Street, Oxford OX2 6DP

Oxford University Press is a department of the University of Oxford.
It furthers the University's objective of excellence in research, scholarship,
and education by publishing worldwide in

Oxford New York

Auckland Bangkok Buenos Aires Cape Town Chennai
Dar es Salaam Delhi Hong Kong Istanbul Karachi Kolkata
Kuala Lumpur Madrid Melbourne Mexico City Mumbai Nairobi
São Paulo Shanghai Singapore Taipei Tokyo Toronto

and an associated company in Berlin

Oxford is a registered trade mark of Oxford University Press
in the UK and in certain other countries

Published in the United States
by Oxford University Press Inc., New York

© Oxford University Press 1958

The moral rights of the author have been asserted
Database right Oxford University Press (maker)

Special edition for Oxbow Books, Oxford
(and their American partner Powell's Books, Chicago)

British Library Cataloguing in Publication Data

Data available

ISBN 0-19-814221-8

1 3 5 7 9 10 8 6 4 2

Printed in Great Britain
on acid-free paper by
Biddles Ltd.,
Guildford and King's Lynn

PREFACE

THIS book owes its beginnings to the sponsorship of the National Association of British and Irish Millers and to their enlightened desire for research into the remote antecedents of their industry. In meeting the challenge of the task thus set before me I have tried to reconcile the claims of classical scholarship with those of twentieth-century technology; to use modern methods in tackling some old problems; and to produce a detailed discussion of the ancient evidence that should yet be intelligible to a reader with 'small Latin and less Greek'. The difficulties of such an undertaking are obvious: I can only hope that my attempt to surmount them has not failed altogether and that this book makes some contribution both to the study of the early history of one of our more important industries and to that of a much neglected but none the less important aspect of the everyday life of classical antiquity.

Fortunately I have been able to rely throughout on the ready help of the Millers' Association and of their research establishment under Dr. T. Moran. This help was by no means confined to the financial sphere, and in expressing my deep gratitude for it I must emphasize that I was from beginning to end left completely free to 'follow the argument wherever it might lead'.

Nor is this the only help that I have received. Dr. G. E. F. Chilver, my former supervisor and tutor, has amidst his many occupations found the time to give me the benefit of his advice and constructive criticism throughout. Professor A. H. M. Jones and Mr. C. T. Stevens have shown an interest in this book which did not end when they had finished examining the D.Phil. thesis on which it is based. Professor I. M. Campbell read the whole of the book in typescript and gave me much valuable advice. Professor I. A. Richmond generously provided detailed information about the water-mills on Hadrian's Wall. Dr. E. Cecil Curwen supplied a photograph and allowed me to use one of his reconstructed querns for grinding experiments, which in turn were made possible by the kindness of the Sussex Archaeological Society and of Mr. E. Pyddoke. Professor Amedeo Maiuri and Dr. Olga Elia helped me at Naples and Pompeii and, like the

Director of the Saalburg Museum (who himself supplied a photo-graph besides much valuable information and assistance), gave me permission to take the photographs without which the first part of this book would be very incomplete. The editors of the *Thesaurus Linguae Latinae* and of Pauly–Wissowa's *Realencyclopädie* placed at my disposal several articles unpublished at the time. Dr. M. V. Taylor, Professor A. Hug, and Professor G. R. Driver patiently answered my inquiries; and Professor W. D. McHardy gave me much friendly advice. To all of these, and to the Delegates and staff of the Clarendon Press, I owe a very great debt of gratitude: the responsibility for the shortcomings of the book is, of course, mine alone.

An apology is due to the reader for the fact that, for technical reasons, some of the longer footnotes had to be relegated to a separate section at the end of the book. The page numbers given in that section refer to the place where the note would have appeared as a footnote; and it is hoped that the cross-references provided will prevent this arrangement from being too incon-venient.

Since the book went to the printers several works relevant to it have been published which could unfortunately no longer be taken into account. This applies especially to the second volume of *A History of Technology* by C. Singer, E. J. Holmyard, A. R. Hall, and T. I. Williams (Oxford, 1956) and to the third volume of *Studies in Ancient Technology* by R. J. Forbes (Leiden, 1956). The recent deaths of Professor V. Gordon Childe and Professor D. M. Robinson are a sad loss to all working in this field, as to many others: this book is indebted to no small extent to the work of these two scholars.

L. A. M.

Cardiff, April 1958

CONTENTS

CONTENTS
PART II. FLOUR

LIST OF TEXT FIGURES

LIST OF PLATES

LIST OF TABLES

ABBREVIATIONS

THE abbreviation of references to Greek and Latin authorities follows the normal conventions, for which the reader unfamiliar with them may be referred to any of the major lexica. (Square brackets indicate pseudepigrapha; Galen is cited by Kühn's edition and Dioscorides by Wellmann's.) The list that follows is confined to those abbreviations that cannot or may not be generally familiar.

AJP	*American Journal of Philology*, 1880– .
Am. Journ. Arch.	*American Journal of Archaeology*, 1895– .
Ann. d. Inst.	*Annali dell'Instituto di correspondenza archeologica*, 1829–85.
Antiq. Journ.	*Antiquaries Journal*, 1921– .
Ἀρχ. Ἐφ.	*Ἀρχαιολογικὴ Ἐφημερίς*, 1910– .
Arch. Pap.	*Archiv für Papyrusforschung*, 1900– .
Arch. Ztg.	*Archäologische Zeitung*, 1843–86.
BE	R. Bennett and J. Elton, *History of Corn Milling*, London and Liverpool, 1898.
Blümner	*see* p. 1, n. 3.
Brit. Sch. Ann.	*Annual of the British School at Athens*, 1895– .
Bull. Arch.	*Bullettino dell'Instituto di correspondenza archeologica* 1829–53, 1856–85.
CIL	*Corpus Inscriptionum Latinarum*, Berlin, 1862– .
Corp. Gl.	*Corpus Glossariorum Latinorum*, Leipzig, 1888–1924.
CQ	*Classical Quarterly*, 1907– .
CR	*Classical Review*, 1887– .
Délos	*see* p. 218, *Note A.*
DS	Ch. Daremberg and E. Saglio. *Dictionnaire des antiquités grecques et romaines*, Paris, 1877–1919.
Frank, *Econ. Survey*	*Economic Survey of Ancient Rome*, ed. T. Frank, Baltimore, 1933–40.
Jasny, *Wheat Prices*	*see* p. 146 and n. 2.
JRS	*Journal of Roman Studies*, 1911– .
Lindet	*see* p. 218, *Note A.*
LS	H. G. Liddell and R. Scott, *Greek–English Lexicon*, 9th ed. by H. Stuart Jones, Oxford, 1940.
LSh	C. T. Lewis and C. Short, *Latin Dictionary*, Oxford, 1880.

ABBREVIATIONS xv

Mém. de l'Inst.	Mémoires de l'Institut de France, Académie des Inscriptions et Belles-lettres, 1815–1911.
Mon. Ant.	Monumenti antichi della Reale Accademia dei Lincei, 1890– .
Mon. dell'Inst.	Monumenti, annali e bullettini dell'Instituto di correspondenza archeologica, 1854–6.
Olynthus	see p. 218, Note A.
PW	A. Pauly, G. Wissowa, and W. Kroll, Realencyclopädie der klassischen Altertumswissenschaft, Stuttgart, 1894– .
Rhein. Mus.	Rheinisches Museum für Philologie, 1842– .
Riv. di Fil.	Rivista di filologia e di istruzione classica, 1873– .
Röm. Mitt.	Mitteilungen des deutschen archäologischen Instituts, Römische Abteilung, 1886– .
Thes. Ling. Lat.	Thesaurus Linguae Latinae, Leipzig, 1900– .
Trans. Am. Phil. Ass.	Transactions of the Americal Philological Association, 1869– .
Voigt	see p. 146, n. 1.

ACKNOWLEDGEMENTS

GRATEFUL acknowledgement for permission to reproduce copyright material is made to Penguin Books, Ltd., for the quotation from Robert Graves's *The Golden Ass* (*Note K*, p. 220); to the Trustees of the British Museum for Plate 1; to the authorities of the Louvre for Plate 2, Fig. *a*; to the late Professor D. M. Robinson and the Johns Hopkins University Press for Plate 2, Figs. *b* and *c*, Plate 3, and Figs. 3 and 4 (p. 45); to the General Direction of the Vatican Museums and Galleries for Plate 5, Fig. *b*, Plate 7, Fig. *a*, and Plate 8; to Dr. E. Cecil Curwen for Plate 11, Fig. *b*; to the Director of the Saalburg Museum for Plate 14, Fig. *c*, and Fig. 12 (p. 123); to the Archaeological Institute of America for Fig. 1 (p. 13); and to Professor G. Daux and the French School at Athens for Fig. 5 (p. 46).

INTRODUCTION

IT is perhaps not too fanciful to interpret the old saying that 'man is what he eats' as meaning, among other things, that the food eaten by a given national or social group in a given period of history provides a good indication of the standard of civilization reached. For if, on the material plane, the history of civilization is the history of man's endeavour to master his surroundings, the development of his methods of providing himself with the nourishment required by his body constitutes a significant part of that history.

The development in question cannot, on the whole, consist in any large change of quantity: famine and under-nourishment apart, the amount of food eaten is, or ought to be, determined by and large by natural necessity. When we speak of an improvement in the human diet we normally mean above all an increase of variety within the diet and greater freedom in choosing the means by which to provide for the body the food that it requires. Improved methods of food production and of transport and commerce have all played their part in liberating man from his dependence upon the chance haul of the day (whether of animals or of plants) and in making it possible for him to some extent to impose his will upon nature.

But in addition to his natural desire for variety in his diet, man also feels the need to cook and otherwise prepare his food before eating it, in order to make it both more palatable and easier to digest. He began to do this in very early times; but ever since then he has continued to try both to make his food more and more attractive and, by the invention of technical aids, to reduce the amount of time and energy spent in ministering to the natural want. This development, too, is germane to the history of civilization: it has not only meant an increase in creature-comforts, but it has made it less necessary to live merely in order to eat. The present study is concerned with some aspects of this development as it affected, during one great period in the history of western civilization, that part of the human diet which is derived from cereals—those grasses which were first gathered in their wild state, and later cultivated, in order that their seeds might be used for food.

One cereal or another has formed the staple basis of the diet in every part of the world ever since agriculture first began. No wonder, therefore, that the changes that have taken place over the centuries have affected cereals more than any other type of food. This book is not concerned with the important place of grain in both economic and political history, on which much has been written elsewhere, but with a few of the less obvious facets of the history of cereal food, which have received less attention in the past. In dealing with the grain-mill and the products supplied by the grain-mill in classical antiquity it confines itself to a narrow field, and something must be said at the outset on how these specialized topics fit into the wider background.

When we give any thought at all to the grain from which our bread is made we tend to think only of wheat, which now provides practically all the bread that is eaten in this country and in those with which we are best acquainted. Yet the properties which make wheat suitable for bread exist—though in greatly varying degrees— in other cereals also, and in large parts of the world other cereals occupy the place taken by wheat in this country. Rye, for example, is still the main bread grain in many parts of Europe, and in several Asiatic countries barley, used elsewhere mainly for brewing and for the feeding of animals, is used for baking. Indeed, even in Britain it is a recent development that has given to wheat the importance it enjoys today.[1]

Nor is it necessarily in the form of bread that cereals are eaten by man. Some crops are used for the feeding of livestock and enter into human nutrition only indirectly; even in the diet of bread-eating societies cakes, pastries, 'pasta', porridge, custard, and the like, have their place; and the various forms in which rice is eaten in the East show that the large part of our food which is derived from cereals can be absorbed in many different ways.

Why, then, is it that both bread and wheat have, in the Western world at any rate, come to occupy so prominent a place? The answers to the two parts of this question are interdependent: bread is regarded as the most desirable basic cereal food, and wheat as the most desirable grain from which to make bread. Both these preferences are, of course, partly irrational, but for both there are also some good reasons.

[1] Cf. Sir W. Ashley, *The Bread of our Forefathers* (Oxford, 1928).

The seeds of all cereals contain, in addition to the germ or embryo, a large amount of 'endosperm'—starchy material which in nature acts as food for the embryo and keeps the young plant alive until it can itself produce starch—and a much smaller amount of husk or 'bran', which is intended to be a protecting coat for the inside of the grain. Both endosperm and bran consist largely of carbohydrates, but with the difference that the carbohydrates of the bran are insoluble in water or in dilute acids or alkalis (which means that they cannot be digested, at least by man), while those contained in the endosperm are soluble and capable of being turned into glucose, the main 'fuel' in our food. It is thus the endosperm that is the primary source of food in the grain, and the endosperm of cereals is the most important single source of carbohydrates in the human diet.[1] (The other chemical constituents of grain—notably fats, proteins, and vitamins—may be ignored for the moment.)

Now animals living on grain can eat and digest it as it comes from the plant, but man's equipment for digesting raw starch is poor, and he therefore finds it necessary to 'pre-digest' cereals by cooking them. This cooking sometimes means no more than a parching or toasting of the grain; but more usually it consists of two essential parts, the addition of water or some other liquid and the heating of the mixture. If such a mixture (containing a sufficient amount of water) is heated to about 140 degrees Fahrenheit the starch swells and gelatinizes, and porridge results. Porridge of this type is both edible and digestible, but it cannot be kept for any length of time and it is always more or less fluid. These are two disadvantages in a basic food, both of which can be overcome if the mixture is baked, and it was probably because of this that bread soon acquired its importance.

Baking involves much higher temperatures—at least 450° F. in the case of the modern loaf—and the mixture (now the 'dough') is made less fluid. Much of the water, moreover, is evaporated during baking, and this, together with the killing of bacilli by the heat, leads to improved keeping qualities as well as to a more solid consistency.

A baked product of this simple type, however, still suffers

---

[1] In modern Great Britain about one-third of the daily calorie 'intake' comes from cereals, and the proportion was probably higher in antiquity when there were no potatoes.

from the disadvantage that, unless it is very thin and therefore insubstantial, it becomes unpalatable and difficult to chew as soon as it has cooled. In all good bread this is avoided by 'leavening', which lightens the loaf and loosens its texture: yeast, or some other substance which in the right conditions gives out carbon dioxide gas, is introduced into the dough to make it 'rise'. But a well-risen loaf will result only if the flour contains enough 'gluten-forming' proteins which, when mixed with water, form an elastic substance that prevents the gas in the dough from escaping. This gluten content, more than any other factor, determines the so-called baking qualities of a flour.

These considerations are relevant here because they help to distinguish between the various cereals. Wheat, barley, rye, oats, rice, millet, sorghum, and maize, in spite of differences in detailed chemical composition and flavour, can all be cooked and used for food in much the same way, except when it comes to making aerated bread. For this, wheat is, owing to the amount and quality of its gluten, far superior to all other cereals, and it is thus no accident that it should have reached the dominant position as a bread grain which it now occupies. Within the wheat family, the species of *triticum vulgare* for similar reasons now provides almost all our bread wheats: the numerous varieties that can be found in a modern miller's catalogue all belong to this one species. This was not always true, and it is still not everywhere true; but the fact that the preference for wheaten bread has in many countries been able to assert itself to such an extent that wheat is now widely eaten where once it was expensive or altogether unavailable provides one example of an advance in the history of nutrition.

In classical antiquity maize was unknown, and some other cereals were exotic and rare, in the Greek and Roman world. Rice was expensive and used mainly for medicines,[1] while sorghum made only a brief appearance in Italy in the first century A.D.[2] Others again, though grown for economic reasons in districts with a less favourable climate than that of the Mediterranean area, were simply not wanted. Oats—an everyday food in central Europe—were, except in the extremes of famine, considered fit only for animals;[3] rye—the closest relative of

---

[1] Cf., e.g., Hor. *Sat*. ii. 3. 155. [2] Plin. *N.H.* xviii. 55.
[3] Ibid. 149, and cf. especially Gal. vi. 523 K.

wheat, and after wheat the best bread grain—also remained a 'northern grain' which did not penetrate south of the Alps until late in the classical period, and then probably in small quantities;[1] and the millets, both common and Indian, were essentially a stand-by in times of shortage, though common millet was used for bread when better grains were not available.[2]

Wheat and barley were thus the two main grains of classical antiquity. But although barley was for a very long time of the greatest importance in the Greek-speaking world both as fodder for animals and as human food, it was, as will be shown later, normally eaten in the form of a 'kneaded thing' ($\mu\hat{a}\zeta a$) rather than bread, and bread made from barley was, as early as the sixth century B.C. described as 'fodder for slaves'.[3] Barley was, moreover, generally considered less nourishing than wheat,[4] and by the fourth century B.C. the preference for wheat and the bread made from it, which can be discerned in Greek literature from early times, had ousted barley from its prominent position in the human diet, with the result that by the time of Alexander the Great wheat had become the 'corn', or main grain, of Greece.[5]

One reason why barley is less suitable for bread than wheat is that its grain, like that of all cereals other than wheat and rye, is normally 'husked' and cannot be freed from its cover-glumes by ordinary threshing.[6] The special hulling operation which such grain must undergo was in antiquity inevitably combined with a roasting of the grain in its husks: this roasting must have largely destroyed the gluten content of the grain, and have made it unsuitable for leavened bread, even if before hulling it contained a sufficient amount of suitable gluten-forming proteins. Barley, with its low protein content, is unsuitable for bread irrespective of this; but there is good evidence to suggest that the place taken by barley in early Greece was in Italy,

---

[1] Cf. *PW* Suppl. viii. 648 ff.

[2] They could still be sown when the failure of other crops had become apparent; cf. in general *PW*, viii. 1950 ff. (Indian millet, in spite of its Latin name *panic(i)um*, was hardly ever used for bread.)

[3] Hipponax of Ephesus *ap*. Athen. vii. 304b.

[4] Cf., e.g., [Arist.] *Probl.* xxi. 2; Diosc. *M.M.* ii. 86 W.; Gal. vi. 507 K. (The *hordearii gladiatores* of Plin. *N.H.* xviii. 72 are not, as has been thought, evidence to the contrary.)

[5] Cf. here *CQ*, N.S., v. 135 ff.

[6] For details see ibid. 129 ff.

---

where barley was always far less important, occupied by a species of the genus wheat which is unsuitable for bread only because it is husked.[1]

The Linnaean genus *triticum* comprises, so far as cultivated wheats are concerned, both some husked and some 'naked' species. All our bread wheats are of the latter type; but when Varro in the first century B.C. tells us that the Roman *pistor*, or miller-baker, was originally a man who 'pounded *far*'[2] or when, a century later, the elder Pliny says that the same *far* was the original food of Latium,[3] the grain mentioned by these writers is one of the husked wheats the cultivation of which has been on the decline since early times. [The word is usually translated as 'spelt', but of the two principal species of husked wheat *triticum spelta* probably did not become known in the Mediterranean area until about the first century A.D., and was never important there: the grain denoted by *far*—and by other words, such as ζειά (ζέα), ὄλυρα, ador, semen (adoreum)—was almost certainly *triticum dicoccum*, or emmer.][4] The chemical make-up of this wheat is such that good bread can be made from it[5]—if the grain can be freed from its husks without roasting; but in early Italy this was impossible, and it is revealing that Pliny can adduce the fact that the Romans for a long time lived on porridge (*puls*) rather than bread as proof for his statement that *far* was originally the staple grain of Latium. Like the 'kneaded thing' of Greece, porridge could be made from a grain that had previously been roasted.[6]

In Pliny's and even in Varro's day the *far* of early Rome had largely disappeared from the human diet, just as barley had done in Greece two centuries and a half earlier, in favour of those wheats which can be freed from their husks on the

---

[1] It is not generally recognized that roasting was normal with husked grains only, nor that barley was far less important in Italy than in Greece. Lack of space makes it impossible to prove these statements here; but cf., for instance, on the question of roasting Thuc. vi. 22, Plin. *N.H.* xviii. 61, and on the place of barley in Italy ibid. 74 and *CQ*, N.S., v. 141.

[2] *ap.* Non. 152. 14 Müll.

[3] *N.H.* xviii. 83.

[4] Cf. N. Jasny, *Wheats of Classical Antiquity* (Baltimore, 1944), pp. 106 ff.

[5] Cf. J. A. LeClerc and others in *Journ. Amer. Soc. of Agronomy*, x (1918), 215 ff.

[6] There is no evidence that husked wheat was ever grown in Greece outside Thrace and Macedonia; cf. A. Jardé, *Les Céréales dans l'antiquité grecque*, i (Paris, 1925), p. 5, n. 9.

threshing-floor and from which good bread can be made. But even then it was not true, as it is nowadays, that practically all bread wheats belonged to the one species of *triticum vulgare*.

The wheat that is still used, especially in Italy, for 'pasta' and the like belongs, not merely to a different species, but to an entirely different 'group': although it, too, is naked, it is botanically more closely related to emmer than to common wheat.[1] 'Macaroni wheat' (*t. durum* Desfontaines), which is today next to *t. vulgare* the most widely grown wheat, derives its name from its hard flinty grain: the centre of its cultivation still lies in the Mediterranean area, and it is probable, therefore, on botanical grounds that it was grown there also in antiquity. Similarly 'rivet wheat' (*t. turgidum* Linn.), another representative of the emmer group, was almost certainly one of the wheats of classical antiquity. But the grain of rivet wheat often resembles that of common wheat both in its plump shape and in its mealy endosperm: botanists did not distinguish this wheat from other naked wheats until the sixteenth century; and it is even possible that *t. turgidum* and *t. durum* did not diverge from their common ancestor before the Middle Ages.

Throughout antiquity two kinds of naked wheat are sharply distinguished by our authorities. Often the distinction appears, on the face of it, to be simply that between autumn- and spring-sown crops, but in fact it goes deeper than that: spring wheat was in antiquity, as it is now, grown in the Mediterranean area in exceptional circumstances only, and our evidence, which cannot be discussed in detail here,[2] suggests that in fifth- and fourth-century Greece the main, autumn-sown, crop belonged to the emmer group, while spring wheat was of the softer *vulgare* type. Later, and perhaps first in Italy, the greater popularity of the soft wheats with the consumer[3] appears to have led to an increase in their cultivation at the expense of the wheats of the

---

[1] Modern botany divides the genus into three groups, according to chromosome number: common wheat and spelt belong to the hexaploid group (42 chrom.), macaroni wheat, rivet wheat, and emmer, to the tetraploid (28 chrom.); for details see Jasny, op. cit., pp. 17 ff. and, on wheat in general, J. Percival, *The Wheat Plant* (London, 1921).

[2] The literary part of this evidence was first assembled by M. Voigt in *Rhein. Mus.*, N.F., xxxi (1876), 105 ff. For a recent discussion see Jasny, op. cit., pp. 53 ff.: the conclusions dogmatically stated in the text differ from Jasny's at several points, but lack of space prevents a detailed exposition.

[3] But not with the farmer; cf. *CR*, N.S., v. 246.

emmer group, though the latter continued to be 'wheat *par excellence*'—*triticum*, in a narrow sense of the word, in Latin;[1] πυρὸς ἄριστος or σεμιδαλίτης in Greek. The result was that in imperial Roman times a mere seasonal classification was no longer appropriate: the soft wheats—*siligo* and σητάνιο [2]—by then included, in addition to spring wheat, a considerable part of the autumn-sown crop, especially in districts like Campania where today, too, *t. vulgare* predominates over *t. durum*, which in many parts of Italy still makes up the main wheat crop.

Both kinds of naked wheat were used for bread in antiquity, but Roman literature leaves no doubt that 'the tender loaf, snowy white, made from soft *siligo*'[3] was thought much more desirable. The colour of this loaf would alone be enough to explain this; for, rightly or wrongly, a wide preference for white grain and white grain products has long been at work all over the world. This preference has affected barley, rice, and maize, no less than wheat, and has helped in modern times progressively to reduce the amount of rye used for bread. Partly it is no doubt an irrational, and often perhaps an unreasonable, preference; but one aspect of it at least is accounted for by the fact that the endosperm of grain is normally much lighter in colour than the bran (though dark colour does not always indicate the presence of bran). In the preparation of food for human consumption the advance of civilization has—again rightly or wrongly—meant that more and more of the work originally done by the digestive organs should be done by other means before the food is eaten. The removal of the indigestible bran from the flour (which can be achieved by sifting, since milling normally leaves the bran in relatively large particles) is a case in point, and it is probably because a white product contains less indigestible material than a darker product from the same grain that there has long been a demand for the whitest possible loaf, a demand which millers have tried to meet by removing from the flour as much of the bran as is technically and economically possible. For the existence of this demand in our time ample evidence is provided by the unpopularity of the darker wartime

---

[1] In its wider sense *triticum* (= 'threshable grain') included all naked wheat, but not the husked species which also form part of the modern genus *triticum*; cf. *CQ*, N.S., v. 140 and notes.

[2] Also σιτάνιος and σιτανίας.

[3] Juv. *Sat.* 5. 70.

loaf, which did not yield to any assurances that the darker bread was more wholesome.[1] The efforts made in ancient times to satisfy this demand form the subject of the second part of this study.

Another reason why bread from *siligo* was preferred to that made from wheats of the emmer group is connected with the consistency of the endosperm: wheats of the *vulgare* type alone yield fine flour by ancient methods of milling. The flinty kernels of *t. durum* are easily reduced to middlings or semolina, and it is largely[2] because this semolina is free from fine flour that *t. durum* is preferred for products, such as 'pasta' and porridge, for which semolina rather than flour is used. (The importance of these products in countries like Italy, where the production of *t. durum* is economically advantageous, may perhaps be due to this.) This semolina, however, can only with great difficulty be reduced further, and even if it is so reduced the quality of the resulting flour is comparatively poor.[3] For bread, on the other hand, fine flour is required, and if fine flour cannot be obtained the texture of the loaf will suffer, even if the grain used is in other respects suitable for bread.

The purpose of reducing grain into smaller particles by milling or simple pounding is to make the starch contained in it more freely accessible to the chemical changes which it must undergo before it can be digested. This process is more essential for baked products than for those that are merely boiled; but even with boiled cereal foods some form of reduction is usual. The milling of grain is probably the oldest of all human arts: it almost certainly goes back to a time when grain was still being gathered from plants growing wild, and for long ages thereafter the 'daily grind', in a very literal sense, was prominent among the less pleasant household tasks. A reasonably fine flour can be produced even by primitive milling methods, and an improvement of these methods does not necessarily mean that the flour

---

[1] Some valuable vitamins are lost by the removal of the bran, and 'polished' rice has in some countries been the cause of beriberi: with white flour this effect is, however, avoided now by artificial 'enrichment'.

[2] But by no means entirely: the chemical composition of the grain is even more important in this connexion; cf. also Jasny, op. cit., p. 43.

[3] Jasny (ibid. 45) points out that *with modern milling methods* hard varieties of *t. vulgare* (but not of *t. durum*) are preferred for bread flour, but that previously the best flours were obtained from the soft *vulgare* varieties.

is any finer, but rather that it is produced with less human
effort and, at least in modern times, that the mill is so designed
as to pulverize the endosperm while leaving the bran in large
particles in order to facilitate its elimination from the flour. It
is the aim of the first part of this book to inquire what progress
was made in this direction during the period of classical
antiquity.

Within the last century or so grain-milling has changed
beyond all recognition. The stone-mill, driven by wind or
water, has given way to the power-driven roller-mill, and this
change was accompanied, or soon followed, by other advances
in milling technique. Not only is the mill itself now driven by
new forms of power, but it is possible today to separate the bran
from the endosperm, and to measure and control the particle
size and constituents of the ground products, in a manner
unheard of two centuries ago. These advances—and especially
the introduction of new motive powers—in many respects re-
semble similar changes in other industries that took place during
the industrial revolution; but the revolution in grain-milling
has attracted remarkably little interest in comparison with
similar changes in, for instance, the field of locomotion. It is
strange to reflect that few people realize that it is by now something of a rarity to find a stone-mill in use in Britain otherwise
than for cattle-food.

In addition to their intrinsic interest as landmarks of progress, revolutions of this kind tend to pose the question how
that which is being replaced itself came into being; for only if
this question is asked and answered is it possible to see these
revolutions in their proper setting. In the field of milling the age
preceding the 'industrial revolution' was that of windmills and
water-mills. Of these the windmill is a creation of the Middle
Ages, whether its origin falls in the seventh[1] or in the twelfth[2]
century: for the invention of the water-mill, on the other
hand, we have the express testimony of classical Rome. But
the working parts of a water-mill need but little adaptation
to make them suitable for wind propulsion, and it is thus true

---

[1] Heringius (*De Molendinis eorumque iure*, 1663, p. 55) quotes a chronicle of
A.D. 718 for the statement that in Bohemia water-mills then began to displace the
earlier windmills.

[2] *Annales des Bénédictins*, cited by Mongez, *Mém. de l'Inst. Royal de France*, iii (1818),
474; cf. Lindet, 1900, p. 41.

to say that in this sphere, as in many others, classical antiquity left behind it the groundwork on which the modern world was to build many centuries later.

Now the wind- or water-driven mill itself presupposes the principle of grinding corn in one machine, consisting of two round stones one of which rotates above the other round a common axle. Only after this principle had been invented did it become possible to employ the muscle strength of animals, the natural forces of wind and water, or indeed any motive power other than unaided human effort, for the work of grinding corn. The main question which the first part of this book sets out to answer is whether it was before or during the period of classical antiquity that the rotary grain-mill was invented: did the thousand years or so preceding the invention of the water-mill see no greater development in milling technique than the fifteen hundred or so that followed it, or was it in the great age of Greece and Rome that the grain-mill underwent its first 'industrial revolution'? An eighteenth-century treatise[1] complains of the 'obscurity and difficulty' by which an investigation of this kind is beset: though much new material has since been discovered, the obscurity and difficulty still remain to offer a challenge to the investigator.

[1] Kramer, *De Iure Principis circa Molas* (Göttingen), p. 5.

PART I · GRAIN-MILLS

I

THE HOMERIC MILL

ANYONE who, without strictly specialized knowledge, sets out to seek some information on the milling methods used in antiquity, turning for this purpose to the best reference works available, is left with the impression that the technique of grain-milling advanced little in the period from the beginning of Greek history (as opposed to prehistory) in the Homeric age to the introduction of water-mills in imperial Rome. It is true that there are in existence several books and articles, dealing either with some aspect of the history of milling or with some particular archaeological finds, in which it is admitted that non-rotary mills were used during the early part of the period:[1] but even these works are, for the most part, rather vague about the origin of the rotary mill which they usually ascribe to 'some forgotten forerunner of Archimedes'[2] in the sixth or fifth century B.C.; and those books to which a classical student who is not a milling specialist is likely to turn have ignored the question altogether.[3] Even the best of these reference books unanimously assume that at some time in prehistory an advance was made over the most primitive grinding appliances, which they identify as the mortar and pestle, and that there was then no further change until the water-mill was invented: the mills mentioned in the Homeric text were 'without doubt not very different, except that they were of ruder make',[4] from the rotary mills found in great numbers at Pompeii or other mills of a similar Roman date. In the four sections of this chapter that follow the various

---

[1] See *Note A*, p. 218.   [2] Curwen, *Antiquity*, xi. 138.

[3] These include Blümner's *Technologie und Terminologie der Gewerbe und Künste bei Griechen und Römern* (vol. i, 2nd ed., Leipzig, 1912), Neuberger's *Technik des Altertums* (Leipzig, 1919), and the articles *Mola* in *DS*, iii. 1960 ff., and Μύλη in *PW*, xvi. 1064 ff. (The latter, published in 1933, ignores not only Lindet and *BE*, but also a fundamental article in Ἀρχ. Ἐφ. 1917, pp. 151 ff., on which cf. below, pp. 44 ff.)

[4] Autenrieth, *Hom. Dictionary* (Eng. ed., London, 1877), s.v. μύλης, well reflecting an attitude which still prevails.

arguments are examined on which this common belief in a
Homeric or pre-Homeric date for the origin of the rotary mill
appears to be based.

1. *The Greek name of the mill.* 'The word μύλη is never found in
the enlarged sense of the Latin *mola* which at times includes
pounding implements in its meaning.'—BLÜMNER.[1] This statement, representative of a widely held attitude, begs the principal
question about the history of the grain-mill in antiquity. It rests
on the implicit assumption that the normal connotation of words
denoting a grain-mill in any language, ancient or modern, is
a contrivance for grinding corn, consisting of two round stones
one of which revolves above, and concentrically with, the other:
any meaning that does not comply with this definition is regarded as 'enlarged'.

This definition does not, of course, cover the mills now in
common use, the rollers of which are not made of stone and do not
revolve concentrically. But, either because the picture evoked by
the words in question in the mind of the layman is still that of the
windmill or water-mill, or because the modern rollers do the
work formerly done by stones covered by the definition, no difficulty is felt in applying to modern mills the names which once
denoted very different machines.

If those who are familiar with modern mills see no objection to
calling them by the same names as earlier mills, it must be
because the function of the machine, and not the particular
method by which it fulfils this function, determines the choice of
name; and if the roller-mill could thus take over earlier names
the same is likely to be true of the windmill and water-mill. Nor
is there any reason why the rotary mills driven by human or
animal power, by which windmills and water-mills were preceded, should not have taken over the names from still earlier
non-rotary appliances—unless the derivation of the words suggests a necessary connexion with rotary motion.

This is not the case: the root of the word μύλη is old and appears in most Indo-European languages, but its original significance is no more than 'apparatus for crushing'.[2] In common use

---

[1] p. 21 (my translation). The masculine form μύλος is late Greek.
[2] Cf. Boisacq, *Dict. étym. de la langue grecque*, s.v.; Walde–Hofmann, *Lat. etym.
Wörterb.*, s.v. *molo*; *O.E.D.*, s.v. Mill; Curwen, *Antiquity*, xi. 134; *BE*, i. 58; and
cognate verbs, e.g. Germ. *zermalmen*.

μύλη probably soon became restricted to 'grain-mill', simply because grain-mills were the best known of these crushing implements;[1] but it (and its equivalents in other languages) always remained capable of being applied, with the appropriate qualification, to instruments for crushing other substances.[2] Similarly 'mill', like its synonyms in other languages, now implies rotary motion.[3] But this is so only because, up to the introduction of roller-milling, mills covered by our definition had become by far the most common type of mill. The approximate date of this second restriction of meaning can be determined only on the basis of the date of the introduction and common acceptance of the rotary mill.[4]

We must not, then, infer from the use of words which are known to have denoted rotary mills at some time, that these words always and necessarily denoted rotary mills; nor must we speak of an 'enlarged sense' when we find such words applied to other implements for the reduction of grain. Yet there are two ways in which linguistic usage can be of help after all: the verbs describing the operation of the mill may give a clue concerning the mode of operation; or else we may be lucky enough to find descriptive epithets added which provide a similar clue.

There are sufficient instances of verbs of turning applied to grain-mills in Roman literature from at least the first century B.C. onwards[5] to enable us to say with certainty that the normal Roman mill was rotary, even if we had no other means of knowing that it was. But it has commonly been overlooked that no such verbs are found in Greek literature before that time.[6] This may be accident, but it probably is not; and for what it is worth it suggests that the normal Greek mill was non-rotary.

[1] Similarly 'flour' means wheat flour, and if we mean, e.g., barley flour we say so.
[2] Cf. our 'coffee-' or 'pepper-mill'.
[3] The extension to 'mills' unconnected with grinding (e.g. the cotton mill) is secondary and quite recent.
[4] A final restriction in the meaning of the word, by which it came to be applied from the mill as a whole to the large stationary lower stone which was its most important part (e.g. Poll. vii. 19; Hesych. s.v.; cf. Blümner, p. 30, n. 1), is natural enough, and the word may well have been used in this way at a time when it also denoted the mill as a whole. (Cf., on the other hand, our extension of 'mill' from the machine to the building in which it is housed.)
[5] For examples see below, p. 67, n. 5.
[6] e.g. τὴν μύλην στρέφειν, περιάγειν, περιελαύνειν. Blümner, who was not aware of this, can quote such verbs only from pseudo-Lucian (Asin. 42) and Pollux (vii. 180), i.e. not before the second century A.D. (p. 38 and n. 7).

Adjectives and other descriptive words are always most likely to be added when more than one kind of the thing in question is known, just because they help to distinguish between different kinds. (The preceding few pages, in which different types of mill were being distinguished, probably contain more such epithets than a whole book on one particular type of mill.) If in Latin we find a contrast between 'pushing-mills' (*molae trusatiles*)[1] and 'turning-mills' (*molae versatiles*), we may safely infer—in spite of common misinterpretations of this contrast—that the 'pushing-mill' was not a 'turning-mill', i.e. that it was non-rotary. A detailed discussion of this contrast must be postponed until later: here it must be pointed out only that the absence of a similar contrast in Greek literature, which may again be due to accident, may also have been caused by the absence of one of the two types in Greece. The remarkable paucity in Greek literature of epithets of all kinds in connexion with the grain-mill must, moreover, give rise to the suspicion that only one main kind of mill was known at any one time; and if so, it is to beg the entire question to say that this mill must have been rotary.

2. *Μύλη*, &c., *in the Homeric text*. Mention has been made of two stages in the restriction of the meaning of the Greek word which originally must have denoted any appliance for crushing. We have next to ask how the text of Homer fits into this development.[2]

In the Homeric poems 'mills' (μύλαι) occur only in two passages of the *Odyssey*;[3] 'millstones' (μύλακες)[4] and 'a piece of rock like a millstone' (μυλοειδὴς πέτρος)[5] are mentioned as missiles, and 'crushed in a mill' (μυλήφατος) is used as an epithet for meal.[6] From these passages it has been inferred[7] that rotary mills must be meant, and they must therefore be considered in some detail.

In a well-known New Testament verse[8] we hear of a mill-

---

[1] From *trusare*, 'to push to and fro', which occurs in Catull. 56. 6. For the contrast see Cat. *Agr.* 10. 4; Plin. *N.H.* xxxvi. 135; Gell. *N.A.* iii. 3. 14; and below, pp. 62 ff.

[2] Nothing need here be said about the old problem of the authorship and date of the Homeric poems: it is sufficient for our purposes that they are without question the oldest extant works of Greek literature.

[3] vii. 104 and xx. 106, 111.

[4] *Il.* xii. 161.

[5] *Il.* vii. 270. For the use of early millstones as missiles cf. Judges ix. 53; 2 Sam. xi. 21; also Virg. *Aen.* viii. 250; Oppian, *Cyn.* iii. 137; Sen. *Ep.* 82. 24.

[6] *Od.* ii. 355. The significance of the second part of the word is not quite certain.

[7] e.g. by Blümner, p. 21; Buchholz, *Homerische Realien*, vol. ii, pt. 1, p. 108.

[8] '... it were better for him that a millstone (μύλος ὀνικός) were hanged about his

stone being hanged about a man's neck. This verse may not refer
to an actual mode of punishment; but when it was written there
must have been millstones in existence which could be hanged
about a man's neck—presumably because they were round and
had a hole in the centre.[1] Homer gives us no similar indication
concerning the shape of the millstones which he mentions as
missiles: all that can be inferred is that the stones in question
must have been particularly hard and heavy, and that they
probably had a recognizable shape which was associated with the
stones commonly used for grinding corn.

The passages in the *Odyssey* in which mills themselves are mentioned are also tantalizingly inexplicit. Although it is in each
case expressly stated that it was for corn that the mills were being
used, it is suggested by the language of the passages in question
that μύλη no longer meant 'grinder generally', and that it was
already capable, without any specifying addition, of denoting a
'corn-grinder'. (This impression is confirmed by the fact that
such an adjective as μυλήφατος could be used elsewhere.) On the
other hand, these passages say nothing to explain the nature of
the mills to which they refer.[2]

When, however, Homer says[3] that one of Odysseus' maids
'halted her mill and spoke a word, a sign to her lord' (ἥ ῥα μύλην
στήσασα ἔπος φάτο, σῆμα ἄνακτι), his language has been thought[4]
to compel the inference that a rotating type of mill is meant. It is
implicitly assumed that 'to bring to a halt' (ἱστάναι) is used only
where a positive effort is required to stop a movement, and that it
cannot be used of the mere leaving-off of the effort which induced
the movement. But all this is mere assumption since the verb in
question simply means 'to cause to stand (still)', and the distinction just mentioned cannot in any case apply to the grain-mill.
There is no doubt that in the passage in question it was the maids
who worked the mills, and there is no mill—rotary or non-
rotary—worked by human power which, with grain between

neck, and that he were drowned in the depth of the sea' (Matt. xviii. 6; cf. Mark
ix. 42, and Luke xvii. 2, where λίθος μυλικός is used).
  [1] But cf. Blümner, p. 30, n. 1.
  [2] The simile of the 'leaves of the tall poplar tree', which is applied to the
activity of Alkinoos' maids in *Od*. vii. 106, must surely refer only to the spinning of
the yarn (the last activity mentioned), just as the word ἥμεναι ('sitting') in the same
line can hardly refer back as far as the mention of the mill in line 104.
  [3] *Od*. xx. 111.
  [4] e.g. by Hug, *PW*, xvi. 1065.

the stones, would require a positive effort to bring it to a halt.[1]

The Homeric text, then, serves to show only that there were in existence when it was written stone appliances of a recognizable shape, commonly used for grinding corn, which were called μύλαι and were probably associated in the popular mind with their usual function. The first stage in the restriction of the meaning of the word had probably been reached—and may indeed have been reached almost as soon as the appliance itself was invented—but there is no indication that the second stage, the emergence of the meaning 'rotary mill', had even been approached.[2]

3. *Mythology*. Another reason for the common belief in the early origin of the rotary mill is that the invention of the grain-mill was ascribed in antiquity to divine or semi-divine intervention.[3] Several different stories appear to have been current, and the invention was variously traced back to Demeter,[4] to Myles the son of Lelex,[5] to Mylas (one of the Telchines) and the Mylanteioi Theoi,[6] and, finally, to Zeus Myleus.[7]

Some of these myths may be late fabrications, made up to explain some traditional name; but at least some of them must be due to the fact that the origin of milling fell in a very early age. Yet the myths must not for this reason be connected with the origin of the rotary mill: it is far more probable that the great discovery for which the credit was given to superhuman beings was the principle of reducing grain to groats, meal, or flour, before it was cooked, than that it should have been some later improvement in the process. A discovery of this kind was parallel to that of the cultivation of grain which was the principal benefit that Demeter was said to have bestowed upon men. In each case the innovation was the superimposition of a craft (τέχνη) upon that which nature provided: what had been wild plants began to

---

[1] Jacobi (*Saalburg Jahrbuch*, iii, p. 79, n. 3) draws attention to the phrase γούνατ᾽ ἔλυσαν ('they have loosened my knees') in l. 118, which can be taken literally if a saddle-quern (below, pp. 9, 19 ff.) is meant.

[2] See *Note B*, p. 218.

[3] Cf. Blümner, p. 21 and notes, where the myths are summarized.

[4] Plin. *N.H.* vii. 191; cf. Polemon *ap.* Ath. iii. 109a.

[5] Paus. iii. 20. 2; iv. 1. 1. Myles appears as 'the inventor of water-mills' in R. Graves's *The Greek Myths* (Penguin Books, 1955), ii. 111.

[6] Hesych. s.vv. Μύλας, Μυλάντειοι, Steph. Byz. s.v. Μυλαντία.

[7] Lyc. 435.

be grown under man's control, and—perhaps even before the beginnings of agriculture—a fine material, white and powdery, easily cooked and digested, began to be produced from the hard unpalatable grain yielded by the plant. It is surely to this innovation rather than to any later technical advance, such as the introduction of the rotary mill, that the myths refer; for no advance, however great, could have matched the original invention in importance.

Writers of the Roman period may, it is true, themselves have thought of the mill as rotary when they related their versions of the myths, since by their time the mill must have been generally thought of as a rotary appliance. But even this may be doubted. For while Pliny[1] tells us that Ceres was adjudged a goddess because she taught men to grind, he also informs us on Varro's authority[2] that turning-mills (molae versatiles) were invented by the Volsinians in Etruria.

Seneca, a near-contemporary of Pliny, was certainly thinking of a mill more primitive than the rotary in his severely rational account of the invention of the art of grinding corn which he quotes from Posidonius, who lived in the early first century B.C.[3] In this account the invention of milling is ascribed to the ingenuity of a man who followed the model provided by nature in the form of the teeth which by their hardness break down the food that is taken into the mouth, and thus facilitate swallowing and digestion. This shows a clear grasp of the essential function of the mill which (like all other implements and activities concerned with the preparation of foodstuffs for human consumption) serves as a preliminary and an aid to the processes of digestion. It also shows incidentally what the original discovery is likely to have been, and that the rotary mill must be thought of

[1] N.H. vii. 191.
[2] Ibid. xxxvi. 135. Varro, 'the most learned of the Romans', was born in 116 B.C.—nearly a century and a half before Pliny—and his antiquarian interests make his evidence important on points such as this. This will be true especially if the event quoted from Varro turns out to have taken place a relatively short time before Varro himself was born.
[3] Ep. 90. 22–23: 'receptas ... in os fruges concurrens inter se duritia dentium frangit, et quicquid excidit ad eosdem dentes lingua refertur. ... hoc aliquis secutus exemplar lapidem asperum aspero imposuit ad similitudinem dentium, quorum pars immobilis motum alterius exspectat. deinde utriusque attritu grana franguntur et saepius regeruntur donec ad minutiam frequenter trita redigantur. ...'

as a refinement parallel to that of the developed baking-oven
which is explicitly mentioned later in the same passage as 'gradually invented'.[1]

4. *References in the Old Testament.* The Homeric poems, then,
give no indication of the nature of the mills mentioned in them,
and the assumption that these mills must have been rotary cannot
be justified on their evidence. It remains to examine some passages in the Old Testament: though outside the scope of the
present inquiry, some of these probably belong to the same
period of history, and earlier studies of our subject—from Heringius in the seventeenth century onwards—have brought them
into the argument.[2] But the fairly numerous references to mills
and milling in the Old Testament provide little that is valuable
from our present point of view: no descriptions are given either
of the appliance on which Sarah made ready 'three measures of
fine meal',[3] or of that on which the manna was ground in the
wilderness,[4] or of the mills of which neither the nether nor the
upper stone must be taken to pledge,[5] except that in this last
case it is clear that the two stones must have differed recognizably
from each other. Nor are other passages[6] more helpful.

The Hebrew word (רֶכֶב) which is used to denote the upper
millstone[7] means primarily 'a chariot' or 'a rider', and is therefore on any interpretation a natural word to use for the upper
millstone which 'rides' on the lower. The action of grinding,
moreover, is never described in any way that might point to a
definite type of mill, and here, as in Homer, it is noticeable that
no verbs of turning occur: the word (טָחַן) used of Samson who
was put 'to grind' in the prison-house[8] and of the young men
who were taken 'to grind' in the Babylonian exile[9] means no
more than 'to reduce something to very small pieces'.

There is, however, a passage in the book of Exodus[10] which
mentions an Egyptian 'maidservant that is *behind* the mill': the
preposition in this phrase, though by no means conclusive evid-

---

[1] 'deinde furni paulatim reperti.'
[2] Cf. Ebert, *Reallex. d. Vorgeschichte*, viii. 324–5. For Heringius cf. above,
p. xxii, n. 1.
[3] Gen. xviii. 6.   [4] Num. xi. 8.   [5] Deut. xxiv. 6.
[6] Isa. xlvii. 2 and Jer. xxv. 10 should be added to those usually quoted.
[7] Deut. xxiv. 6; Judges ix. 53; 2 Sam. xi. 21.
[8] Judges xvi. 21.   [9] Lam. v. 13.
[10] xi. 5.

ence by itself, is most natural, and the words can be taken literally, if this passage is connected with certain Egyptian statuettes of which more will be said later.[1] These statuettes show a well-known early type of grain-mill, the 'saddle-stone' or 'saddle-quern', consisting of a sloping slab of stone *behind* which the worker (usually a woman) kneels with a second and smaller stone, the grain-rubber or 'rider', in her hands, to grind the grain by rubbing the 'rider' up and down on the sloping lower stone. This is the only pointer which the Old Testament provides to the nature of the mills mentioned in it, and for what it is worth it indicates a non-rotary type.

From the evidence reviewed in this chapter it is indeed safe to infer that all grain-mills of classical antiquity—from the earliest to the latest—shared one common principle: on all of them 'the grain was crushed between two stones of which the upper was mobile, the lower immobile'.[2] But the further inference, that this community of principle included rotary motion, is not equally justified. Once the idea that mills must necessarily be rotary is discarded, there is nothing in the evidence reviewed so far to suggest that the mills to which it refers were rotary. This evidence does not, it is true, tell us much about the nature of the mills concerned, but it gives no grounds for accepting the established view that they were essentially similar to the mills used in imperial Rome. For positive evidence we must look elsewhere.[3]

[1] See below, p. 29.

[2] Blümner, p. 22. The lower stone was, of course, immobile only in the sense that it was stationary during grinding (as it has been with practically all stone mills at all times), while the upper stone was moved to crush the grain: the primitive stage, where natural rock *in situ* was used as a bed for grinding, had by Homer's time—and by the time when Deut. xxiv. 6 was written—clearly been superseded.

[3] Nothing has been said about the Minoan 'Linear B' material, the decipherment of which is at present (1957) attracting much attention. Although some relevant words appear to have been identified, the nature of the available material is such that it can provide no help in the present context.

II

THE DONKEY

ENOUGH may have been said to suggest that any inferences of the kind discussed so far are likely to be double-edged, and that it is only from archaeological finds of actual grinding implements that something more decisive can be expected. But before we turn to such finds there are a few further points which need discussion, if only because they have been brought into the argument to prove the early existence of rotary mills, and have found their way into the reference books. The two most important of these points are in one way or another concerned with donkeys, either in name or in effigy. The donkey must figure prominently in any study concerned with ancient milling methods; but we must be on our guard against interpreting either its classical names or pictorial representations of the animal, wherever they appear in connexion with milling, as necessarily referring to donkey-mills, merely because donkeys were undoubtedly used for turning mills in Roman days. The mistaken interpretations here to be discussed are due to neglect of this precaution.

The Greek word for 'a donkey'—ὄνος—was regularly used, from at least the fifth century B.C. onwards, to denote the upper millstone.[1] From this usage it has been inferred, even by those whose interpretation of the evidence discussed in the last chapter is free from the usual mistakes,[2] that mills driven by donkeys must have been known at least as early as the fifth century B.C.—and mills driven by animals must *ipso facto* be rotary. But granted that it is a remarkable coincidence that the name 'donkey' should have come to be applied to the upper millstone if it was not driven by a donkey,[3] it may well be still more remarkable to suppose that the name was transferred from the animal to the stone it drove. And the transference was very complete: for a passage in Herodas,[4] written in the third century B.C., shows that

---

[1] See *Note C*, p. 218.　　　　　　　[2] e.g. Curwen, *Antiquity*, xi. 137.
[3] It seems impossible to believe that this is a case of etymologically unconnected homonyms.
[4] 6. 83. That ὄνος in the phrase ὄνου λίθον ἀλοῦντος, 'when the "donkey" grinds

the word ὄνος was also used of the upper stone of a mill worked by a woman.

The figurative meanings of ὄνος cover a wide range; but it is not necessary to assume (with Liddell and Scott) that they are all derived from the 'ass as a beast of burden'. It is difficult to see how either the meaning of 'spindle or distaff'[1] or that of 'beaker or wine-cup'[2] can be traced back to this source; and the origin of the meaning 'windlass'[3] is also doubtful. That the word acquired the latter meaning because the windlass was usually driven by an ass is improbable;[4] and while it is conceivable that this meaning is derived from the 'ass as a beast of burden', it may be well to remember that the ass is famous also for its long ears,[5] and in the case of Herodotus' 'wooden donkeys' (ὄνοι ξύλινοι) two 'ears' may well have served as guides to the rope.

It is hard to see what characteristic of the donkey it was that made its name appropriate to the upper millstone. Some upper stones of non-rotary mills are known which have protuberances or 'ears', serving as handles,[6] at either side; and it may be that these 'ears', which seem to have appeared at about the time at which the word ὄνος came to be applied to the upper millstone,[7] gave rise to this usage (although the 'ears' on these mills were horizontal rather than vertical). But this is admittedly mere speculation, and it may be wisest to admit that we do not know why the upper millstone should have been called 'donkey'. In view of the other figurative meanings of the word, however, it would at any rate seem rash to assume that the name must have been due to the driving animal: the dangers of such an assumption are well illustrated by our 'donkey-engine' and the pitfalls into which it might lead future archaeologists.[8]

But if it is right to say that a transference of name from the

stone' ([Arist.] Probl. 964ᵇ38), which is used of the mill working without grist in it, also refers to the stone and not to the animal is generally admitted.

[1] Poll. vii. 32; x. 125; Hesych. [2] Ar. Vesp. 616; see Rogers, ad loc.

[3] Hdt. vii. 36; Hippocr. Fract. 31; Arist. Mech. 853ᵇ12.

[4] The windlass mentioned in the Hippocrates passage was certainly not driven by an ass. [5] Cf. Apul. Met. vi. 32; ix. 15.

[6] Cf. below, p. 42. Handles were often called 'ears' in Greek; see LS s.v. οὖς 11. 1.

[7] If the interpretation of the mills in Xen. Cyr. vi. 2. 31 put forward later in this chapter (below, p. 17) is correct, it may be significant that ὄνος = 'upper millstone' is first quoted from the writer who mentions these mills.

[8] Heringius (p. 69) even thought that the ὄνος must have been the lower stone 'because it remains idle like a donkey'! Cf. also below, p. 16.

driving animal to the stone it drove is unlikely, a somewhat paradoxical conclusion follows. For if ὄνος in the meaning of 'upper millstone' is really unconnected with the animal driving the mill, it must have become difficult to continue using the word for the stone when donkeys did appear, since it would not have been easy to speak of 'a donkey turning a donkey'. The millstone in the Greek text of the Gospel[1] is no longer called 'donkey' (ὄνος) but 'donkey-driven' (μύλος ὀνικός), and this change from noun to adjective may not be accidental. The noun ὄνος is last used for the upper millstone by Herodas in the third century B.C. and in the Aristotelian *Problems*, which may be slightly earlier or considerably later.[2] But so far from establishing the employment of the donkey with the mill for the third century B.C. and earlier, this usage may even serve to indicate that the donkey-driven mill could not have been in existence at that time.

The second point at which the donkey enters into our search for the origin of the rotary mill is rather different but no less important; for on the commonly accepted view of it it provides a sure *terminus ante quem* for the invention of the donkey-mill. By a remarkable error a Megarian bowl, belonging to a class known as 'Homeric' and dating from the third or second century B.C., has been taken to show, in the reliefs appearing on it, 'the working of a mill of the Homeric age'.[3] The name of these bowls— presumably the origin of the anachronism—is due to the fact that they usually, though not always, illustrate scenes from the Homeric poems; and as evidence for Homeric times they are analogous to an illustration in a fourteenth-century manuscript which shows Samson working at a complicated medieval treadmill:[4] if only this error were at stake the bowl would hardly be worthy of discussion, but we shall here be concerned with a somewhat different point of interpretation.

This bowl was first published in 1914.[5] More recently another copy of a bowl from the same mould has been found, from a discussion of which[6] the drawing reproduced in Fig. 1 is taken.

[1] Matt. xviii. 6; cf. above, p. 4, n. 8.
[2] Its reappearance in the medieval lexicographers is irrelevant.
[3] See *PW*, xvi. 1071. On the date of this bowl cf. Parsons, *Hesperia*, v, p. 87, n. 2.
[4] Cf. *BE*, i. 56.
[5] By Versakis, Ἀρχ. Ἐφ. 1914, pp. 50 ff. The correct interpretation of the two non-rotary mills on it is due to Kourouniotes, ibid., 1917, pp. 151 ff.
[6] By Rostovtzeff, *Am. Journ. Arch.* xli. 86 ff. The two copies of the bowl are now

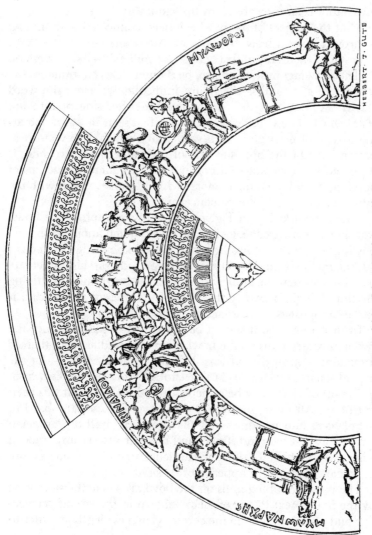

MYΔWOPΘI

TIMHPOS

HMAΔOI

MYΔWПΔΡXHS

HERBERT · J · GUTE

Fig. 1. 'Homeric' bowl from Thebes now in the Louvre

This bowl has figured in nearly all modern articles on ancient milling, and, so far as the point here at issue is concerned, it has invariably been interpreted in the same way.

That the subject of the bowl is indeed connected with milling is proved conclusively by two of the words—ΜΥΛΩΝΑΡΧΗΣ ('master of the mill') and ΜΥΛΩΘΡΟΙ ('millers')—that appear on it. The drawing must, of course, be thought of as continuous: the 'master of the mill' is the figure immediately below the word ΜΥΛΩΝΑΡΧΗΣ, and the two figures on either side of him are ΜΥΛΩΘΡΟΙ. These 'millers' are, as was first seen in 1917, operating a type of non-rotary mill with which we shall have to deal presently.[1] On the opposite side of the bowl, however, there is supposed to be depicted, according to the general consensus of opinion, 'a mill of Pompeian form with its donkey':[2] it is with the latter that we shall here be concerned.

When the drawing in Fig. 1, with a photograph of the bowl, was shown to an archaeologist who knows much about 'Homeric' bowls of this type but has little specialized knowledge of ancient milling methods (and has therefore no prejudices), his immediate reaction was that the donkey shown on the bowl 'might be doing anything'. This is exactly the view of the present writer, and it can be supported by reasoned argument.

In this connexion it should be noted first of all that, once the two non-rotary mills on the bowl are recognized as such, there is something—occupying at least half the available space—for the legend ΜΥΛΩΝΑΡΧΗΣ–ΜΥΛΩΘΡΟΙ to refer to: the donkey, from this point of view, may be attached to a third mill, but this need not be so. All those, moreover, who have discussed the bowl in detail have had to admit that the supposed 'mill of Pompeian form' is at best very indistinct; and it is hard to see any trace of a harness by which the donkey is attached to it. This point is more significant than might appear at first sight.

The two undoubted mills on the bowl are—like the sieve held by the figure next to one of them—shown in the wrong perspective and at right angles to the correct view,[3] evidently in order to

at Athens and in the Louvre respectively. (Rostovtzeff gives references to other discussions of the Athens copy.)   [1] Below, p. 44.

[2] Childe, *Antiquity*, xvii. 22, sharing the generally accepted view.

[3] The characteristic upper stones are shown in a 'plan' view instead of the correct 'side elevation': this will become clear to the reader from the discussion of such mills in Chapter VII.

make it quite clear what they are; and we might therefore expect the same crude method of representation to have been applied also to the 'donkey-mill'. Yet this supposed mill is obscured to at least half its height by the donkey—in spite of the fact that on ancient pictorial representations of animal-mills, which have come down to us in comparative plenty, it is almost invariably the mill that is shown in full, and if anything is obscured it is the animal. At least seven of the monuments in question are alike in this respect: they will be discussed in detail in their proper context.[1]

This rule was broken only if, for some special reason, the donkey had to be given prominence, as in a graffito from the Palatine[2] which illustrates a donkey at work rather than a donkey-mill. But in such a case the harnessing was shown clearly, and the mill was elevated above the donkey, so that, although behind the donkey, it might still be seen in full.[3] In view of the way in which the other mills on our bowl are shown, it seems certain that this practice would have been followed here too if, for some reason, the donkey had to be placed in front of its mill.

That there was a reason for showing the whole of the donkey is sufficiently obvious from the drawing, though we cannot now know the details with any certainty. 'Homeric' bowls usually illustrate epic scenes; but even where they do not, as in this case, it has been convincingly argued[4] that they depict some literary subject, rather than mere scenes from everyday life. In the present case the words appearing on the bowl are alone enough to suggest that the subject was a literary one, and it may well have been a scene from a mime of the kind familiar from Herodas, which enjoyed great popularity in the third and second centuries B.C. This scene appears to have contained two main subjects, separated on the bowl by the two figures brandishing what look like clubs. One is governed by the legend ΜΥΛΩΘΡΟΙ and shows the 'master of the mill', two non-rotary mills, and a man with a sieve; the other is governed by the word ΚΙΝΑΙΔΟΙ—and the donkey appears in the ΚΙΝΑΙΔΟΙ half.

---

[1] Blümner, pp. 40 ff., figs. 14–18, 20–21; cf. below, pp. 77 ff.
[2] See below, p. 83 and Fig. 9.
[3] A Pompeian wall-painting (Blümner, fig. 23) of the feast of the Vestalia, when the asses were the heroes of the day, is not strictly relevant here, since it shows the mill at rest with two donkeys in the foreground well away from it. But here again the mill is raised and no part of it is obscured.
[4] By Rostovtzeff, loc. cit.

With the loss of the literary text the full explanation of the bowl has, of course, also been lost. Of the two words not connected with mills, τιμωρός normally means 'avenger' and may mean 'executioner',[1] while κίναιδος probably has a meaning—'catamite'—which, in the form cinaedus, it commonly has in Latin,[2] and which in Greek can be traced back to the early fourth century B.C.[3] (That the subject was obscene is obvious from the drawing.)

Now in Latin the word asellus, 'little ass', is used with a similar meaning quite frequently, and Petronius in the first century A.D. mentions the cinaedus and the asellus in this sense in the same chapter.[4] There is, moreover, good evidence that this meaning of 'ass' is of Greek origin;[5] and if a human cinaedus was called an 'ass' it was because the animal itself was reputed to have similar characteristics. That this was so is clear from the bowl, and it is confirmed elsewhere[6]—and it may have been these characteristics that made its name appropriate for the upper stone of a saddle-quern.

We cannot be certain about the structure that is shown behind the donkey on the bowl, but it may well represent the panniers (κανθήλια) mentioned by Aristophanes,[7] lifted from the back of the ass and, like other objects on the bowl, turned through a right angle for greater clarity. Alternatively the KINAIΔOI half of the bowl may be connected with certain itinerant priests of the Syrian Astarte who, according to a much later narrative, were not only themselves cinaedi but at times carried their goddess on the back of an ass with a similar reputation.[8] Whatever the explanation, the appearance of a donkey on this Megarian bowl provides no more evidence for the existence of the donkey-mill

[1] Cf. Polyb. ii. 58. 8.

[2] e.g. Plaut. Asin. 627; Catull. 16. 2; 25. 1; Juv. Sat. 2. 10.

[3] Plat. Gorg. 494e (cf. schol. ad loc.); Aeschin. i. 131, ii. 99; Herod. 2. 74; &c.

[4] Satyr. 24; cf. Juv. Sat. 6. 334; 9. 92; Epist. Imp. Aug. ap. Gell. N.A. xv. 7. 3; and Thes. Ling. Lat. s.v.

[5] See Script. Hist. Aug. Comm. 10.

[6] Cf. [Luc.] Asin. 56 (also 28, 32–33); Apul. Met. iii. 24 (also iv. 23, vii. 21); and, for the relations between an ass and human cinaedi, [Luc.] Asin. 35–38. There is also a Sanskrit name for an ass (gardabha-) which probably means 'the lascivious beast'.

[7] Vesp. 170.

[8] The resemblances between this part of the bowl and the narrative in Apul. Met. viii. 26 ff. or [Luc.] Asin. 35 ff. are most striking: the mills in these stories are undoubtedly rotary, but the bowl may well depict a version of the same tale three to four centuries older.

in the early hellenistic period than does the name ὄνος for the upper millstone for classical Greece.

To end this chapter one other piece of 'evidence', not connected with donkeys, requires a brief discussion. Xenophon (c. 430–c. 354 B.C.), who provides the earliest evidence for ὄνος as the upper millstone, elsewhere includes 'hand-mills' (χειρόμυλαι) among the equipment necessary for an expeditionary force, 'for they are the least heavy among the implements used for grinding corn' (τῶν σιτοποιικῶν ὀργάνων).¹ This appears to be the only extant passage in classical Greek in which a word for a hand-mill occurs,² and it is commonly thought that it must refer to rotary 'querns' of a type familiar from later times.³ But this is far from certain. The text, first of all, is itself doubtful: one of the two groups of manuscripts reads 'mills' (μύλας) for 'hand-mills' (χειρομύλας), and if this is accepted no difficulty arises. (The words stressing their light weight may have been added by the scribe who changed 'mills' to 'hand-mills'.⁴) But even if 'hand-mills' is correct, Xenophon is only contrasting a comparatively light portable mill worked by unaided human effort with a heavier one aided by some kind of mechanical contrivance. This interpretation can be accepted on the basis of some archaeological evidence to be discussed presently,⁵ without the assumption that these hand-mills were rotary.

¹ Cyr. vi. 2. 31.
² All the references which I have been able to find are later than the earliest extant rotary hand-mills; cf. Blümner, p. 31, n. 2 and LS s.vv. χειρομύλιον, -μυλον, -μυλος. (LXX Num. xi. 8, where μύλος is used, should be deleted from Blümner's note.)
³ See, e.g., Holden, ad loc., and Blümner, pp. 31–32. Childe (Antiquity, xvii. 24) has correctly pointed out that rotary motion cannot be inferred from the passage; yet Storck and Teague (Flour for Man's Bread, p. 82) again imply that Xenophon's hand-mill was a rotary quern, and their statement that 'the quern was in use in many parts of the Mediterranean world by the fifth century B.C.' (p. 81) is largely based on this assumption.
⁴ The difficulty is that these words appear also in those MSS. reading μύλας.
⁵ Below, pp. 42 ff.

III

FINDS OF EARLY CORN-GRINDERS

NOTHING in the evidence discussed so far has yielded any certain trace of the existence of the rotary mill before Roman times. Whether it is justifiable to infer that rotary mills did not exist, cannot be decided before all the relevant evidence has been examined: at this point it would appear that the answer, if it is to be found anywhere, will be found among the archaeological remains of the period.

Archaeologists have on the whole been much more careful in arriving at their conclusions than have those who have discussed our subject in more general terms. The main accusation which must be brought against them is that, with very few exceptions, they have shown a complete lack of interest in grain-mills. Frequently a find is either not reported,[1] or it is mentioned, even in a full excavation report, in so summary a manner that the reader cannot know what type of grain-mill is being described—or even whether it is a grain-mill at all.

A further difficulty arises from inaccurate stratigraphical reporting[2] which often makes it impossible now to date objects that could have been dated if greater accuracy had been employed. Some years ago attention was drawn to the possibility of using mills themselves as a standard for dating other finds:[3] if this suggestion could be followed up the grain-mill would not only become more interesting to archaeologists than it appears to be at present, but it would, owing to its intimate connexion with daily life, itself provide a good illustration of the stage of civilization which it would help to date. Some beginnings have been made in this direction;[4] but meanwhile the available evidence is much less than would be desirable for a discussion such as this,

[1] See Childe's comments on this in *Antiquity*, xvii. 19.

[2] For an archaeologist's observations on this cf. Deonna, *Délos*, xviii, p. ii.

[3] See Curwen, *Antiquity*, xi. 133. Curwen's remarks relate to rotary querns, to Britain, and to a period later than that here under discussion; but they are equally applicable in the wider context.

[4] Cf. especially the writings of Curwen, Childe, and Robinson, referred to in *Note A*, p. 218.

and less even than might have been provided by the material already discovered.

The discovery of objects relevant here began with Heinrich Schliemann (1822–90) who, whatever the faults of his method, can still be called the father of modern archaeology. The finds made by Schliemann in most of his numerous excavations were brought to bear on the history of milling before the end of the nineteenth century by a few writers who saw that many of the traditional views could not be reconciled with these finds:[1] yet the old views continued to survive, and several more decades were to elapse before the archaeology of early Greece began to take its rightful place in the history of the corn-mill.

Schliemann's chronological placing of his finds in relation to the Homeric poems can no longer be accepted;[2] but for our present purposes this is not vital, since it will be sufficient here to accept these finds (or at least the less early among them) as belonging to a stage of civilization in prehistoric Greece and Asia Minor which is commonly known as Mycenaean. The objects which Schliemann rightly identified as corn-grinders are described by him clearly and in considerable detail—far more detail than is supplied by many of his otherwise more scientific successors:

[They] are either of trachyte . . . or of basaltic lava, but by far the larger number are of the former material. They are of oval form, flat on one side and convex on the other, and resemble an egg cut longitudinally through the middle. Their length is from 7 to 14 and even as much as 25 inches; the very long ones are usually crooked longitudinally; their breadth is from 5 to 14 inches.[3]

Schliemann—and in this he is followed by Dörpfeld, who succeeded him—at first thought that these remains represent both upper and lower stones of 'saddle-querns'[4] of the type briefly described in Chapter I in connexion with the book of Exodus and certain Egyptian statuettes, and illustrated below in Plate 2,

[1] See Lindet, 1899, pp. 419–20; *BE*, i. 9 ff., 30 ff.; but cf., e.g., Blümner and *PW*.
[2] The Homeric Troy was identified by Schliemann with the second settlement at Hissarlik; Dörpfeld identified it with settlement vi, and Professor Blegen's recent expedition with settlement viiA. For the rest Dörpfeld's distinction between the various strata (*Troja und Ilion*, p. 31) is still in the main accepted; cf. Blegen and others, *Troy*, i (Cincinnati, 1950), p. 22.
[3] *Ilios* (Eng. trans., London, 1880), p. 234; cf. p. 275. Dörpfeld (*Troja und Ilion*, pp. 387, 399) adds some square stones and some of a quite irregular shape.
[4] Lindet's *pierre à écraser*. On the word 'quern' cf. Curwen, *Antiquity*, xi. 134.

Figs. *b, c*. According to the shape of their axes Dörpfeld distinguished nine types among these stones,[1] and he reports finds of six
of these types from Troy.[2] These differences may, however, be due
largely to wear or to the original shape of the stone blocks, and
it is difficult either to regard them as typologically significant or to
recognize from them which were upper and which lower stones.
(This last point can be decided only on the basis of their relative
sizes.)

Stones of this kind were found in very great numbers in Troy
ii–v, the prehistoric settlements of the early and middle Bronze
Age. Some were found also in settlement vi, and one stone found
in this stratum 'was set in a clump of earth, about 0·50 m.
[= *c*. 1 ft. 8 in.] high, in such a way that its long axis was inclined at an angle of approximately 25 degrees. In front of this
clump the ground was firmly trodden down, and a small area
exactly below the lower end of the millstone was surrounded by a
wall of earth about 5 cm. [= 2 in.] high, evidently in order to
receive the meal as it fell from the sloping stone.'[3] This discovery
leaves no doubt concerning the nature of at least the lower stone:
it corresponds exactly with what is shown by the statuettes.
Schliemann himself found similar stones at the 'Tumulus of Pro-
tesilaus' in the Thracian Chersonese,[4] and at Tiryns,[5] Mycenae,[6]
and Thymbra,[7] and he mentions them also from Silesia and
Saxony, from the terremare of the stone and bronze ages in
Italy, from museums in Italy, Switzerland, and France, and
from Holyhead in the British Isles.[8] Other finds have been reported from prehistoric sites at Corinth, in Achaea and Thessaly,
on the islands of Delos, Thera, Cos, and Cyprus, and elsewhere.[9]

[1] According to whether (i) their long axis and (ii) their short axis is (*a*) straight, (*b*) concave, or (*c*) convex.
[2] Viz. long axis straight with short axis straight or convex; l.a. concave with s.a. straight, concave, or convex; both axes convex.
[3] Dörpfeld, *Troja und Ilion*, pp. 399–400.
[4] *Troja* (Eng. trans.), p. 257.
[5] *Tiryns* (1886), p. 80.
[6] *Mycenae and Tiryns* (1878), p. 77.
[7] *Ilios*, p. 711 (cf. index).
[8] Ibid. 234, 451; *Troja*, p. 44.
[9] Cf., e.g., Wace and Thompson, *Prehistoric Thessaly, passim* (see index); Evans, *Palace of Minos*, ii. 13. The references are well collected in *Délos*, xviii. 123–4. Some stones from Palaikastro which are described as rotary mills by Dawkins (*Brit. Sch. Ann.* xi. 268) are quite insufficient to show that rotary mills existed in Crete in the period to which they belong.

On the same prehistoric sites, and not only at Troy, 'rudely cut, nearly globular stone instruments' of basaltic lava, granite, quartz, diorite, porphyry, or other kinds of hard stone, were found by the thousand:[1] that these belong to the same stage of civilization as the stones just described is proved by their presence in the same places and by their absence where the saddle-quern is absent.[2] Schliemann, who was at first reluctant to connect these stones with the grinding of corn, later consistently described them as 'grain-bruisers': though never explicit on the point, he must have thought that they sometimes took the place of the upper stone of the saddle-quern.

If he was right in this belief grain must, at least sometimes, have been reduced on the saddle-quern by pounding rather than rubbing. But this is not what the Egyptian statuettes suggest, and, apart from these globular stones, all the evidence of extant stones, and of figures depicting similar stones in use, leads to the conclusion that on the saddle-quern grain was rubbed and not pounded or 'bruised'. Otherwise the lower stones ought to have a mortar-like cavity in the centre, produced either by use or by some form of preparation before use: in fact even badly worn stones do not show this.

Dörpfeld[3] explained Schliemann's 'grain-bruisers' as tools for removing rough edges on various types of material, ascribing their spherical shape to wear. (Stones of almost any original shape would tend to become spherical as their corners were knocked or worn away.) For the reasons given it seems safe to follow him— and Schliemann's own first thoughts—in believing that the globular stones were unconnected with the grinding of corn, and that stones essentially similar in shape to the lower stones (though smaller and less wide in relation to their length) were used as rubbers on the saddle-querns that were the grain-mills of prehistoric Greece and of primitive civilizations everywhere.[4]

[1] *Ilios*, p. 236.
[2] Ibid. 573.
[3] *Troja und Ilion*, p. 387.
[4] A single instance of what may have been another form of upper stone, with a flat grinding surface, is described by Dörpfeld, *Troja und Ilion*, p. 399, fig. 393 (cf. Schliemann, *Ilios*, fig. 1809): in the absence of parallel examples it is still impossible to say whether this interpretation is correct.

IV

MORTARS

SIDE by side with the millstones discussed in the last chapter Schliemann also found stone mortars and pestles.[1] Since these have, rightly or wrongly, been connected with the grinding of corn something must be said at this point about the mortar and its relation to the mill. Before the importance of the saddle-quern in the history of milling was recognized the mortar always figured prominently in this discussion. It was usually thought of as the immediate predecessor of the rotary mill, though it was admitted that it survived side by side with the mill until a very late period.[2] With the recognition of the saddle-quern it became at once relegated to a far less important place; but even now it cannot be omitted altogether.

Among the words which are usually grouped together as meaning 'a mortar', there is a clear distinction in both Greek and Latin between two parallel groups.[3] One of these is represented by *mortarium* in Latin and by θυεία and ἴγδις in Greek, the other by *pila* in Latin and by ὅλμος in Greek. 'Mortars' of the first of these groups were used like mixing-bowls in the modern kitchen:[4] cheese, garlic, or even hemlock, could be crushed in them occasionally, but that was not their essential purpose. Since the mortar is 'a vessel . . . in which ingredients are pounded with a pestle' (*O.E.D.*), the *mortarium* was, paradoxically enough, not a mortar, and it may therefore be dismissed from the argument.

The other group deserves more careful attention here; for it is certain that the appliances denoted by ὅλμος and *pila* were primarily employed for crushing. A simple proof of this is pro-

---

[1] See, e.g., *Ilios*, p. 235.
[2] So, e.g., Blümner, pp. 13 ff.
[3] Even in the medieval glossaries, *Corp. Gl.* iii. 270. 8 alone fails to observe this distinction which Blümner (p. 14, n. 6) was the first to notice.
[4] Cf. especially Ar. *Nub.* 676 (where the θυεία is a primitive 'mixing-trough' or κάρδοπος), *Ran.* 124, *Pl.* 719; Chrys. Tyan. *ap.* Ath. xiv. 647f *fin.*; Cat. *Agr.* 74, 75, 76; [Virg.] *Moret.* 116. In Ar. *Pax*, 230 ff. the θυεία is used for the preparation of an 'olio' or salad (μυττωτός, Lat. *moretum*), together with an ἀλετρίβανος: in the same passage Cleon is the ἀλετρίβανος that *stirred up* all Greece (ἐκύκα, l. 270).

vided by the frequent mention of the pestle together with this type of mortar—ὕπερος with ὅλμος in Greek,[1] *pilum* with *pila* in Latin.[2] It is with the use of these appliances that the rest of this chapter will be concerned.

We know from certain Greek terracotta figures and vase-paintings[3] that in the ὅλμος and *pila* (which might be either of wood[4] or of stone[5]) an up-and-down movement was employed for the pestle; and this can only mean that pounding rather than rubbing or grinding was aimed at. This is confirmed by the lever attachments which have been used with mortars in modern times[6] and, according to a plausible reconstruction of the apparatus of which certain stones found on Delos formed part,[7] also in antiquity. It is suggested also by the phrase 'twisting the pestle' which, like 'twisting the club', became proverbial for wasting one's labour since the ὕπερος was properly used for pounding.[8]

While the mortar was used for pounding, grain was, as we have seen, almost certainly ground by rubbing as soon as the saddle-quern came into use, and on all stone-mills thereafter. Yet mortars and grain-mills are constantly found together on sites of varying ages; they are mentioned together in papyri;[9] and mortars are referred to by writers as late as Pliny and even later[10]

[1] Or possibly ὕπερον; cf. *LS*, and Hes. *Op.* 423, Hdt. i. 200, Luc. *Hermot.* 79, &c.

[2] Cat. *Agr.* 10. 5, &c.; cf. Blümner, p. 15 and notes. The *pistillum* which frequently appears in company with the *mortarium* was probably no more a 'pestle' than the *mortarium* was a mortar, but rather a tool for crushing and mixing ingredients in cookery. So also the Greek δοῖδυξ which accompanies the θυεία: the ὕπερος-*pilum* never appears with the θυεία-*mortarium*, nor the δοῖδυξ-*pistillum* with the ὅλμος-*pila*.

[3] See Blümner, p. 19, figs. 3 and 4.

[4] Hes. *Op.* 423; Ar. *Vesp.* 238; Plin. *N.H.* xviii. 112; &c.

[5] Eust. *ad Il.* xi. 147, p. 835. 48; Cat. *Agr.* 10. 5: 'pilam ligneam i . . . pilas ii' (which seems to imply that the 'normal' *pila* was not made of wood; cf. Plin. loc. cit.). Metal, too, was used; see *PW*, xvi. 319 ff.

[6] See Meringer, *Wörter und Sachen*, i. 3 ff.; Storck and Teague, p. 47 (both with illustrations); cf. Polyb. i. 22. 7 and Walbank, ad loc.

[7] Hock, *Schumacher Festschrift*, 1930, pp. 80–84; *Délos*, xviii. 125–6: but it is doubtful whether these machines were connected with milling. The rival arguments based on Hes. *Op.* 424 by Lindet and Meringer are beside the point: Hesiod's ἄξων was merely a pole for a wagon.

[8] See *LS* s.v. ὕπερος. (Luc. *Hermot.* 79 describes another futile way of using a mortar—that of pounding water in it.)

[9] Cf. *Olynthus*, viii. 330 and 335–6. (But it cannot be certain that the mortars found at Olynthus are ὅλμοι rather than θυεῖαι: it is noteworthy that no pestles were found with them, though wooden pestles may have been used.)

[10] Plin. *N.H.* xviii. 112; and cf. below, p. 25.

for processes connected with the reduction of grain. It has commonly been taken for granted that mills and mortars were used
side by side in the same establishments and for the same purpose,
on the grounds that the mortar was cheaper and that it was
capable, as only quite advanced mills were, of producing different
grades of ground product:[1] in view of the important difference
between the pounding action of the one and the rubbing action
of the other, neither of these reasons seems convincing.[2]

'Corn-crushers', used in the Palaeolithic period first on hollows in the natural rock and later on portable mortars, were
probably the first implements ever used for grinding corn.[3] But
as regards classical antiquity there is a problem in the survival
of the mortar after the advance to the saddle-quern, and later to
the rotary mill, had been made. Throughout the history of the
grain-mill the less advanced type usually disappeared soon after
the more advanced had come into use: the mortar, which for a
long time outlasted all new inventions, does not fit into this line of
development, and we must surely ask what it was that enabled it
to survive.[4]

One proviso must at once be made: the mortar, like the donkey,
must not be associated with milling automatically, since it was
obviously a very handy implement with a wide variety of uses.[5]
A terracotta figure shows something much larger than grain
being pounded in it;[6] by various writers it is connected with drugs,
pulse, fodder, and dried fish;[7] and it was used also in a great
number of ways entirely unconnected with food.[8]

Yet it is abundantly clear that the mortar was often used for
grain;[9] nor can it be doubtful that, at least in Italy, it was long

---

[1] Cf. Blümner, p. 17.
[2] Lindet (1899, p. 424) rightly pointed out that different verbs were used in
Greek and Latin for 'pounding' in a mortar and 'grinding' in a mill (though he
wrongly placed *pisere* in the latter class).
[3] Cf. *BE*, i. 3 ff.
[4] This problem has often been overlooked altogether; but it was recognized—
though not solved—by, e.g., Lindet and Maurizio (*Anzeiger für Schweizer Alter-
tumskunde*, 1916, p. 14).
[5] Different pestles were sometimes used in the same mortar; cf. Cat. *Agr.* 10. 5.
[6] Blümner, fig. 4.
[7] Hdt. i. 200; Paus. v. 18. 2; Eust. *ad Il.* xi. 147, p. 835. 48; Hesych. and Suid.,
s.v. ὅλμος.
[8] Cf. Meringer, loc. cit. (esp. p. 28).
[9] Cf., e.g., the papyri referred to above; Cat. *Agr.* 14. 2; Varr. *L.L.* v. 138; Plin.
N.H. xviii. 112; and *PW*, xvi. 319. The purpose of the ὅλμοι which the 'bread-

used instead of a mill for grinding wheat where only small quantities were needed: Cato in listing the fixtures needed for a *villa* mentions 'a little mortar in which to crush wheat',[1] while he prescribes mills of various types for larger establishments.[2] It may even be that this became more common as mills developed and increased in price. At one time every family of any size must have owned at least one saddle-quern: as mills became more expensive only large households could continue to afford their own, while the smaller came to rely on commercial establishments. For the little that was still ground at home these smaller households may well have preferred a mortar with its variety of uses to a saddle-quern that would stand idle most of the time.[3] (Yet the meal produced in a mortar must have been very coarse.) It is also possible that the use of the mortar was more widespread in Italy than in Greece: the only direct evidence comes from Italy, and though this may be due to the accident of preservation, it may, as we shall see, have other causes.

But all this cannot account for the presence of mortars in the same place with mills, and the question why two implements of such different stages of development should have been used together has still to be answered, though it has become less formidable. The most obvious answer to this question is that the two were used for different operations, and this answer, which curiously enough does not seem to have occurred to modern scholars, is supported by the ancient evidence, particularly for Roman times. Again and again the *pila* is connected with *far* and ζειά—those wheats that needed a hulling operation to remove the *outer* husk before they could be ground: it is the mortar that appears to have been the appliance regularly used for hulling these grains after they had undergone their preliminary roasting or parching. Pliny actually tells us that wooden mortars were used in order that the grain might not be broken prematurely,[4] and

sellers' (ἀρτοπώλιδες) in Aristophanes, *Vesp.* 201, 238, have as almost the sign of their trade is not certain: *LS*, apparently without much evidence, give for these passages the special sense of 'kneading-trough'.
[1] *Agr.* 14. 2: 'paullula pila ubi triticum pinsat.'
[2] Ibid. 10. 4; 11. 4.
[3] This may have been true especially in the interval between the invention of the animal-mill and that of the rotary quern—if they were invented in this order; cf. below, Chapter XIV.
[4] *N.H.* xviii. 112; cf. ibid. 97: the breaking of the grain was, of course, the function of the mill.

an 'emmer-pestle' (*pilum farrarium*), mentioned by Cato for an establishment which also had mills,[1] was undoubtedly used in this way.

Originally, it is true, this operation may have been combined with, or followed by, a rough crushing of the grain in the same mortars, and in the production of *alica* (emmer groats)[2] the mortar was probably, even in the first century A.D., the only implement employed.[3] But it is unlikely that it was used for the manufacture of meal and flour in any considerable quantities after even the simplest types of mill had been invented: it is certain at any rate that the mortar was at all times associated particularly with the husked grains, and among these especially with *far*;[4] and St. Augustine even remarks that *far* cannot be prepared without a pestle.[5] Now *far* was the main grain of early Italy, and it is probably no accident, therefore, that our evidence for the employment of the mortar is more plentiful for the Roman than for the Greek part of our period. (Yet the mortar was used also for barley:[6] here again it must have been employed mainly for hulling, but here again it was, in the manufacture of *tisana*,[7] used also for a rough crushing of the grain.) It is interesting to remember in this connexion that the Latin word *pistor*, which came to denote a miller-baker, literally meant 'pounder', because originally a *pistor* was 'one who pounded emmer'[8]—presumably in a mortar.[9]

The mortar, then, could maintain itself side by side with even quite advanced mills simply because it had a function different from that of the mill. This answer to our problem seems obvious once it is pointed out, and it receives confirmation from a number of sources. The explorer David Livingstone, for instance, after

---

[1] *Agr.* 10. 5.

[2] Cf. below, p. 148.

[3] Cf. Plin. *N.H.* xviii. 112, where the operations of hulling and crushing are, however, clearly distinguished.

[4] Cf., e.g., Varr. *ap.* Non. 152. 12 M., *R.R.* i. 63, *L.L.* v. 138; Plin. *N.H.* xviii. 97, 112, and sec. 99 (where the difference between *acus* and *palea* must relate to that between husked and naked grain); Serv. *ad Aen.* i. 179 (where the mention of parching shows that husked grain is meant).

[5] *de Civ. Dei*, vi. 9: 'neque far conficitur sine pilo.'

[6] See esp. Plin. *N.H.* xviii. 73; Gal. vi. 501 ff. K.; and the anonymous *Laus Pisonis*, l. 17. (Piso's name was thought to derive from *pisere*, 'to pound'.)

[7] Cf. below, p. 147.

[8] Cf. above, p. xviii, and below, p. 69.

[9] See *Note D*, p. 218.

describing the saddle-quern as he found it in use in Africa, continues thus:

The corn is pounded in a large wooden mortar . . . with a pestle 6 ft. long and 4 in. thick. The pounding is performed by two or three women at one mortar.[1] ... By the operation of pounding with the aid of a little water, *the hard outside husk of the grain is removed, and the corn made fit for the millstone* [i.e. the saddle-quern].[2]

Similarly the use of the mortar is quoted in modern times for hulling rice in the Far East,[3] and a seventeenth-century work[4] shows a mortar with lever attachment on the same plate with, and subsidiary to, an elaborate hand-mill. The purpose of this semi-mechanical mortar, which, as we have seen, had its parallels in antiquity, is described as follows:

Where millet or other produce of the same kind [i.e. husked grain] is to be peeled or pounded a rounded block of wood with iron attached to its lower side[5] may be fitted up with a lever and treadle, and the grain may then be peeled with it in a hollow tree formed like a mortar. This is so well known that it is unnecessary to describe it at length.

Mortars were thus used for peeling husked grain (and for a purpose quite distinct from that of the mills in the same room), and this employment of them was so common in the seventeenth century that it did not need detailed description.[6]

A ninth-century map of the monastery of St. Gallen in Switzerland[7] provides a link in time between this modern evidence and that of antiquity. This map shows a mill divided into three parts. The first is the 'place for parching the grain' (*locus ad torrendas annonas*),[8] the second contains the *pilae*,[9] and the third the *molae*: once again the distinction between the mill and the mortar is clear, and it is highly probable, from its geographical location,[10] that this installation was intended for husked wheat.

[1] For a Greek parallel see Blümner, p. 19, fig. 3.
[2] *Zambesi*, p. 542 (quoted by *BE*, i. 112): my italics.
[3] Lindet, 1899, p. 423; cf. *BE*, i. 113.
[4] G. A. Böckler, *Theatrum Machinarum Novum* (Nuremberg, 1673), fig. 10 and text (my translation); cf. Lindet, 1899, p. 423 and fig. 7.
[5] Cf. the *pilum praeferratum* of Plin. *N.H.* xviii. 97, on which see Blümner, p. 16, n. 2.
[6] Cf. also, for millet in modern Rhodesia, A. I. Richards, *Land, Labour, and Diet in N. Rhodesia* (Oxford, 1939), pp. 91–92.
[7] See Meringer, pp. 23–24.
[8] Cf. the φρύγετρον and κοδομεῖον of Poll. vi. 64, which was, however, probably a *vessel* for roasting grain; see Blümner, p. 11, n. 4.
[9] Not *mortaria*—even in the ninth century.
[10] Switzerland has long been the centre of the cultivation of *triticum spelta*.

It is, of course, impossible to prove for every instance in which mills and mortars are found together that they were used for different purposes, and it would be surprising if such proof were possible. But it is so unlikely that mills and mortars were used side by side for the same purpose, and the use of the mortar for hulling (together, perhaps, with some further reduction of *husked* grain) is so well established, that it may probably be inferred from its presence in the same place with a mill that husked grain was in use in that neighbourhood. If this inference cannot be regarded as quite certain it is because it is just possible that the mortar may have been used for a first operation in actual grinding. An operation of this kind might be employed in order to flatten the grain and thus to facilitate the work of the mill; but there is no evidence that 'naked' wheat was subjected to such an operation in antiquity.[1]

It appears, then, that the appliances commonly classed together as mortars fall into two groups of which only one was primarily used for pounding. Mortars of this group—the ὅλμος and the *pila*—were employed, among their many other uses, in the preparation of grain for human consumption. For small quantities they may have served instead of a mill; but where more advanced mills were available the basic difference in the mode of operation makes it most unlikely that mortar and mill were used for the same purpose. In these cases the mortar appears to have been used predominantly on husked grains with the primary object of removing the outer husks. The place of the mortar in the history of milling after the most primitive epoch is a far less prominent one than has commonly been thought,[2] and it can at this point be dismissed from the present discussion, although its variety of forms and uses presents a fruitful subject for separate investigation.

[1] The 'hollow engine' (*cava machina*) mentioned for grain by Ovid, *Fast.* vi. 381, was probably not a mortar: the words may equally well describe a mill; cf. the ' "lap" of the mill' (*gremium molarum*) in [Virg.] *Moret.* 23.

[2] Storck and Teague, op. cit., p. 48, again note that 'the mortar was a side path, leading to a dead end'; but they again fail to tackle the problem of its survival side by side with advanced mills.

V

TERRACOTTA FIGURES

THE mortar, then, stands outside that line of development which in classical antiquity led from the saddle-quern described in Chapter III to the mechanical water-driven mill, and we must now ask when the first significant advance over the saddle-quern was made. The primary evidence for an answer to this question must clearly come from extant millstones, but a valuable addition to this evidence is provided by terracotta figures of various periods depicting the grain-mill at work. Before the stones themselves are discussed something must be said about these figures which were completely misunderstood by those who took it for granted that only rotary grain-mills were known during our period.

Ever since the importance of the saddle-quern was recognized, certain statuettes found in Egyptian tombs, from the third dynasty (c. 3000 B.C.) onwards, have been universally identified as depicting the biblical 'maidservant that is behind the mill'. One of these statuettes, on view in the British Museum, is shown in Plate 1, Fig. a, and Bennett and Elton's *History of Corn Milling*[1] gives details of many others. Though belonging to different periods of Egyptian history all these statuettes are essentially alike. A human being—usually a woman, but sometimes a man—is shown kneeling on both knees behind a slab of stone with a flat upper surface. This stone is set either horizontally level or, much more frequently, at an angle of 15 degrees or so, sloping away from the human figure whose knees are usually very close to the higher end of the stone. The figure itself is bent forward from the waist. Its arms are straight and its palms are bent grasping the two ends of a movable upper stone which rests on the sloping slab just described with its length across the width of the latter. The posture of the figure is such that the full weight of the upper part of the body is brought to bear on the stone in its hands. The upper stone is usually rather less long than the lower stone is wide; it is shaped rather like a 'Vienna loaf'—approximately a half-cylinder,

[1] i. 38 ff.

tapering away conically at the ends where it is grasped by the hands. At the lower end of the large stone there appears in several instances a hollowed recess which, if it is right to see in these figures saddle-querns with their operators, must have been intended for the reception of the ground product.

One indication that this explanation of these figures is correct comes from their relation to others[1] which obviously depict the baking of some kind of cake or bread, and on one of the Gizeh figures of the sixth dynasty the two activities are going on side by side. In addition to this the survival of the saddle-quern in primitive countries provides further evidence: Livingstone's sketch of a negro woman using a saddle-stone in nineteenth-century Africa shows 'no practical variation from the form of the statuettes of the time of the Pharaohs';[2] Bennett and Elton give other modern parallels from various primitive parts of the world far distant from each other (including America in the eighteenth century); and there are even more recent witnesses to the fact that this method of grinding is still being employed today in some regions and societies as it was in others when they reached the same stage of civilization many centuries ago.[3] Everywhere the saddle-quern was the first major improvement on the original 'rock-crushers',[4] bringing with it the change from pounding grain to rubbing it between two stones. Although stone-mills were later to develop in many ways, this new principle was not finally superseded until the roller-mill came into use in the nineteenth century: it was only then that the Iron Age really began in milling.

In view of the similarity between saddle-querns belonging to very different epochs and parts of the world there is nothing unreasonable in the claim that the stone which Dörpfeld reports as having been found *in situ* at Hissarlik[5] provides an example from real life of that which is depicted by the Egyptian statuettes just described. If, moreover, analogous figures are found in classical Greece it may safely be inferred that they, too, represent the same activity.

[1] See *BE*, i. 46–48; cf. Storck and Teague, p. 67.
[2] *BE*, i. 83; Livingstone, *Zambesi* (1865), p. 544.
[3] See, e.g., A. I. Richards, *Land, Labour, and Diet in N. Rhodesia*, p. 103 and n. 2, where very hard work on the saddle-stone is said to produce about 10 lb. of coarse millet meal per hour.
[4] See above, p. 24, and *BE*, i. 3 ff.
[5] Cf. above, p. 20.

A Theban terracotta group (now in the Louvre) of the latter part of the sixth century B.C.[1] may well be relevant here, although it has also been thought to illustrate the kneading of the dough. In 1899 Lindet described it as

un groupe de quatre personnages, hommes ou femmes, occupés à manœuvrer un objet qui peut être évidemment un fragment de pâte à pain ou de pâte céramique, mais qui peut être également une pierre destinée à écraser le grain,

and this is a fair statement of the case. In addition to these four figures the group contains a flute-player—and for corn-grinding musical accompaniment is particularly well attested in ancient literature:[2] but since other occupations (including kneading) were at times similarly accompanied,[3] this point cannot be pressed, and Lindet's doubts must still prevail.

The British Museum possesses a small working doll of terracotta (Plate 1, Fig. *b*) which is also in a posture similar to that of the Egyptian statuettes.[4] Since the legs are missing (and were probably never there), it is impossible to say whether this figure, too, is meant to be kneeling. The board behind which the worker (in this case a woman) appears has raised ledges round three of its sides and is therefore rather different from the normal saddle-stones. Since, moreover, the woman's hands were empty when the model was found, the question of interpretation becomes even more difficult than usual, and the Museum authorities themselves do not wish to have the rolling-pin which they have since supplied by way of reconstruction considered as more than a guess. The date of this figure, which comes from a grave in Kameiros on the island of Rhodes, has been definitely established as the middle

---

[1] Blümner, pp. 63–64 and fig. 25; Lindet, *Rev. Arch.* 1899, pt. ii, p. 419; Poittier, ibid., pt. i, p. 11, fig. 8; Perrot–Chipiez, *Histoire de l'art dans l'antiquité*, viii, p. 138, pl. 1; *DS*, iv. fig. 5695.

[2] Cf. Blümner, p. 32, notes 4–5; *PW*, xvi. 1068. The evidence, which unfortunately does not contain a reference to the flute, includes a well-known 'mill-song', reported by Plutarch (*Conv. Sept. Sap.* 14, p. 157e): ἄλει, μύλα, ἄλει· καὶ γὰρ Πιττακὸς ἄλει, μεγάλας Μυτιλάνας βασιλεύων. ('Grind, mill, grind; for Pittacus too did grind, though he ruled great Mytilene.')

[3] Blümner (p. 64, n. 3) quotes an Etruscan custom of 'kneading, boxing, and flogging to the music of the flute' from Alcimus (*ap.* Ath. xii. 518b); cf. K. Bücher, *Arbeit und Rhythmus*[2] (Leipzig, 1899), pp. 42, 52, 60 ff. (esp. 61), 88, 319, and LXX *Eccles.* xii. 4.

[4] This figure has not apparently been published before in connexion with milling or breadmaking.

of the fifth century B.C., and another figure from the same place
and of the same date, also in the British Museum,[1] which shows
a woman *standing* behind a raised basin and kneading dough, suggests at any rate that the subject of milling and breadmaking is
one which can legitimately be expected on a terracotta of this
type.[2]

In this case, as with the group discussed before it, it is impossible to arrive at any certain conclusion; but it is at least possible
that they depict the age-old custom of grinding corn on a saddle-
quern. Another terracotta figure, moreover, which is now in the
Louvre, is so similar to the Egyptian statuettes that it can be
accepted as certainly relevant here.[3] This figure (Plate 2, Fig. *a*)
comes from Thebes and belongs to the third quarter of the sixth
century B.C. It shows a headless man sitting on his heels and
leaning over a sloping stone which, although the details of the
man's activity are indistinct, can hardly fail to be a saddle-stone :
if so, this terracotta shows the saddle-quern in use in Greece
during a period well within the memory of many of those who
fought in the Persian wars.

Bennett and Elton considered the kneeling position (on both
knees) of most of the Egyptian statuettes a certain indication that
it is milling which is depicted,[4] and the parallel modern evidence
supports this contention. The posture of the worker is a fair
criterion since a person kneeling in this way can most easily bring
substantial weight to bear on the stone for long periods. Even if it
is impossible with some of the Greek figures, owing to the absence
of the lower limbs, to be certain of the position, and even if the
worker is not kneeling in every case, it is relevant to ask with regard to any given figure whether its position is such as would be
natural if it were desired to bring pressure to bear on the stone.
In this way the three pieces here discussed can be distinguished

---

[1] B 234; with it cf. Blümner, figs. 27 and 28.

[2] The golden figure of what was thought to be his 'baking girl' (ἀρτοκόπος) which
Croesus sent to Delphi (Hdt i. 51. 5) deserves mention at this point.

[3] This figure is mentioned by Lindet (1899, p. 419 and n. 2) who describes it as
the figure of a woman and as belonging to the fifth century. The details given in the
text, which were ascertained after cleaning, have been kindly supplied, together
with the photograph, by Mlle Simone Besques-Mollard of the Department of
Greek and Roman Antiquities at the Louvre. (Apart from Lindet's mention of it,
the figure has not to my knowledge been published.)

[4] i. 46: some of the figures in the British Museum do not, however, conform to
this rule.

PLATE I

a. EGYPTIAN 'MAIDSERVANT BEHIND THE MILL'
Wooden model from Asyut, *c.* 2000 B.C.
British Museum

b. WORKING MODEL OF WOMAN AT SADDLE-QUERN (?)
From Kameiros (Rhodes), mid-fifth century B.C.
British Museum

PLATE 2

a. MAN AT SADDLE-QUERN
Terracotta from Thebes, third quarter of sixth century B.C.
Louvre

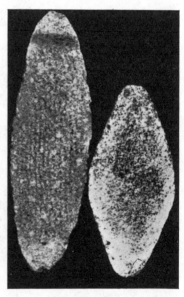

b. LOWER MILLSTONE FROM
OLYNTHUS

c. UPPER STONES OF SADDLE-
QUERNS FROM OLYNTHUS

from others—such as the kneading woman mentioned a little earlier and a group in the National Museum at Athens[1]—where the figures are standing. (In the last case it is, in spite of the presence of a sieve, certain from the finished loaves shown that it is kneading which is depicted.) This Athens group, incidentally, yields a further criterion which is perhaps rather more fruitful: in all figures which are more or less certainly connected with kneading some kind of basin or trough[2] is present, and the absence of this in a terracotta which otherwise could be connected with either milling or baking may be taken as evidence that it is milling which is being shown.

The evidence of the terracottas, once again, is far from plentiful. Such as it is, it suggests that the saddle-quern was in use in classical Greece in its primitive form. But once again the question whether it can be argued from silence that the saddle-quern was the only grain-mill then in use must be left unanswered for the present.

---

[1] Blümner, p. 62, fig. 24.

[2] Perhaps the θυεία and κάρδοπος respectively; cf. above, p. 22, n. 4.

VI

THE SADDLE-QUERN IN CLASSICAL GREECE

SOCRATES, according to Xenophon,[1] advised one Aristarchus to get rid of the poverty imposed upon him by refugee relations by using them for various trades, among which breadmaking is included,[2] just as Ceramon and others had done with their slaves, becoming wealthy in consequence. Aristarchus objects that as free people his relations cannot be employed in this way. Socrates' reply to this objection need not concern us: the passage shows clearly that there were in Athens by the end of the fifth century B.C. men who had grown rich by running bakeries. It goes without saying that these men were looked down upon by those with a 'liberal education',[3] and it is clear from this passage that it was unusual to employ anyone but a slave for the actual work[4]—but the commercial bakery had clearly come into being. Plato provides another reference to a commercial baker,[5] and the existence of this trade is implied also by the references to 'bread-sellers' (ἀρτοπώλιδες) in Aristophanes,[6] since the wares which these women sold must have been produced on a commercial scale.[7]

Beyond the few facts vouchsafed to us by Xenophon, Plato, and Aristophanes, we know nothing about these bakeries—nor is it possible to say whether or no they were confined to Athens at this

---

[1] *Mem.* ii. 7. 3 ff.

[2] ἀρτοποιΐα. (The list also includes ἀλφιτοποιΐα; cf. below, p. 149.)

[3] The degree of contempt presumably depended on how far they demeaned themselves by doing more than invest in the business. Some of them probably ranked among the independent craftsmen or δημιουργοί, on whom see *PW* s.v.

[4] The 'breadmakers from the mills' whom Nicias required for the Sicilian expedition in 415 B.C. (Thuc. vi. 22) were to be compelled to serve for hire, and were therefore almost certainly not slaves. But this was probably an exception, and elsewhere breadmakers (σιτοποιοί) are usually women, and normally women slaves. Criminals may also have been used, but this again may apply only to condemned slaves; cf. Blümner, p. 33, n. 2, and references there.

[5] *Gorg.* 518b (ἀρτοκόπος, cf. below, p. 38, n. 3).

[6] *Vesp.* 238; *Ran.* 858.

[7] In an Aristophanic fragment the bread shop (ἀρτοπώλιον) is 'the abode of the baking ovens' (*Fr.* 1 = 155 *ex* Ath. iii. 112e).

early time—but their existence at Athens in the fifth century
B.C. is certain.[1] At the same time, however, slave bakers, milling
their owners' grain, must still have served in many of the larger
households. This had long been the practice in many parts of the
world, and the baker at Pharaoh's court whose dream is interpreted in the book of Genesis[2] has his later oriental counterparts
in the 'baking girl' whose statue was sent to Delphi by Croesus,[3]
in the baker whom Cyrus gave as a present,[4] and in the bakers
who were to be found among the slaves of the Persian generals
Mardonius[5] and Tiribazus.[6]

But not all the evidence comes from the east: when Priam's
daughter Polyxena in Euripides' *Hecuba*[7] mournfully expects
that her fate after the fall of Troy must include the making of
bread in the house of one of the Greek chiefs, we are not only
reminded of the slaves whom Homer[8] mentions as so engaged, but
we are surely justified in taking the passage as some evidence
also for Athens in the late fifth century B.C. This is confirmed by
a more direct reference to a baking girl (σιτοποιός) in one of Theo-
phrastus' *Characters*, written approximately a century later.[9]

The position in fifth-century Athens, then, was very similar to
that which the excavations at Pompeii have shown to have existed
in the cities of Italy in the first century A.D. Large households still
had their own mills and bakeries, but those too small for this were
catered for by commercial miller-bakers. That the two trades of
milling and baking must have gone together in the fifth century,
as they did in Roman days, seems self-evident: it was only the
advent of the mechanical windmill and water-mill, the location
of which is determined by natural conditions, which made the
separate mill an economic necessity. As long as the baker can
himself economically produce the flour he needs as and when he
needs it, the combination of the mill with the bakery has obvious
advantages.

At Pompeii some twenty bakeries—some of the domestic,

---

[1] The passages here quoted all belong to the fifth or early fourth century B.C.:
similar references become increasingly common later.

[2] xl. 1 ff. (ἀρχισιτοποιός, LXX). [3] Hdt. i. 51. 5.

[4] Xen. *Cyr.* v. 5. 39. [5] Hdt. ix. 82. 1. [6] Xen. *An.* iv. 4. 21.

[7] l. 362. [8] *Od.* vii. 104, xx. 105 ff.

[9] iv. 7, and cf. Plaut. *Merc.* 396, 416. There are several fifth- and fourth-century
references to the mill as a building (μυλών; cf. Blümner, p. 36, n. 2); but there is
never anything to show whether it was within the household or part of a commercial establishment.

others of the commercial type—have been discovered by excavation. In the Greek world, with one possible exception, not a single commercial mill has yet been found that could belong to an age earlier than that of imperial Rome. (The possible exception is a site in southern Attica[1] where so many millstones were found together in one place that the existence of a commercial mill in that place becomes very probable. If an inscription referring to the site has been rightly interpreted,[2] this mill, which appears to have been connected with religious worship, must go back to at least the first half of the fourth century B.C., though some of the objects found there may be considerably less old.) Our task here would be much easier if one of the bakeries mentioned in literature—such as that of Thearion, which seems to have enjoyed special fame (or notoriety)[3]—were to be found. Meanwhile the existence of the commercial mill-bakery must be allowed for as a factor contributing to the comparative scarcity of material from other places; for the concentration of much of the milling and baking in a few establishments diminishes the chances of finding milling implements by excavation.

Yet such finds are by no means unknown. Schliemann long ago mentioned the discovery in the earliest debris of the Athenian acropolis of saddle-stones similar to those which he found elsewhere,[4] and stones of the same kind have been found on many later sites also. It would be tedious, and quite unnecessary, to give details of all these finds: a few of the archaeological discoveries made in Greece will be enough to show that the saddle-quern was not merely a relic of the remote past at the time when Thearion's baking-ovens provided Aristophanes' bread-sellers with their wares.

Among excavated sites of the right age (and, incidentally, among those most fully reported) a prominent place is taken by Olynthus on the mainland of the Chalcidic peninsula, largely because the destruction of the city in 348 B.C. gives a reasonably

[1] Boundazeza; see J. H. Young, *Hesperia*, x. 190. The excavation report was written in the belief that rotary and non-rotary mills were commonly used side by side: it does not provide any conclusive evidence for the early existence of the former.

[2] *Hesperia*, vii. 1 ff. with Ferguson's comments (esp. on line 46), ibid. 57.

[3] It is mentioned both in the Aristophanic fragment and in the passage from Plato's *Gorgias* cited above.

[4] See, e.g., *Tiryns* (Eng. trans., 1886), pp. 80–81.

certain fifth- or fourth-century date to the objects brought to light by the excavations. For articles found there in any considerable number this date can be taken as quite certain, since objects which are plentiful among the remains can hardly either have reached the site after it had become deserted, or have been of great antiquity when the city was destroyed.

On this basis a classical date may confidently be assigned to the saddle-querns of which by 1938 fourteen examples had been found at Olynthus,[1] side by side with a rather different and more advanced type of grain-mill which will be discussed presently. The lower stones of these querns are indistinguishable from those of the more advanced mills, except that in one case the two stones of a saddle-quern were found together. These lower stones, illustrated in Plate 2, Fig. *b*, are remarkably constant in size, their length varying between 18 and 24 in., their width between 12 and 18 in., and their thickness between 2 and $2\frac{3}{4}$ in. Their shape is more regular than that of earlier examples, and they also, for the most part, show one important innovation: they are 'regularly, but not always, striated with incised lines: sometimes in a herringbone pattern, sometimes at right angles to the length, sometimes in both directions'.[2]

Though absent on some stones of Roman date, these striations are common to later millstones of all types, and they are familiar to us from modern stone-mills where they are invariably present. On rotary mills striations have a triple purpose: they give the stones a better grip on the grain by keeping their pores free from clogging; they enable the mill to cut rather than crush the grain at its first contact with the stones, thus keeping the bran in larger pieces; and they help to control the speed at which the grist passes through the mill. The first two of these functions apply also to non-rotary grinders: the last was less important in the case of the saddle-quern, since the same result could be achieved by adjusting the slope of the lower stone. Yet the herring-bone pattern in which the striations appear on some of the Olynthian stones could hardly have been due to the other two factors, and must have helped to regulate the flow of the grist, especially when, in the more advanced Olynthian mills, the stones were no longer set at a slope.

The occurrence of these striations on some of the stones found

[1] Robinson and Graham, *Excavations at Olynthus*, viii. 326.   [2] Ibid. 329.

at Olynthus is helpful, incidentally, for the interpretation of some literary passages. Aristophanes[1] mentions a 'good newly-cut mill-stone, sharp enough to crush my temper', and Herodas[2] in one of his mimes speaks of the cutting of an upper millstone (ὄνος) for the small sum of four obols. In both cases it is probably the re-cutting or 'dressing' of an old stone, rather than the provision of an entirely new one, that is meant.[3]

The upper stones of the Olynthian saddle-querns (see Plate 2, Fig. c) are $15\frac{1}{2}$–$21\frac{1}{2}$ in. long, $5\frac{1}{4}$–8 in. wide, and 2–$4\frac{1}{2}$ in. thick. They are flat on one face and convex on the other, and thus re-semble 'an egg cut longitudinally through the middle' to which earlier examples are compared by Schliemann,[4] though the egg has in the course of development become somewhat elongated. In some cases wear of the central part of the grinding surface leaves the ends projecting like handles (see left of Fig. c).[5] Here again striations—longitudinal in this case—are sometimes, though not always, found:[6] from the literary evidence, where the dressing of the 'donkey' is more prominent than either that of the mill as a whole or that of the lower stone,[7] we should expect grooving more often on the upper than on the lower stones, but the finds and literary passages in question are too few to be decisive on this point.

Other saddle-stones have come to light in the recent American excavations of the Athenian agora, where specimens that had evidently been discarded are sometimes found among the rubbish in disused wells. Researches into the *tholos* (the official banqueting house) and its predecessors have brought to light some saddle-querns among debris belonging to the late sixth century B.C.,[8] and

[1] *Vesp.* 648.

[2] 6. 84. Blümner, who believed that donkey-mills must have existed when Herodas wrote, yet shows convincingly that this passage has nothing to do with mill-donkeys (p. 30, n. 5).

[3] This 'dressing' was probably the function of the μυλοκόπος or ὀνοκόπος; see LS. The Latin equivalent is *molicudus* (*Corp. Gl.* iii. 308. 55; 530. 8), but some medieval writers thought μυλοκόπος meant 'miller' (*moliarius*, ibid. ii. 373. 63)—presumably because ἀρτοκόπος means 'baker'; cf. above, p. 34, n. 5 and Blümner, p. 31, n. 1. [Jahn thought the 'donkey-cutter' (ὀνοκόπος) was a whip!]

[4] See above, p. 19.   [5] *Olynthus*, viii. 326.

[6] The fact that striations are present even on some badly worn stones shows that they must have been periodically renewed, and thus illustrates what Aristophanes and Herodas are likely to have meant.

[7] i.e. the μύλη, in both senses of the word; cf. above, p. 3, n. 4.

[8] H. A. Thompson, *Hesperia*, Supp. 4 (1940), p. 25; the date is discussed ibid., p. 28.

a well filled up about a century later has yielded some samples of what in the excavation report are described as millstones:[1] that these, too, were saddle-stones is made clear later in the report[2] where it is clearly stated that the broken millstones found in levels associated either with the archaic buildings on the site or with the *tholos* itself are 'of the simple saddle-quern type which was in common use with little change from the neolithic period well into classical times'. They are cut from a 'highly abrasive dark coloured igneous stone',[3] and their shape appears to have been very similar to that of the stones found at Olynthus. The two specimens of which details are given in the report are fragmentary, and some of their dimensions are doubtful; but those which can be ascertained fall within the limits quoted from Olynthus. A similar lower stone, of the late sixth century, was found in 1937 during excavations on the northern slope of the Athenian acropolis,[4] and its size, too, agrees with the Olynthus limits, while a variation in thickness between its two ends suggests that, like the prehistoric stones, it was set at a slope when used. A 'circular mill' found in the same place was probably not a mill at all, and was interpreted as such only because it was not known that a circular mill belonging to the sixth century B.C. would be a very remarkable discovery.

Delos, too, provides examples of the saddle-stone, both from its prehistoric settlements and from those of the Graeco-Roman era. The dating of these examples is much less certain than that of the finds discussed hitherto; but the prehistoric stones from Delos are similar in every respect to those reported by Schliemann, and the later examples closely resemble the stones just described. The lower stones are again rectangular, either of constant thickness throughout or sloping from one end to the other, and sometimes show striations similar to those found at Olynthus; nor do the sizes of either the upper or the lower stones differ materially from those of stones found elsewhere.[5] (The variations in both size and shape are, however, rather greater than elsewhere, but this is only to be expected from a site which extends

---

[1] Ibid. 96.   [2] Ibid. 143.   [3] Ibid. 144, and fig. 104.
[4] O. Broneer, *Hesperia*, vii. 209: length 19·1 in.; width 15·2 in.; thickness 2·6–3·3 in.
[5] See *Délos*, xviii. 124–6 and plates 48–49, where the following dimensions are given: length of lower stones 13·8–25·6 in., width 10·2–18·5 in., thickness 1·4–2·8 in.; length of upper stones 10–16 in., width 4–8 in.

through many centuries.) Only one type of stone found on Delos must briefly be discussed because the accepted interpretation of it seems to be wrong.

Certain Delian stones, of lava and approximately hemispherical, have deep grooves in them which evidently served for the attachment of a wooden handle or something similar. Now upper stones of non-rotary mills with wooden handles to facilitate the to-and-fro movement are by now well known and will be discussed presently. These stones, however, and other similar stones found elsewhere, have been explained[1] as being, as it were, the upper stones of saddle-querns used for pounding rather than rubbing. They would then be like the pestles of the semi-mechanical mortars mentioned earlier[2] which were suspended and counterbalanced in order to relieve the operator of the need for lifting the pestle after each blow.

The similarity between the material of these stones and that of the normal upper millstones gives this explanation some plausibility; and it is indeed possible that they were used for some kind of pounding operation. Pounding on the saddle-stone is, however, both in itself unlikely and completely unsubstantiated by the signs of wear on the stones that have been found; and the grooving of the lower stones would become utterly pointless if they were used in this way, since none of the purposes for which stones are grooved could then be achieved. The action of pounding (πτίσσειν and pinsere; often, as has been shown, connected with the hulling of husked grain) was always clearly distinguished from that of grinding (ἀλετρεύειν and molere) :[3] for the suspension theory to become plausible so far as the saddle-quern is concerned the two activities would have to be confused, and this confusion is not borne out by the evidence. The reconstruction itself may well be correct, but if so, it was certainly not the lower stone of a saddle-quern on which these suspended hemispherical stones were used.

One other type of upper stone must here be mentioned. Among a large number of 'millstones' (presumably lower stones of the usual kind) found in the milling establishment in southern Attica mentioned earlier, two complete and several fragmentary upper

[1] By Hock, *Schumacher Festschrift*, 1930, pp. 80–84.
[2] Above, pp. 23, 27.
[3] Cf. Meringer, *Wörter und Sachen*, i. 3 ff. and above, p. 24, n. 2.

stones were found of a type equipped with fingerholds.[1] That these stones were grinders is made probable by the grooving of their flat surfaces and by the place where they were found. They do not differ essentially from the ordinary saddle-quern, but are merely a somewhat peculiar form of it, due perhaps to nothing more than the idiosyncrasy of one particular mill-owner: no parallel finds have been made elsewhere.

The examples here quoted should suffice to show that the ordinary saddle-quern, made rather handier by the elongation of the upper stone and by the introduction of grooving on both stones, was widely used in Greece until well into classical times and perhaps until the end of the classical era. The details that have been given of some of the specimens found will make it possible to understand the development which the saddle-quern underwent at some time before the fall of Olynthus, at a time when in all probability it was itself still in common use.

[1] J. H. Young, *Hesperia*, x. 190 and fig. 11d. (The dating of the discoveries is uncertain owing to the circumstances in which they were made.)

VII

THE 'HOPPER-RUBBER'

I N a pseudo-Virgilian poem, in which the operation of a rotary hand-quern is described, 'the left hand is bent on serving, the right on the work of the mill' :[1] one hand gradually fed the grist into the quern while the other turned the stone, and in this way grinding could continue for some time without interruption. It was different with the saddle-quern which required both hands for its operation: only a little grain could be put between the stones at a time, and whenever the mill was empty the worker had to stop for a moment to renew the supply. That this frequent stopping was felt to be inconvenient is shown by a development of the saddle-quern which took place in Greece and the distinguishing feature of which is a slit in the upper stone. This slit, together with a cavity in the stone, evidently served as a hopper from which the grain could feed into the mill automatically.

Except on some rotary querns, hoppers were to become the invariable rule later with animal and mechanical mills of all kinds, for the simple reason that it is wasteful to employ human labour for a task which can equally well be performed by a box with an opening in its lower side through which the grain can by gravity feed into the mill in a controlled flow. In the case of the saddle-quern the provision of a rather more primitive hopper marks a step forward in the development of the mill by diminishing, however slightly, the amount of human labour needed to produce a given amount of meal.

In the Greek world this development took two forms one of which is logically prior to the other, though the available evidence does not show whether it is prior also in time. The 'earlier' of these two forms, illustrated in Fig. 2, is a very simple adaptation of the ordinary saddle-quern. The upper stone is widened and a cavity made in it large enough to receive a fair quantity of grain. A slit is then made at the bottom of this 'hopper' (its exact width being a matter for experiment) through which the grain can gradually feed into the mill to be ground. The hopper

[1] *Moretum* 25: 'laeva ministerio, dextra est intenta labori.'

itself is round or nearly so, and the stone has two lateral projections in line with the ends of the slit by which it can be grasped.[1]

Stones of this type have been found at Priene[2] and on Delos:[3] they are distinguished by their rounded shape and by their stone 'handles', for which two slots are substituted on the rectangular

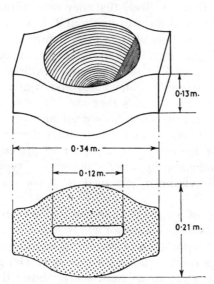

FIG. 2. 'Hopper-rubber' from Priene

stones of the 'more advanced' (and much more common) type of which a few specimens from Olynthus are shown in Plate 3, Figs. *a* to *d*. These slots were connected with a contrivance, to be described presently, for facilitating the miller's work which had the incidental effect of making the mills in which these slotted stones were used less easily portable than either the saddle-quern or the 'earlier' form of 'hopper-rubber'.[4] With this innovation the mill became a fixture for the first time since hollows in the

---

[1] Childe (*Antiquity*, xvii. 22) compares these 'handles' with those of certain saddle-querns of the Iberic Iron Age found in Catalonia (*Anuari d'Estudis Catalans*, vi. 647, fig. 49); cf. also above, p. 38, and Plate 2, Fig. *c*.

[2] Wiegand–Schrader, *Priene*, p. 393.

[3] *Délos*, xviii. 126: only one example, 9·4 in. long and 5·1 in. wide.

[4] This convenient name was given to both the types here under discussion by Childe, loc. cit.

natural rock were used for grinding corn. If, therefore, it is not
the ordinary saddle-quern which, in the passage discussed earlier,
was called a 'hand-mill' by Xenophon,[1] it is probably the 'early'
hopper-rubber: by contrast with the more developed form,
where the hands did not actually touch the stone, it may well be
thus described, and the two types of hopper-rubber are so similar
in appearance that it is likely that they were in existence at the
same time. The need for a portable mill, in circumstances like
those described by Xenophon, was evidently still felt after the
invention of the fixed grinding-machine, just as later the rotary
hand-quern remained in use for many centuries after the invention of animal-mills, water-mills, and windmills. It is this
consideration which suggests that the logically prior form of
hopper-rubber was not necessarily prior in time. A rectangular
stone found on Thera,[2] similar to the 'more developed' type but
fitted with handle-grips of stone instead of the usual slots, also
lends colour to the assumption that the 'earlier' type may well be
a secondary development designed to make the hopper-mill
portable.

The purpose of all these stones, which have been found in
great numbers, was unknown for a very long time. The merit of
their correct interpretation probably belongs to Flinders Petrie[3]
who in 1888 was quite certain what they were. During the following twenty-five years or so most writers ignored Petrie's discoveries,[4] and the stones in question were explained as sieves[5]
or even as windows.[6] It is only since Kourouniotes[7] showed the
connexion between the 'more advanced' of the two types and the
two non-rotary mills on the 'Homeric' bowl, which had recently
been published, that the function of these stones has been generally
understood.

On this bowl the two millers (ΜΥΛΩΘΡΟΙ; see Fig. 1, p. 13) are
each standing by a mill which rests on a table, and are operating
this mill by means of a long handle which is pivoted behind the

---

[1] Cyr. vi. 2. 31; see above, p. 17.
[2] Thera (ed. H. v. Gaertringen), iii. 181, fig. 193.
[3] Tanis, ii. 27; cf. BE, i. 53. (Childe ascribes the correct explanation to Elton,
who, however, expressly disclaims it.)
[4] e.g. Lindet and Blümner, but not BE. As recently as 1933 these stones were
again ignored in PW, xvi. 1069.
[5] Cf. below, p. 59 and n. 3.
[6] See DS, iii. 1034, and Monumenti Antichi dei Lincei, xxiii. 731.
[7] Ἀρχ. Ἐφ. 1917, p. 153.

PLATE 3

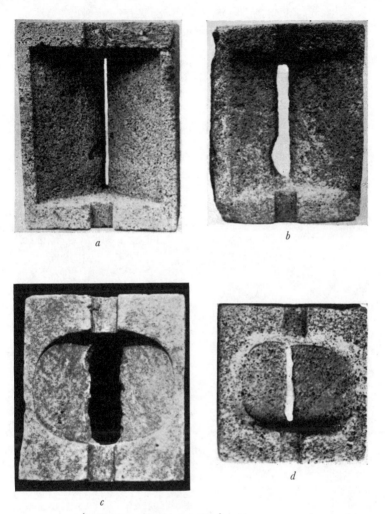

a

b

c

d

'ADVANCED HOPPER-RUBBERS' FROM OLYNTHUS

stones.[1] The upper stones to which these handles, or levers, are attached are of the type illustrated in Plate 3, Figs. *a* to *d*, and shown diagrammatically in Fig. 3: since they are, like other

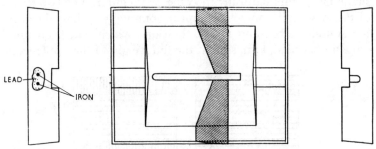

FIG. 3. Upper stone of 'Olynthian' grain-mill

objects on the bowl, turned towards the spectator for greater clarity (cf. above, p. 14), their shape, which resembles Plate 3, Fig. *c*, is distinctly visible. The characteristic slots cannot be seen, since the lever lies across them; but holes and traces of iron-and-lead fastenings on some extant stones of this kind (see Fig. 3)

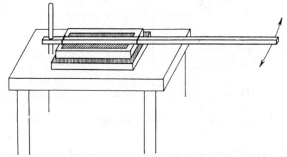

FIG. 4. Diagram to illustrate operation of 'Olynthian' grain-mill

show beyond doubt that it was the function of the slots to receive such a lever, which at times was probably held in position by iron clamps.

A diagrammatic reconstruction of a mill of this type appears in Fig. 4: as indicated by the arrows, the mode of operation

---

[1] The lever was probably known as κώπη (cf. *LS* s.v. 6) and the lower stone perhaps as τράπεζα; see Poll. vii. 19 and the papyri quoted by Robinson, *Olynthus*, viii. 330 (cf. 335), but cf. also *Note E*, p. 219.(In a fourth-century inscription κῶπαι must refer to persons and may mean 'mill-hands'; see Ferguson, *Hesperia*, vii. 57.)

must have been a to-and-fro movement sidewise, covering a sector of the circle of which the pivot was the centre. The upper stone was now rather larger than it had been formerly, and its shape had, quite naturally, become rectangular. The two stones of this new mill, moreover, appear commonly to have been set horizontally level, and not at the slope which had been usual with the saddle-quern, so that the full weight of the upper stone

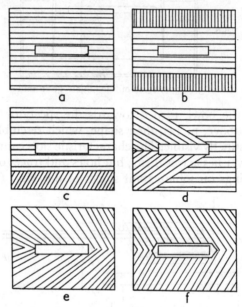

FIG. 5. Grooving patterns on 'Olynthian' hopper-rubbers

was brought to bear on the grain. The flow of the meal out of the mill was controlled by the herring-bone grooving of both stones with which we are already familiar, and Fig. 5 shows how the development of the grooving patterns was influenced by this consideration.

The provision of the lever and pivot for the upper stone represents a development far more important than would appear at first sight: in combination with the grooving of the grinding surfaces of the stones, this new arrangement meant that the mill had now become a 'machine' which by its construction controlled the particle-size of the meal it produced, irrespective of the skill and diligence of the operator.[1] It is true that this control was by no means complete, since both the length of the 'stroke' and the speed of operation still depended on the worker; but here for the first time we find a mill which controlled its own feed[2] and, by means of the striations on the stones, the discharge of the ground products. The weight of the upper stone, moreover, which was no longer supplemented by that of the human body, determined the weight that was brought to bear on the grain, while the lever-and-pivot contrivance gave at least some mechanical assistance to the force applied by the operator. (Of the two limiting factors only one—length of 'stroke'—was eliminated by the invention of the rotary mill worked by man or animal: the speed of operation was controlled only when the motive power became mechanical and the rate of revolution could be regulated by a system of gears.[3])

The problem of how to make a single machine out of the two separate millstones by attaching the upper stone to the lower obviously had to be solved before the mill could become rotary. We shall see later that the solution of this problem was probably delayed by the difficulty of fitting the stones together in such a way that the grist could be introduced while the mill was at work. The contrivance here under discussion was a rudimentary attempt to overcome this difficulty, and for this reason, in addition to those just mentioned, the name 'mill' here acquires a meaning much closer to its modern meaning than when it referred to the saddle-quern, which was no more than a pair of separate stones.[4] The peculiar importance of the lever-mill for the present inquiry lies in the fact that it represents the most important specifically Greek contribution to the history of corn-milling.

[1] This, of course, only applies to the meal as it leaves the mill proper: the flour could in any case be graded (subject to a suitable size of bran particle) by the use of a sieve or sieves after grinding, though the relative amounts of coarse and fine flour that could be separated by sifting would depend on the particle size of the meal.

[2] But again only partially, since wear of the grinding surfaces must have tended to widen the slit; cf. Plate 3, Figs. b and c.

[3] The optimum speed of a rotary hand-quern can only be found by experiment: at different speeds even a good quern is inefficient.

[4] It is noteworthy in this connexion that the Hebrew word for a mill (saddle-quern) in the Old Testament is a dual (רֵחַיִם): a literal translation of Deut. xxiv. 6 is 'No man shall take to pledge a pair of millstones or (even) a "rider".'

A secondary, but perhaps archaeologically significant, conclusion follows from this. It is often pointed out that it is difficult
to distinguish between the lower stones of the ordinary saddle-
querns and those of the hopper-rubbers. The pattern of grooving
may, however, afford a criterion by which the two can be distinguished, since it is only with the arrival of the lever-operated

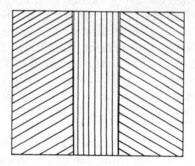

Fig. 6. Common grooving pattern on
lower stones of 'Olynthian' mills

mill that the herring-bone arrangement acquires significance.
With the earlier types of mill the operator was able—by hand or
by means of the upper stone—after grinding to push the meal
from between the stones with little inconvenience: now the worker must have stood well away from his mill, and a pattern of
grooving which guided the meal from the stone at the right time
must have considerably helped him in increasing his output. A
grooving pattern, therefore, such as that shown in Fig. 6, which
appears to have been designed with this object in view, may perhaps safely be taken to indicate that the stone in question was
used in a lever-operated mill.

The truth of this theory will be tested only when the criterion
here suggested is borne in mind in the excavation of sites where
upper stones of both the old and the new type are found:[1] that
there was a standard pattern of striation is, however, clear already,
and even a writer who considered this an 'unimportant detail'
was struck by the close similarity in this respect between stones—

---

[1] The position is, however, complicated by the possibility that the herring-bone
pattern may, *after* its invention with the lever-operated mill, also have been used
with portable mills.

upper stones in this case—from various sites.[1] This similarity,
which extends beyond the grooving patterns to all other characteristics of the stones, may be due to a common centre of manufacture from which the stones were exported to the sites where
they are now found. There is a suggestion that these stones were
known as 'Theran', and the evidence for the existence of a centre
of manufacture on the island of Thera has been well discussed
in the Olynthus excavation report.[2] This evidence is weakened
to some extent by the realization that the grooving pattern is
not as unimportant as has been thought (so that the similarity
between the stones in this respect is rather less likely to be due
merely to the caprice of one manufacturer), and the suggestion
is in any case only tentative. But the possibility remains, and the
theory may be confirmed as further evidence becomes available.

It now remains to give some details of this type of stone and of
what is known of its distribution over the Greek world. That the
lever-operated hopper-rubber was the principal grain-mill of
Greece in the classical era is made highly probable by the frequent
occurrence of stones belonging to it among the excavated remnants of Olynthus which must belong to this period. (This type
of mill will therefore from now on be referred to as 'Olynthian'.)
Thirty-one specimens of the upper stone had been found in the
excavations up to the year 1938.[3] They are described in the report
as being remarkably uniform in size and general characteristics;
made of hard black porous lava, and measuring from 0·42 to
0·57 m. [= 16·5–22·4 in.] in length, 0·36 to 0·47 m. [= 14·2–
18·5 in.] in width, and 0·08 to 0·16 m. [= 3·1–6·3 in.] in thickness.[4] Their hoppers are either rectangular or oval, the former
being rather more common.[5] The slit at the bottom of the hopper
varies from 0·15 to 0·42 m. [= 5·9–16·5 in.] in length and, when

[1] Robinson, *Olynthus*, viii. 330. Even the two parallel lines along the slit, which
Robinson thought particularly unimportant, are not without significance, since
they would help in starting the outward flow.
[2] Ibid. The 'Theban' mills mentioned in the Egyptian papyri quoted by Robinson surely support his argument, in spite of the fact that a textual corruption is
improbable: a 'foreign' name, such as 'Theran', may well have been corrupted by
popular usage into a well-known local one.   [3] Ibid. 327.
[4] One exceptional stone is 0·225 m. [= 8·9 in.] thick. The comparatively great
variation in thickness is easily accounted for by wear and recutting.
[5] Robinson comments that the two types are contemporaneous and that the
rectangular shape gives greater capacity in specimens of the same size. As against
this the oval would give greater weight to the stone and might be preferred for this
reason.

unworn and unbroken, from 0·015 to 0·03 m. [= 0·6–1·2 in.] in
width. The grinding surfaces are usually, but not invariably,
striated in a herring-bone pattern. (According to the report all
the stones may once have been striated, and the exceptions may
be due to wear coupled with bad maintenance.) The handle by
which these stones were worked is shown by the slots in the stones
to have been from 0·055 to 0·07 m. [= 2·2–2·8 in.] wide and at
least 0·02–0·03 m. [= 0·8–1·2 in.] thick. One example shows
the stumps of iron rods by which the handle was more firmly
held in place, but ordinarily no such fastening was used.[1]

The lower stones, of which twelve specimens (some possibly
belonging to ordinary saddle-querns) had been found at Olynthus
by 1938, were not conspicuously larger than the upper, and tended
to be thinner. According to the report they measure 0·45–0·59 m.
[= 17·7–23·2 in.] in length, 0·30–0·45 m. [= 11·8–17·7 in.] in
width, and 0·05–0·07 m. [= 2·0–2·8 in.] in thickness. That they
were thinner than the upper stones is not surprising since their
weight would be immaterial provided that they were secured in
some way to the table.

It was hardly necessary, owing to the way in which the mill
was worked, for the lower stone to be much longer than the
upper, but it might have been expected to be substantially wider.[2]
The fact that this was not generally so can only be explained by
supposing that the movement of the upper stone was small, and
therefore probably rapid, and that even so the upper stone would
at either end of its arc protrude beyond the edge of the lower, thus
carrying some of the meal off the stone at each stroke. (This
would always be the meal which had been between the stones
longest and had worked its way outward.) Since the upper stone
necessarily described an arc in its movement, the lower stone
might also be expected to be trapezoidal rather than rectangular,
so that it could be set with its narrow side near the pivot: one
specimen of this shape has in fact been discovered at Olynthus,
but it is exceptional.[3]

   [1] For details see Robinson, pp. 328–9. Traces of fastenings have also been found
on Delos and elsewhere.
   [2] Of the only pair found together at Olynthus both stones are 0·51 m. [=20·1 in.]
long. The full width of the lower stone is unfortunately not preserved. Of a pair found
at Priene the lower stone is 0·07 m. [= 2·8 in.] larger both in length and in width.
   [3] The grooving pattern, too, seems to have been influenced by this consideration;
cf. Fig. 5e.

The two stones were, as we have seen, usually arranged in a horizontally level position. A variation on this is shown by some Delian stones[1] where both the upper and the lower stones taper in thickness either lengthways or sideways, the two tapers offsetting each other so that the top of the mill was still level while the meal could run down a slope. Grooves in a herring-bone pattern would, however, make this unnecessary, and there is no evidence that it was at all usual.

A hopper-rubber found at Caulonia in the Greek part of southern Italy, which was once wrongly interpreted as a window,[2] shows that stones of this type were known at least as early as the sixth century B.C. From then on they became very widespread throughout the Greek world. From 'Great Greece' finds are reported from Sesso Orlando[3] as well as Caulonia; in 'Old Greece' they come not only from Delos and Olynthus but from Priene,[4] Eretria,[5] Demetrias,[6] Methana,[7] Thera,[8] Phaestos,[9] and Aegina;[10] and similar discoveries are recorded from the Greek settlements of Tanis and Naukratis in Egypt.[11] Stones from outside Greece are generally of rougher workmanship, which distinguishes them sharply from the uniformity of the Greek stones and makes it likely that they were merely local imitations of the latter. Such stones are reported from Gordion in Phrygia,[12] from Tell Halaf in northern Syria,[13] and from Alishar in central Asia Minor.[14]

There is thus abundant evidence for the widespread use of the lever-mill in the Greek world. That we can now with certainty

---

[1] Ἀρχ. Ἐφ. 1917, p. 153, fig. 2; Délos, xviii, fig. 154.
[2] Monumenti Antichi, xxiii. 731.
[3] Ibid.; cf. Childe, Antiquity, xvii. 21.
[4] Wiegand-Schrader, Priene, p. 329, fig. 474; p. 393, figs. 524–5.
[5] Ἀρχ. Ἐφ. 1917, p. 153.
[6] Stählin–Meyer–Heidner, Pagasai und Demetrias (Berlin, 1934), pp. 130–1, fig. 26, and plate xxi B, C.; cf. below, p. 52.
[7] Mitt. d. dtsch. arch. Inst., Ath. Abt., xxxiv. 347–8 and plate xxv. 3.
[8] Thera, iii. 179, 181, figs. 193, 195.
[9] Mon. Ant. xiv. 475–7, fig. 84b.
[10] Childe, Antiquity, xvii. 21.
[11] BE, i. 53; Flinders Petrie, Tanis (1888), ii. 27.
[12] Körte, Gordion, p. 176.
[13] von Oppenheim, Der Tell Halaf (Leipzig, 1931), p. 181, plate 49b, c; Eng. trans. p. 206.
[14] von der Osten, The Alishar Hüyük, Season 1927, pt. i (Univ. of Chicago Oriental Inst. Publ. 6), p. 112 and fig. 106 (where the slit is described as due to wear), and E. F. Schmidt, Seasons 1928–9, pt. ii (O.I.P. 20), pp. 76–77 and fig. 116 (where such a mill is described as rotary!).

reconstruct it we owe to the perspicacity of Kourouniotes; for although the correct explanation of the finds as millstones had been found independently, their mounting is shown only on the 'Homeric' bowl. Many incorrect suppositions about their use as millstones had been made before Kourouniotes wrote, and some of these can still be found even in quite modern reference works.[1]

We have seen that these mills must have come into being before the end of the sixth century: they certainly continued in use at least until the third century B.C., as is shown both by the 'Homeric' bowl and by their occurrence at Demetrias which was founded in 294; and they probably did not die out until considerably later.[2] That the bowl does not prove the existence of the rotary mill in early hellenistic times has already been suggested, and the question of the origin of the rotary mill must still be left open. But there is at least some evidence that the life of the 'Olynthian' mill was prolonged; for when Aulus Gellius[3] tells us that Plautus was at one time engaged in working the 'pushing-mill' (*mola trusatilis*), and when Cato[4] contrasts this 'pushing-mill' with the donkey-mill (*mola asinaria*), we may now say that it is most probable that the 'Olynthian' mill, which had been so common in earlier days, still survived in the second century B.C., and that in Roman Italy it was then described as a 'pushing-mill' by contrast with the 'turning-mill' which had by then come into use.[5] The description would certainly have been apt, and it is tempting to suppose that the mills which appear so frequently in Plautus' plays, and the mills at which Plautus himself is said to have worked, were similar to those shown on the 'Homeric' bowl which in all probability illustrates a literary subject closely akin to a Plautine comedy.

[1] e.g. K. Galling. *Biblisches Reallexicon* (Tübingen, 1937), col. 387.
[2] Those found by Boak and Petersen in the Fayûm are early Roman; see *Olynthus*, viii. 330.
[3] *N.A.* iii. 3. 14; cf. below, pp. 63 ff., where the interpretation of this passage is discussed in detail.
[4] *Agr.* 10. 4; 11. 4.
[5] This is suggested by Childe, *Antiquity*, xvii. 22; but cf. also below, p. 64.

VIII

GREEK ROTARY MILLS

IN the preceding chapters we found a number of reasons for
questioning the common belief that grain-mills were rotary,
and remained essentially unchanged, throughout classical
antiquity. Once this belief is called in question, much of the
evidence that is commonly used to support it is seen to be of remarkably little value in upholding it, and the literature of the
period in particular, down to early hellenistic times, yields none
of the indications for the existence of the revolving mill which it
has been thought to yield. It now remains to discuss certain
archaeological finds of the hellenic and early hellenistic eras
which have compelled even those who have assessed at its true
value the evidence discussed so far to believe that 'the existence of
rotary mills in Greece . . . may be regarded as archaeologically
established'.[1]

Before these finds are discussed it must once again be pointed
out that the accepted belief may itself have influenced our knowledge of archaeological discoveries. On the one hand investigators, unaware of the weak foundations on which this belief is
based, may well have described as rotary grain-mills objects
which they would not have so described had they known the
true position.[2] On the other hand it is possible also that rotary
grain-mills have failed to be reported because they were mis-
takenly thought to be too ordinary to deserve mention.

Olynthus, because of the comparatively certain date of its
finds, once again provides the most important piece of evidence.
A fragmentary 'mill' has been found there which is compared in
the report to the mills still used in Macedonia and is described
as follows:[3]

A smaller rough section, 1·19 m. [= 46·9 in.] in circumference,

---

[1] Childe, *Antiquity*, xvii. 23. (But Childe, too, considers the 'Homeric' bowl
proof positive for the existence of the donkey-mill in the third century B.C.)

[2] Analogous mistakes have been made in the translation of literary texts: the
Vulgate version of Exodus xi. 5, for instance, has a 'maidservant who is *at* [not
behind] the mill' (*ancilla quae est ad molam*).

[3] *Olynthus*, ii. 55 and fig. 146; cf. viii. 331. (Wording slightly adapted.)

goes below; a larger section with a raised broad outer edge and
grooved inside goes above. It has a deep cemented square hole in the
middle. The height is 34 cm. [= 13·4 in.], of the upper section 25 cm.
[= 9·9 in.], the upper diameter 51 cm. [= 20·1 in.].

The photograph is unfortunately rather poor, and the main
evidence for interpreting this unique find as a rotary grain-mill
appears to be in the existence of similar mills in modern Macedonia. It is unfortunate also that the stones are fragmentary and
that it is impossible, for instance, to say how this 'mill' was
turned.

The square hole in the upper stone is certainly remarkable.
Its only advantage over a round hole (which would surely have
been much easier to bore) would be its better grip on a handle
inserted in it;[1] but its purpose cannot have been to receive such
a handle since there would then be no possibility of introducing
the grist without lifting the heavy upper stone from the lower
every few seconds. The general shape of the stones, moreover,
although apparently paralleled in modern Macedonia,[2] would be
unique for a grain-mill in antiquity. For ancient support for this
interpretation the report has to rely on the supposed, but probably non-existent, donkey-mill of the 'Homeric' bowl on the one
hand, and on the Pompeian mill on the other: but the Pompeian
mill was, as we shall see, entirely different in its construction.[3]

To the present writer the description of these stones suggests
not a mill but rather, perhaps, a contrivance that might be used
for the turning of a gate. The upright post to which the gate was
to be fixed could be securely sunk in the upper stone, and, being
held in position by means of the raised band on this stone, it
could then be turned about the lower stone. The large diameter
of the stones may not be quite consistent with this conjectural
suggestion, and other explanations are no doubt possible: but the
possibility that an explanation on these lines may turn out to be
correct is well illustrated by the converse example of the hopper-
rubbers which were long thought to be windows and by parts of a
water-mill which were once interpreted as belonging to a lift-and-
swing bridge.[4] Views expressed in the Olynthus report cannot be

---

[1] But on rotary querns even the handle sockets are usually round.

[2] The comparison is not illustrated in the report.

[3] The 'intermediate forms found at Delos', which are also mentioned, are themselves probably of Roman date; see below, p. 92.

[4] *Proc. Soc. Ant. Newcastle-upon-Tyne*, 2nd ser., ii. 178 ff.; cf. below, p. 136.

lightly disregarded, and the interpretation of these stones as a grain-mill cannot be rejected outright: but the difficulties of working such a mill would have been formidable; for it left unsolved the very problems which, as we shall see, in all probability delayed the invention of the rotary mill.[1]

The upper stone of a much more handy type of mill is reported[2] from below the Athenaeum at Syracuse in Sicily from a layer between the Siculan and the archaic Greek. It is described as 'a large disc, 38 cm. [= 15·0 in.] in diameter, of extremely porous lava,[3] and of a thickness of 5·5 cm. [=2·2 in.] at the circumference and 9 cm. [= 3·5 in.] at the centre'. This stone has near its outer edge a socket for a vertical handle, which is surrounded, like the central hole, by a raised moulding. When this stone is described as belonging to a 'hand-mill' (χειρομύλη) the description is almost certainly right, though not in the sense in which the word was used by Xenophon.[4]

A considerable amount is known about the development of hand-querns of this type,[5] and the difficulty here is that this stone is such that without stratigraphical evidence it would be taken as belonging to the first century B.C. at the earliest. Childe[6] confesses 'to a certain hesitation in accepting the excavator's stratigraphical observations in attributing such a quern to the seventh century B.C.': encouraged by Childe's authority the present writer feels compelled to follow his example.

'A conical-shaped piece of lava, measuring about 0·40 m. [= c. 16 in.] in height by about 1·30 m. [= c. 51 in.] in girth at its base, which probably formed a millstone for grinding corn or other matter,' was found among the ruins of Motya, a Phoenician colony in Sicily, destroyed in 397 B.C.[7] This stone is highly reminiscent in both shape and material of the common lower stones (metae) of rotary mills of the Pompeian type; yet it seems again insufficient proof for the existence of such a mill in the fifth century B.C. The stone is not characteristic enough to put it beyond

[1] In the case of isolated objects, like these stones, it is, of course, possible that they found their way to the site of Olynthus after the city's destruction; but this hardly affects the issue.
[2] By Orsi, Mon. Ant. xxv. 568 and fig. 159.
[3] A hard porous stone was particularly suitable for mill-stones since it could never become smooth by wear; cf. below, p. 91.
[4] Cf. above, pp. 17, 44.
[5] Cf. below, Chapter XIV.   [6] Antiquity, xvii. 22–23.
[7] Whitaker, Motya (London 1921), pp. 283–4 and fig. 63.

doubt that it formed part of a mill; even if it was a *meta* it may
belong to a later occupation of the site of which several indications
have been found;[1] ordinary saddle-querns 'have been found in
abundance all over the island';[2] and again the investigators may
not have known what a rarity a fifth-century rotary mill would be.

The same tendency to assume too readily that a stone must
have formed part of a rotary mill is illustrated by the way in
which a circular stone found in 1937 during the excavations on
the northern slope of the acropolis at Athens has been interpreted.[3]
This stone measures 0·65 m. [=25·6 in.] in height by 0·60 m.
[= 23·6 in.] in diameter, and is hollowed out with an inner
diameter of 0·43 m. [= 16·9 in.] at the top; it is described as a
mill, but apparently only because it was found (in a well filled
up at the end of the sixth century B.C.) immediately above a flat
lower stone of the usual shape. There is nothing at all to show
that it was connected with grinding, or that it formed part of a
rotary mill. Similar stones have been found elsewhere,[4] and even
if they were connected in some way with grinding and baking it is
impossible to assume that they were employed as rotary mills
side by side with the 'Olynthian' type and for the same purpose.
A rotary mill, moreover, cannot consist of a lower stone which is
hollowed out and filled (or all but filled) by the revolving upper
stone: if only a little grain were introduced into such a mill at any
one time the advantages of rotary motion would be offset by the
need for never-ending stoppages in order to retrieve the meal, and
if it were to be filled with grain efficient grinding would become
impossible. We saw with regard to the Olynthian mill how care-
fully the inward flow of grain and the outward flow of meal were
controlled by the design of the stones. Rotary mills of all types
show the same preoccupation with this feature, and it is therefore
possible to say that no hollow drum can at any time have been
used—except, perhaps, in an unsuccessful experiment—as the
lower stone of such a mill; as the upper stone it can have served
only if it shows effective provision for the flow of grain into the mill.

Once the supposed donkey-mill on the 'Homeric' bowl is seen
in its proper light, there is thus remarkably little archaeological
evidence pointing to the existence of the rotary grain-mill in

---

[1] Whitaker, op. cit., p. 96.　　　　　　　[2] Ibid. 284–5 and fig. 64.
[3] *Hesperia* vii. 209.
[4] Cf., e.g., Whitaker, p. 282.

pre-Roman days.[1] The present survey would, however, be incomplete without some discussion of the use of the rotary principle with grinding appliances in other industries. Childe[2] quotes two instances of this, and feels compelled by them, in conjunction with the stones just discussed, to regard the existence of rotary mills in Greece and Sicily as proved.

Of these two examples one may safely be regarded as established for the fifth or early fourth century B.C.: five more or less

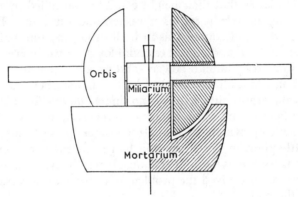

FIG. 7. Olive-mill (*trapetum*) as described by Cato

complete stones (*orbes*) belonging to olive-crushers (*trapeta*)[3] have been found at Olynthus[4] of which (in sharp contrast to the 'handmill' discussed a little earlier) both the date and the interpretation are beyond serious doubt.

The reconstruction of the *trapetum* is assisted by a passage in Cato's work *On Agriculture*[5] which is far more explicit than anything that has come down to us about grain-mills: two *orbes*, each of which formed a segment of a sphere, revolved on their edges in a large stone basin (*mortarium*) with a fixed thick stone pillar (*miliarium*) in its centre. The *orbes* were pierced in the middle and revolved round an axle which was supported on the central pillar (see Fig. 7). Further detail may be omitted here; for in the

---

[1] The Levantine evidence quoted by Childe (*Antiquity*, xvii. 23–24) does not contradict this.　　　　　　　　　　　　　　　　　　　[2] Ibid. 23.

[3] Not 'presses' (*pace* Childe, loc. cit.), which were non-rotary and different appliances altogether. (The exact form of the Latin word is doubtful; cf. *LSh.*)

[4] *Olynthus*, viii. 338.

[5] 20 ff.; on the whole subject cf. Drachmann, *Ancient Oil Mills and Presses* (Copenhagen, 1932).

present context we are concerned with only one point which may help to explain the use of this rotary appliance for oil at a time when the non-rotary 'Olynthian' mill was used for grain: it was essential in the case of the *trapetum* that the *orbes* should be suspended above the bottom of the *mortarium* at a distance which would ensure that the oil could be removed from the olives without being spoiled by crushed kernels.[1] This suspension was most easily achieved by balancing two *orbes* on opposite sides of a central pillar so that their height could be controlled by raising or lowering the axle by means of washers under its centre. Rotary motion, which, of course, was in itself in no way unusual,[2] was therefore natural and almost essential for the *trapetum* even when it was worked by human power—and we know that the *trapetum* was often, if not always, worked by two human beings.[3] In the case of the grain-mill there was no similar motive for making it rotary: here the main advantage of a revolving mill was that it made the employment of animals (or water) possible, and there was little point in this if the mill had to be stopped every few moments for emptying and refilling. It will be noticed that the *trapetum* had not solved the problem of continuous flow into and out of the mill.

It is true that the *trapetum* is less common at Olynthus than the grain-mill characteristic of that site: it is, however, sufficiently common—and the absence of any other appliance for crushing olives[4] is sufficiently marked—to enable us to regard the *trapetum* as the normal implement for crushing olives at a time when without doubt the Olynthian lever-mill was the usual appliance for grinding corn, whether or no we suppose the rotary mill to have existed side by side with it. The rotary *trapetum*, therefore, does not prove the simultaneous existence of the rotary grain-mill.

The second rotary grinding appliance that must be discussed is connected with the extraction of metal from ore. Among the appliances used for crushing mineral ore in the silver mines of

[1] That this consideration was prominent in antiquity is well shown by Drachmann, p. 9; cf. Pallad, *R.R.* xii. 17. 1; Colum. xii. 51. 2, 52. 6, 54. 2; Blümner, p. 342; Jacobi, *Saalburg Jahrbuch*, iii. 87; and below, p. 119.
[2] The potter's wheel, e.g., had long been in use; cf. Childe's chapter on 'Rotary Motion' in Singer, Holmyard, and Hall, *A History of Technology*, i (Oxford, 1954), pp. 87 ff.
[3] Cf. Blümner, p. 339, fig. 119, and p. 342 with n. 3.
[4] As opposed to pressing, which was the second of two distinct operations in the process of oil extraction.

Laurium in Attica a mill was found which, according to the report,[1] was exactly similar to the grain-mills of the 'hour-glass' type familiar from the Roman site of Pompeii. Since the Laurium mines were most intensively exploited in the fifth and early fourth century B.C. it seemed natural to take this mill as belonging to that period, on the assumption that one ancient mill was very much like another. But the silver mines at Laurium were reworked to some extent in the first century A.D.,[2] and the very similarity of the mill found at Laurium to those found at Pompeii, which was destroyed in A.D. 79, makes it highly probable that it belongs to the same period. We know from stones found on Delos that the 'hour-glass' mill was preceded by other types of donkey-mill, and we know from Pompeii and other contemporaneous sites that in the first century A.D. the 'hour-glass' type had become more or less universal: it is surely unlikely, therefore, that the donkey-mill in its Pompeian form had existed in the fifth or fourth century B.C., only to be followed later by more primitive types and to re-emerge after the lapse of five centuries.

Elsewhere the Laurium report speaks of sieves used in the same industry for sifting ore that had been crushed in the donkey-mill.[3] An illustration shows that these 'sieves' were identical in shape and dimensions with the Olynthian hopper-rubbers (which were undiscovered when the report was written), and there can be no doubt that they were in fact grinding implements. The great period of the Laurium mines roughly coincided with the century that preceded the destruction of Olynthus, and it now seems certain that 'Olynthian' stones were then used at Laurium for crushing ore: the solitary donkey-mill clearly belongs to the first century of the Christian era. It follows that the existence of the rotary grain-mill in the age here under discussion can be inferred neither from the donkey-mill found at Laurium, nor from the rotary *trapeta* used at Olynthus, nor yet from those excavated stones which are commonly interpreted as rotary grinders.

We saw at the outset that an unprejudiced review of the evidence that has come down to us from ancient Greece is possible only if the common belief that the grain-mill remained essentially

[1] Ardaillon, *Les Mines de Laurion* (Bibl. École française à Athènes 77), pp. 61–62, fig. 19; cf. Cloché, *Les Classes, les métiers, le trafic* (1931), p. 34, fig. 14a.
[2] Cf. O. Davies, *Roman Mines in Europe*, p. 250, and *Oxford Class. Dict.*, s.v. Laurium.
[3] Ardaillon, pp. 68–69, fig. 22.

unchanged from Homeric times until the period of the Roman principate is called in question, and if the origin of the rotary mill is treated as the main problem for which an answer is sought in our evidence. If we use the remains of one period to fill in the gaps in the evidence bearing on a much earlier period, we need to have reasonable grounds for supposing that in the relevant respects the two periods were similar if we are to avoid serious mistakes. In the case of the grain-mill the evidence for considerable parts of our period is so scant that the rigorous application of this principle is bound to leave us with unanswered questions: yet this method of approach provides the only hope of arriving at the truth, either now or in the future.

Following this approach we found that there is little basis for the established belief so far as early Greece is concerned. Here, as in other early societies, the corn was laboriously rubbed by hand between the two stones of the saddle-quern which represents grain-milling at nearly its most primitive. Neglect of the saddle-quern was probably the most important single mistake made in earlier studies of our subject.

When the saddle-quern was finally superseded the rotary mill still did not immediately come into being, and we found little in the literature, the art, and the material remains of the classical Greek and early hellenistic world to support the widespread conviction that revolving grain-mills must have been known by the fifth or early fourth century B.C. The recognition of the 'Olynthian' mill, in particular, which is so recent that it has not yet found its way into any of the works of reference which the non-specialist may be expected to consult, has thrown an entirely different light on that part of our period. Such evidence for the early existence of the rotary mill as was accepted by even the most critical students has crumbled away on closer investigation, and there now remains nothing but silence in reply to our question—with one exception: Pliny[1] quotes Varro for the statement that turning-mills were invented at Volsinii in nothern Italy.

Arguments from silence are notoriously unpopular, and they must be especially so in a subject in which the evidence is far from plentiful. Neither the lack in Greek literature of the con-

---

[1] *N.H.* xxxvi. 135 'idem [sc. Varro] molas versatiles Volsiniis inventas [tradit]'; cf. below, p. 66. (The exact location of the Volsinii in question is immaterial here.)

trast, of which traces are found several times in Latin, between a 'turning-' and a 'pushing-mill', nor the fact that the Greek mill is never spoken of as turned, nor the absence of any reference to the rotary mill in the art of the period can by itself be conclusive: the archaeological finds might seem to allow rather more certainty, but even here we found grounds for guarding against hasty conclusions.

Yet the argument must by its very nature be largely one from silence, since we cannot expect the invention of the rotary mill to be foreshadowed before the event. The one statement, moreover, that we possess from after the event may well be thought to lack the compelling authority needed to settle a question which concerns the ancient world in general and not only Italy: had Varro's general outlook been wider, or had he placed the invention outside Italy, we might feel more certain that his evidence is to be believed. But even if we must be prepared for our present verdict to be upset as further evidence comes to light, we may, for the moment, well feel inclined to give more credit to Varro's statement than it has received for a long time,[1] and to look for the origin of the rotary mill farther west, and much later, than is usual. Even if much of the argument that has led to this conclusion has been negative, it will not have been useless if it has cleared the way for further investigation and perhaps even for the discovery of the material needed to overthrow it.

[1] Childe and *BE* take Varro's statement more seriously than most recent writers (e.g. Storck and Teague, p. 81).

IX

'PUSHING-MILLS' AND 'TURNING-MILLS'

THE universal silence concerning the rotary mill is broken almost immediately once the question is approached from the Roman side: Cato the Censor, who lived from 234 to 149 B.C., in his book *On Agriculture* mentions grain-mills in two places,[1] and in each case the donkey-mill is among the mills mentioned. Among the equipment needed for an olive-yard of 240 *iugera* [= c. 150 acres] Cato lists one donkey-mill (*mola asinaria*), one pushing-mill (*mola trusatilis*), and one Spanish mill (*mola hispaniensis*); and for a vineyard of 100 *iugera* [= c. 62½ acres] he requires, among other things, three donkey-mills and one pushing-mill. The fact that a mill-donkey is in each case listed among the animals to be provided[2] shows clearly that Cato's *molae asinariae*, unlike the 'donkeys' (ὄνοι) of the Greek mills, must have been animal-driven: but if so, they must also have been rotary, since it would hardly have been possible to persuade a donkey, or any other animal, to work a non-rotary appliance.

Cato does not explicitly say that the mills in his lists were to be used for grain, and their occurrence among the requisites for an olive-yard and a vineyard might suggest that they were intended for the primary products, oil and wine. But although mills were used for crushing olives, grapes for wine were trodden by the feet;[3] and even for oil Cato recommends the *trapetum* in preference to the oil-mill (*mola olearia*),[4] although Columella thought the oil-mill superior to the *trapetum*.[5] The oil-mill, moreover, was at all times constructed differently from the grain-mill, and it is unlikely that *mola* by itself (without an epithet, such as *olearia*)

---

[1] 10. 4 and 11. 4. [2] See *Note E*, p. 218. [3] Cf. *PW*, iii. 1337 ff.
[4] The *trapetum* does not occur in Cato's list, but is probably included among *vasa olearia instructa iuga v* in 10. 2, since elaborate details are given later of the appliances needed for the preparation of the oil as distinct from the growing of the olives (chaps. 12–13, 18, 20 ff.).
[5] xii. 52. 6. (In Varr. *R.R.* i. 55. 5 the *trapetum* is called an oil-mill, but it is certain that the *mola olearia* was normally an appliance distinct from the *trapetum*; cf. Drachmann, op. cit., pp. 41 ff.)

could denote any but the commonest type of mill, namely that used for corn. Hence it seems safe to follow the assumption, which is universally made, that the mills listed by Cato were meant for grain, and were needed to make his establishments as nearly self-sufficient as possible.[1]

The approximate date of Cato's book is 160 B.C.,[2] and in this date we have at last a comparatively certain *terminus ante quem* for the invention of the rotary mill: since, moreover, Cato could mention it without explanation, the donkey-mill was by 160 B.C. probably no longer a complete novelty. On the other hand the rotary mill had not by Cato's time altogether replaced earlier types of mill: it was suggested in the last chapter but one that *mola trusatilis* may have been the Latin name for the Olynthian lever-mill, and if so, the situation to be inferred from Cato's catalogues is very similar to that which is usually—though probably incorrectly—supposed to be depicted on the Megarian bowl. But this explanation of the name *mola trusatilis* is not beyond controversy, and it must therefore at this point be discussed in some detail.

Outside Cato's two lists the only place in which this name (or indeed the word *trusatilis*) occurs is a much-discussed passage in Aulus Gellius' *Attic Nights*, written about the middle of the second century A.D., where the author purports to relate, from one of Varro's lost works, some facts about the life of the comic poet Plautus. This passage may have its roots in the period of Latin literature before Cato, and it therefore deserves careful attention here. It runs as follows:[3]

Varro and several other writers have related that he [Plautus] wrote the *Saturio*, the *Addictus*, and a third play of which I cannot now recall the name, in a *pistrinum* [mill-bakery; but cf. below, p. 69] at a time when he had returned to Rome in poverty after losing in commerce all the money he had made in work concerned with the stage, and when, in order to earn a living, he had hired out his labour to a *pistor* for turning the mills which are called *trusatiles*.

---

[1] See *Note F*, p. 219.
[2] See, e.g., McDonald in *Oxford Class. Dict.*, s.v. Cato.
[3] *N.A.* iii. 3. 14: 'sed enim Saturionem et Addictum et tertiam quandam, cuius nunc mihi nomen non suppetit, in pistrino eum scripsisse Varro et plerique alii memoriae tradiderunt, cum pecunia omni, quam in operis artificum scaenicorum pepererat, in mercatibus perdita inops Romam redisset et ob quaerendum victum ad circumagendas molas, quae trusatiles appellantur, operam pistori locasset.'

The same events are referred to in slightly different terms by St. Jerome (*c.* A.D. 348–420) in his Chronicles for the year 553–4 of the city of Rome (201–200 B.C.), in a passage which is probably based on a lost book *On Poets* by Suetonius (*c.* A.D. 69–140) :[1]

Plautus from Sarsina in Umbria dies at Rome. In want of the means of subsistence he had hired himself out to a *pistor* for work at the hand-mills, and in his free moments there he was wont to write plays for sale.

The trustworthiness of these passages in their bearing on Plautus' life and civic status has often been discussed,[2] but here we are concerned with a more limited question: in the phrase 'turning the mills which are called *trusatiles*' we have, on the face of it, a reference to rotary mills concerning a period earlier than Cato, and in view of the verb used by Gellius the name *mola trusatilis* is often explained as denoting

a large mill with two handles, which two men, ordinarily slaves, pushed upon in order to turn the mill; contrasted by Cato with *molae asinariae* which had one handle to which a horse or an ass was attached and *drew* the mill around.[3]

The two types of mill here distinguished are illustrated by two Pompeian mills in the Museo Nazionale at Naples (Plate 4, Figs. *a* and *b*)[4] which have been reconstructed in accordance with the same theory. But the only evidence, apart from Gellius' verb, for the reconstruction of the mill in Fig. *a*, and for its identification as a *mola trusatilis*, is the occurrence at Pompeii of stones exactly similar to those of the typical donkey-mill described below, but of much smaller dimensions. The two sizes are shown side by side in Plate 5, Fig. *a* :[5] the difference between them

---

[1] Suetonius, ed. Roth (1902), p. 291, l. 17: 'Plautus ex Umbria Sarsinas Romae moritur; qui propter annonae difficultatem ad molas manuarias pistori se locaverat, ibi quotiens ab opere vacaret, scribere fabulas ac vendere solitus.'

[2] Cf., e.g., F. Leo, *Plautinische Forschungen*[2] (Berlin, 1912), pp. 70 ff.; F. Marx, *Ztschr. f. d. österr. Gymnasialwesen*, 1898, pp. 385 ff. (esp. 396).

[3] J. C. Rolfe in the Loeb edition of Gellius, ad loc. For the same view cf. Lindet, 1900, p. 24; Blümner, p. 31, n. 4.

[4] The photographs were taken by permission of Professor Amedeo Maiuri. The '*mola trusatilis*' is shown in use in Maiuri's *Pompeii* (Eng. trans.[5]; Rome, 1947), plate 33, fig. 62.

[5] From the Pompeian bakery in the Vico Storto (VII. ii. 22); cf. Maiuri, op. cit., fig. 61.

PLATE 4

a. RECONSTRUCTED '*mola trusatilis*' AT NAPLES

b. RECONSTRUCTED '*mola asinaria*' AT NAPLES

PLATE 5

a. TWO SIZES OF POMPEIAN MILL

b. RELIEF FROM THE VIGNA DELLE TRE MADONNE IN THE MUSEO CHIARAMONTI

must be distinguished (as it easily can be by the diameter of the mill) from the difference, occasioned by wear, between new and old mills of the same original size.[1]

If we are not prepared to suppose that mills of the smaller of these two types were worked by young donkey foals, in order that these might earn their keep as early as possible,[2] we should indeed have to admit that they must have been worked by human beings. But even if they were, they were certainly not called *molae trusatiles* in the second century A.D., when Gellius wrote: it is clear, not only from the absence of the word *trusatilis* in Latin literature after Cato apart from the present passage, but also from the wording of this passage[3] and from that of the parallel Suetonius passage (where the word is avoided), that the name *mola trusatilis* had dropped completely out of use at a time little later than that of the destruction of Pompeii in A.D. 79. It seems inconceivable that mills which we know to have been in existence such a short time before Suetonius and Gellius wrote[4] should have borne a name so obviously strange to these two writers. Nor does it seem likely that the mills which Cato called *molae trusatiles* should have survived in use during the two or three centuries during which their name became obsolete.

Gellius, therefore, probably copied the word *trusatilis* from the source he consulted about Plautus' life. That source was almost certainly Varro, who in turn may have found the word in Plautus, though it does not occur in any extant Plautine play. But if so, Gellius did not know any more about the nature of the *mola trusatilis* than do his modern commentators: the mills of his own day were rotary, and, like many modern writers, he may well have failed to realize that non-rotary mills had ever existed. He may therefore well have spoken of the turning of the *mola trusatilis* without knowing that by using the verb *circumagere* he became guilty of an anachronism.

The same conclusion—that Gellius' reference to turning does not prove that the *mola trusatilis* was rotary—can also be reached on more positive grounds. *Trusare*, from which *trusatilis* is derived,

[1] See *Note G*, p. 219.
[2] Young animals may have been so used: there is no evidence one way or the other. On the whole question see below, pp. 97 ff.
[3] Marx (p. 396), on grounds which from the present point of view are unprejudiced, says that the word *trusatilis* was 'evidently unfamiliar' to Gellius.
[4] Suetonius was old enough to remember the destruction of Pompeii.

means 'to push frequently' or 'to push to and fro' :[1] by an exactly
similar formation the verb *versare*, 'to turn frequently', produces
the adjective *versatilis*, and we have seen that references are found
in Latin literature both to a *mola trusatilis* and to a *mola versatilis*.
The two are nowhere in extant writings found side by side with
each other, but the analogous formation and the implied contrast have often been commented upon,[2] though it has usually
been overlooked that if turning is contrasted with another activity
the other activity cannot itself have been a form of turning: if
the explanation of *mola trusatilis* which was quoted a little earlier
were correct, the mill contrasted with the 'pushing-mill' ought
to be not a 'turning-mill' but a 'drawing-mill'.[3] With the identification of the Olynthian mill the contrast between pushing and
turning has gained a new meaning, and if we could be sure that
some one ancient author intentionally used this contrast there
could now be little doubt as to what it meant. Fortunately we
know that one author did in fact use both words. *Molae versatiles*
are mentioned by Pliny, in a passage to which reference has already been made, where Varro is reported as saying that they
were invented at Volsinii.[4] But Gellius, too, is quoting Varro,
and Varro, whether or no he was himself quoting Plautus, must
therefore have used both words somewhere in his writings. It is
improbable that Pliny and Gellius are quoting from the same
work of Varro; but we can be sure that Varro mentioned both
molae versatiles and *molae trusatiles*, and he must surely have been
conscious of a contrast between them. This contrast must have
been that between rotary and non-rotary mills.

There is thus much less real doubt about the meaning of the
word *trusatilis* than about many other questions in this field: if
Gellius' reference to turning is rejected as anachronistic, the
contrast between the 'pushing-mill' and the 'turning-mill' is
easily and naturally explained, and the disappearance of the
word *trusatilis* in later Latin is accounted for. The *mola trusatilis*
will, moreover, fit into its natural place in the hellenistic history
of milling as a non-rotary lever-mill of the kind familiar from
Olynthus.[5]

[1] Catull. 56. 6.　　　　　　　　　　[2] See, e.g., *BE*, i. 66, 128.
[3] *Mola tractatilis*: the word *tractatilis* is not found, but it could easily have been
formed in exactly the same way as *trusatilis* and *versatilis*.
[4] See *Note H*, p. 219.
[5] On Cato's 'Spanish' mill see below, p. 110.

X

MILLS AND MILLERS IN PLAUTUS' COMEDIES

THE earliest certain reference to the rotary mill that we have discovered so far belongs to about the year 160 B.C. If it could be shown that Varro derived his contrast between a *mola trusatilis* and a *mola versatilis* from one of Plautus' plays, this date could be moved back to before the death of Plautus, which probably occurred in 184 B.C.:[1] unfortunately we cannot be sure that Varro derived his information from this source. Yet Plautus is, as far as extant works are concerned, the only major Latin author earlier than Cato;[2] and he often speaks of the mill and of its use in the punishment of recalcitrant slaves. [In the extant comedies mills are mentioned five times,[3] and the 'mill-house' (*pistrinum*) ten times.[4]] Can anything be gathered from Plautus' plays about the nature of these mills?

One point emerges immediately: except in one passage of the *Asinaria*, which will be discussed presently, Plautus never—either directly or indirectly—speaks of a mill as being turned. The fact that references to turning do not appear in Greek literature until very late was mentioned earlier; but the general paucity of evidence made it seem inadvisable to rely on it. If Plautus' mills were rotary, his silence is more surprising; for later writers, many of whom have otherwise much less to say about mills, often contrive to show quite incidentally that their mills were turned.[5]

On the accepted view, that Plautus' mills were rotary mills of the Pompeian type, it is odd that the slaves who worked these mills should have had their feet fettered:[6] all humanitarian considerations apart, this can hardly have been conducive to efficiency

---

[1] This is the date given by Cicero (*Brut.* 60): St. Jerome places Plautus' death in 200 B.C.; cf. above, p. 64.

[2] Terence, his only possible rival, did not produce his first play until 166 B.C.

[3] *Bacch.* 2, *Men.* 975, *Pers.* 22, *Poen.* 1152, *Pseud.* 1100.

[4] *Bacch.* 781, *Capt.* 808, *Epid.* 145, *Most.* 17, *Poen.* 827, *Pseud.* 494, 499, 500, 534, 1060; a further reference in *Pers.* 420 is doubtful.

[5] See, e.g., Ov. *Fast.* vi. 318, [Virg.] *Moret.* 26 and 39, Juv. *Sat.* 8. 67, Apul. *Met.* vii. 15, Auson. *Epist.* 21. 34, [Luc.] *Asin.* 42, *Anth. Pal.* ix. 20. 5–6, 301. 3.

[6] Plaut. *Most.* 19, &c.; Ter. *Phorm.* 249; cf. *BE*, i. 102, 199.

if these slaves spent their time walking or running round a mill. If, moreover, the reconstruction of the smaller Pompeian mill as a slave-mill is correct, and if in Plautus' day such a mill existed side by side with the donkey-mill, we might expect some allusion to the 'asinine' nature of the occupation among Plautus' many jokes about milling: but again there is nothing of the kind, outside the one exceptional passage in the *Asinaria*.

In this passage[1] a slave threatens his young master, whom he is for the moment treating as a quadruped,[2] that he will hand him over to the *pistores*, there to be beaten as he runs; and, in view of other passages where slaves are sent to work a mill, this is almost certainly an allusion to the driving of a rotary mill. If the play is genuine, this is the earliest literary reference to an animal-driven mill that has come down to us.

The proviso regarding the authenticity of the *Asinaria* must be added because two French editors of the play[3] find many reasons for denying its Plautine authorship and for placing it somewhat later than Plautus' death; but their arguments have found little favour with other scholars.[4] The number of extant Plautine comedies agrees with the number quoted by Gellius[5] from Varro, and very strong reasons are needed if one of the extant plays is to be regarded as non-Plautine: the arguments that have been brought forward are hardly strong enough, but they serve to show that the *Asinaria* is in many ways exceptional, and may well be the latest among the surviving plays of Plautus.[6]

On this basis the *terminus ante quem* provided by Cato for the introduction of the rotary mill can now be replaced by the date of Plautus' death,[7] about twenty-five years earlier. We saw earlier that the animal-mill is referred to by Cato in a way which suggests that it was no longer a novelty when he wrote: the situation of the *Asinaria* passage, on the other hand, would gain

[1] 708–9: 'nam iam calcari quadrupedo agitabo advorsum clivom,
      postidea ad pistores dabo ut ibi cruciere currens.'
[2] This is important: it means that the passage does not in any case provide evidence for a *slave-driven* rotary mill; cf. below, pp. 97 ff.
[3] Havet and Freté (Paris, 1925).
[4] See, e.g., Ernout's edition (Paris, 1932), p. 80. [5] *N.A.* iii. 3. 3.
[6] Yet Sedgwick (*AJP*, lxx. 376 ff.) and Buck (*A Chronology of the Plays of Plautus*, Baltimore, 1940) regard the *Asinaria*, just because it shows many abnormalities, as the earliest of Plautus' plays (212 or 207 B.C.); cf. also della Corte, *Riv. di Fil.*, N.S., xxix. 289 ff.
[7] Or rather the date of the composition of the *Asinaria*; but we do not know how long before his death Plautus wrote the play.

in comic interest if the donkey-mill had but recently been introduced when the play was performed.

The reference to a donkey-mill has not hitherto been included
among the reasons for considering the *Asinaria* to be exceptional
among Plautus' plays; but there is one among the arguments
that have been used which also concerns us here: in an earlier
scene of the play a *pistor* is mentioned who sells bread and has
presumably also baked it.[1] Now *pistores* who combined milling and
baking in their businesses were common enough in later times;[2]
but according to Pliny[3] they first became known at Rome during
the war with Perseus (171–168 B.C.), about fifteen years after the
probable date for Plautus' death.[4] In view of this, the appearance
of a bread-baking *pistor* in one passage, and one passage only, of
a Plautine play has rightly been thought remarkable.

Pliny may have misapplied the date he found in his source; but
his statement cannot be ignored altogether, and if it is correct, the
pistores mentioned by Plautus—and the *pistor* for whom Plautus
himself is said to have worked—cannot have been miller-bakers,
but must have borne the name in a different and more primitive
sense. Pliny himself evidently knew that the date he gives is later
than Plautus, and that the occurrence of anything inconsistent
with it in Plautus' writings needs explanation;[5] and he also tells
us what he took to have been the state of affairs before the war
with Perseus: he goes on to say that before the change the citizens
(or rather their womenfolk) had baked their own bread, and
quotes the Augustan jurist Ateius Capito for the statement that
the rich had in earlier times had their bread prepared for them
by their cooks, while the name *pistor* had been reserved for those
whose work was the pounding of emmer.[6] This view is confirmed

---

[1] 200: 'quom a pistore panem petimus.'   [2] See, e.g., *PW*, xx. 1821 ff.

[3] *N.H.* xviii. 107: 'pistores Romae non fuere ad Persicum usque bellum annis
ab urbe condita super DLXXX.' It is clear from what follows that *pistores* in the sense
of 'miller-bakers' are meant. (Note incidentally that the date does not depend on a
mere numeral in the text.)

[4] Overbeck–Mau, *Pompeii*[4], p. 387, and *PW*, loc. cit., comment on the Pliny
passage as if the date mentioned in it were early in the *third* century B.C.

[5] He goes on to say that Plautus mentions an *artopta* in the *Aulularia* [l. 400], and
that this has caused disagreement among the doctors about the authenticity of the
line in question: the *artopta* was a baker's implement, and Pliny seems to have been
surprised by its appearance in Plautus.

[6] 'Ipsi panem faciebant quirites mulierumque id opus maxime erat, sicut etiam
nunc in plurimis gentium. ... certumque fit Atei Capitonis sententia cocos tum panem
lautioribus coquere solitos pistoresque tantum eos qui far pisebant nominatos.'

in very similar terms by two passages which the fourth-century
grammarian Nonius Marcellus quotes from Varro;[1] and Virgil's
commentator Servius, a contemporary of Nonius, provides further
confirmation.[2] All these writers thought that the name *pistor*
was derived from the pounding (*pinsere* or *pisere*) which had been
the work of the early *pistores*; and, unlike many ancient etymo-
logies, this derivation is clearly correct.

In reliance on Pliny's statement, the word *pistor* is in Plautus'
plays usually taken to mean 'miller, not baker'.[3] This is obviously
inadequate for the *Asinaria* passage in which a *pistor* sells bread,
and if Pliny's date—and the authenticity of the play—is accepted,
some other explanation must be found for this passage. Only one
such explanation suggests itself: Plautus may here be following
his Greek original[4] more closely than usual, or he may at least be
describing Greek rather than contemporary Roman usage. This
assumption gains some support from the Greek tone of the
passage as a whole[5] and from the fact that the words in question
are spoken by a procuress (*lena*) whom Plautus may have wished
to present as a real Greek while romanizing his other characters.
In Athens, as we have seen, the trade of miller-baker existed as
early as the fifth century B.C.[6]

But even if the bread-selling *pistores* of the *Asinaria* are not
accepted as evidence for contemporary Italy, it is still difficult to
assume—as Pliny himself evidently did—that the change from the
earlier to the later meaning of the word *pistor* took place at the
time of the war with Perseus. Pliny implies that during the period
of the *pistores* in the earlier sense there was no commercial bakery,
and that pounded emmer (*far*) was the national food, while
bread, though not unknown, was a luxury: this had undoubtedly

---

[1] p. 152. 12 Müll.: 'PINSERE, tundere vel molere. Varro Ταφῆ Μενίππου: "nec
pistorem ullum nossent, nisi eum qui in pristino pinseret far."—idem de Vita
Populi Romani lib. i: "nec pistoris nomen erat nisi eius qui ruri far pinsebat.
nominati ita eo quod pinsunt."' (*Pistrino* is almost too easy a correction of *pristino*.)

[2] *ad Aen.* i. 179: 'quia apud maiores nostros molarum usus non erat, frumenta
torrebant et ea in pilas missa pinsebant, et hoc erat genus molendi, unde et pin-
sores dicti sunt, qui nunc pistores vocantur.'

[3] e.g. Gray on *Asin.* 709 (ignoring the difficulty of l. 200!) and *Trin.* 407; Lindsay
on *Capt.* 160 (London, 1900); &c. (The word also occurs in *Capt.* 807, *Curc.* 483,
Epid. 121, *Poen.* 266.)

[4] The *Onagos* of Demophilus.

[5] The Greek word *oenopolium* is used for 'a wine-shop' in the same line, but
nowhere else in Latin.

[6] See *Note I*, p. 219.

been true once, but it was no longer true when Plautus wrote. At the time when the commercial *pistores* merely 'pounded *far* in mortars' the product of their work can have served only for porridge,¹ which must therefore still have been the staple food of Italy: those who could afford to eat bread must have had the grain for it ground in their own households, by the women mentioned by Pliny.² The grain itself, moreover, was in all probability different from the emmer used by the commercial 'pounder', since the baking qualities of emmer would be largely destroyed during hulling.

In Plautus' plays, on the other hand, we hear very little of porridge (*puls*),³ while bread is mentioned frequently;⁴ and when in one of the plays⁵ a master expresses his relief at the running-away of a slave because it saves him two loaves of bread a day, the 'bread age' must indeed have started—unless we are to suppose that Plautus is in every case describing circumstances other than those which he saw around him: but it is one thing to make this assumption for one particular passage, and for a certain reason, and quite another to do so for a whole group of instances scattered all over the extant plays. The change at the time of the war with Perseus cannot, then, have been the complete change from the old *pistores* to the new: yet Pliny undoubtedly found this date in his source, and the question arises what change it was that did take place then. The interpretation of *pistor* in Plautus⁶ as 'miller' implies that grain was ground, but not baked, commercially in Plautus' day: can this be accepted?

The later *pistor* undoubtedly combined milling and baking in his establishment, and we have seen that this is natural as long as the capacity of the mill is too small to supply more than one bakery, and as long as the mill is not, like the water-mill, tied to a particular location. Bread may indeed have occasionally been baked at home from flour that had been bought; but the

¹ Cf. above, pp. xvii ff.   ² Cf. also Plaut. *Merc.* 396.
³ *Pultem* (from *pultare*, 'to beat') is used in a pun in *Poen.* 729: the word *puls* does not occur otherwise, though in *Most.* 828 and *Poen.* 54 the words *pultiphagus* and *Pultiphagonides* ('porridge-eater') are used in the mouths of Greeks to describe the barbarian Romans.
⁴ *Asin.* 142, 200; *Aul.* 195; *Bacch.* 580; *Cas.* 310; *Curc.* 367; *Men.* 917; *Pers.* 471; *Poen.* 729; *Trin.* 254; *frag.* 2 (Lindsay).
⁵ *Pers.* 471. Aristophanes would certainly have spoken of ἄλφιτα—i.e. *polenta* — in similar circumstances.
⁶ Except, of course, in *Asin.* 200.

discoveries at Pompeii show that this was unusual in the first century A.D.,[1] when the smaller households bought their bread while the larger had their own mills and bakeries.[2]

Yet the *pistores* in the earlier sense of the word may well have had commercial establishments from which they sold unbaked meal or groats produced in mortars; but since these products were used for porridge and not for bread, this does not mean that in early Rome people bought flour for home breadmaking.[3] By Plautus' day, on the other hand, bread had become the staple food and the *pistor*'s establishment contained mills as well as mortars: indeed the words *pistrinum* and *mola* are almost synonymous in Plautus when connected, as they usually are, with the punishment of slaves,[4] and Plautus never in his extant works mentions a mortar (*pila*). We cannot always be certain whether these *pistrina* were commercial or within the household, and a slave who is sent to the *pistrinum* or to the *molae* might merely be assigned to fatigue duties without being banished from his master's home:[5] but when a slave is being handed over to the *pistor(es)*[6] he is probably being sent out of the household, and the *pistor* to whom Plautus himself gave his services must surely have had a commercial establishment.[7]

The *pistores* of Plautus' day were still predominantly rural,[8] and this alone makes it unlikely that they baked bread for subsequent transport into the towns. It looks, therefore, as if, after mills had been introduced and added to the pounding implements which had given the *pistores* their name, these *pistores* were for a time millers in something like the modern sense, with establishments in which flour was produced and sold for home breadmaking. Yet even quite small households had maids to grind the corn,[9] and the practice of buying flour was probably

[1] But the flour prices given by Pliny (cf. below, p. 171) show that flour must have been sold sometimes.
[2] See *Note J*, p. 219.
[3] With barley this practice could still be found in the second century A.D. (cf. Apul. *Met.* vii. 15); but barley again, though admittedly milled by then and not merely pounded in a mortar, was probably not used for baking.
[4] Cf., e.g., *Pseud.* 499–500 with ibid. 1100.
[5] e.g. *Bacch.* 781, *Men.* 975, *Most.* 16 ff., *Poen.* 1152.
[6] e.g. *Asin.* 709, *Epid.* 121.
[7] Certain similarities in wording between the statements of Gellius and Suetonius are noteworthy in this connexion; cf. Marx, loc. cit. (above, p. 64, n. 2).
[8] See esp. *Most.* 16 ff.
[9] Cf. Plaut. *Merc.* 396; Lucilius, *frag.* 1055 (Warmington).

never universal: commercial bakers who did not mill their own flour appear to have been unknown throughout Roman history. It must be admitted that this argument is highly conjectural; and if there was such an intermediate stage between the time when porridge was the staple food and the beginnings of commercial baking, it must soon have been followed by the introduction of bakeries at Rome, which was probably the event to which Pliny refers. These bakeries appear from the outset to have followed what had long been the practice of many households, by milling their own flour. The political circumstances of their introduction—if the connexion with the war against Perseus is more than merely temporal—must remain obscure; but it may be well to remember that Plautus is said to have worked at the 'pushing-mill', and that this 'pushing-mill' was almost certainly a lever-mill of the Olynthian type. In view of the possible absence of donkey-mills shortly before the date given by Pliny, and their certain presence within a few years of it, it seems conceivable that the time of the war against Perseus was also the time of the introduction of the donkey-mill to Rome. Perhaps the new mills were even brought by the new *pistores*, from wherever the latter may have plied their trade before they came to Rome.[1]

---

[1] Overbeck–Mau (op. cit., p. 387), though mistaken about the date and mistaken in the belief that the rotary mill goes back to Homeric times, yet reach this conclusion—impossible as it is on their premisses.

XI

THE POMPEIAN DONKEY-MILL

THE preceding chapters have shown that the rotary donkey-mill was certainly known by 160 B.C., and probably by about 185 B.C. For its earlier existence there is not one compelling piece of evidence, although, on the other hand, there is no proof that it did not exist before then. It is true that in Plautus it is still the maid or the slave who is needed for grinding corn,[1] and that in Cato we find the mill-donkey for the first time: yet we must be prepared to find, as new evidence becomes available, that the donkey-mill existed earlier than we are at present entitled to believe. The time of its probable introduction into Italy was one at which so many foreign ideas and practices found their way there that it would be rash to assume that the animal-mill was invented locally, and invented near the time when we first meet it. The fact that the distribution of this mill during the next few centuries was centred on Italy lends some plausibility to the statement, quoted by Pliny from Varro, that the revolving mill was an Italian invention—especially if the donkey-mill was the first revolving mill to be invented:[2] even so, Varro's evidence on this point is not necessarily reliable.

In Italy the donkey-mill was soon to become the grain-mill *par excellence*. The examples found at Pompeii alone run well into three figures, and this type of mill was by no means confined to Pompeii.[3] Its common occurrence gave rise to the view that, apart perhaps from the rotary hand-mill, it was *the* grain-mill of classical antiquity in general. In earlier chapters we saw how misleading this view has proved; but it has meant also that descriptions of the Pompeian mill are plentiful in modern writings.[4] These descriptions rely largely on the many extant stones;

---

[1] Always with the exception of *Asin.* 200. (Whether slaves were ever used to drive animal-mills will be considered later; see pp. 97 ff.)
[2] The contention that it was invented before the rotary hand-quern is discussed below, pp. 103 ff.   [3] Cf. below, pp. 91 ff.
[4] It may suffice to mention the full description in Overbeck–Mau, pp. 387–8; cf. also Blümner, pp. 27 ff., Tissot, *Géographie de la province romaine d'Afrique* (1884), i. 314, and almost any dictionary of antiquities.

but the donkey-mill is the easier to describe because it can be seen in operation on a number of graffiti, gems, wall-paintings, and reliefs of the period, from the crude scribbling of a child in the *paedagogium* at the foot of the Palatine Hill[1] to the fine workmanship of a fragmentary relief in the Vatican Museums which was

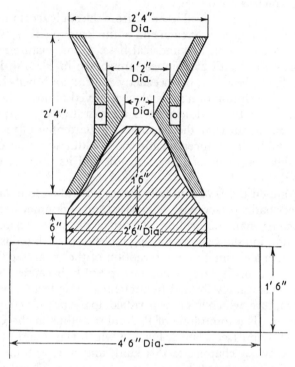

FIG. 8. Section through the stones of a 'normal' Pompeian mill. The measurements are taken from a mill in the Casa di Sallustio

found in 1826 in the Vigna delle tre Madonne outside the Porta Giovanni at Rome and is reproduced in Plate 5, Fig. *b*.[2]

The material and shape of mills of this type are highly uniform; but their sizes vary considerably. There is a 'normal' size, of which approximate measurements are given in Fig. 8, but stones

[1] See below, p. 83 and Fig. 9.
[2] The date of the relief is uncertain, but probably late; cf. Amelung, *Skulpturen d. vatik. Mus.* i. 637, no. 497, plate 68, and Blümner, fig. 16 and p. 41, n. 2, where earlier references to it are assembled.

both larger and much smaller are occasionally found. (The diameter of the upper stone, for instance, may vary from less than 1 ft. 6 in. to over 3 ft.) They are all made of a dark grey, very hard, and highly porous lava,[1] and each mill consists of a lower stone, the *meta*, which is normally solid, and an upper stone, the *catillus*, which is hollow.[2]

The *meta*, which derived its name from the conical columns that were the turning-posts at each end of the Roman circus, is in the shape of a cone with a cylindrical base. (Some examples, from the Vicolo dei Vettii at Pompeii, are shown in Plate 6, Fig. *a*.) The profile is, however, never exactly conical, and 'bell-shaped'[3] is an apt description of it: it is always curved almost spherically near the top; the middle part is comparatively steep; but it flattens out again near the bottom. The flattening of the lower part is usually less noticeable and may be due to wear; but the curve higher up cannot be accidental, and its purpose will be discussed presently.

At Pompeii the *meta* is usually let into a walled foundation—often very badly preserved[4]—which is round and somewhat larger in diameter than the cylindrical part of the stone.[5] Sometimes this foundation shows signs of being tapered inwards on its upper face to form a channel for the reception of the meal (see Plate 6, Fig. *b*); but this is rare at Pompeii, possibly because a similar channel was usually formed by attaching some form of wooden superstructure, which has now perished, to the outside edge of the foundation. The tombstone of P. Nonius Zethus in the Chiaramonti Museum (see Plate 7, Fig. *a*),[6] which was found at Ostia, clearly shows a channel of this kind, and among some debris in one of the courtyards of the Museo Nazionale at Naples a *meta* can be seen with a channel made of lava and of one piece

[1] On the material of these stones cf. also below, p. 91.

[2] These names (cf. *Dig.* xxxiii. 7. 18. 5) are certain and have found common acceptance since 1861 (Jahn, *Ber. d. sächs. Ges. d. Wiss., phil.-hist. Kl.*, 1861, p. 341, n. 192). Before then many fanciful interpretations had been offered, and one of these survives in *LSh* s.v. *meta*.

[3] Tissot, loc. cit.

[4] In sharp contrast to most of the actual *metae*: the rubble of which the foundations were made was obviously cheaper than lava, and it was more economical to raise the mill in this way than to let it into the floor.

[5] But this foundation is not always present and is missing on all the stones in the mill at Ostia; cf. below, p. 93 and Plate 10, Fig. *b*.

[6] Cf. Amelung, i. 778, no. 685, plate 84, and Blümner, fig. 17 and p. 43, n. 2. (For the inscription see *CIL*, xiv. 393.)

PLATE 6

a. Metae OF ANIMAL-MILLS AT POMPEII

b. FOUNDATION OF POMPEIAN MILL

PLATE 7

b. *Catillus* WITH LETTERS AT OSTIA

a. SARCOPHAGUS OF P. NONIUS ZETHUS IN THE MUSEO CHIARAMONTI

with the stone itself.[1] The upper face of the foundation often shows remains of a plaster facing which was obviously intended to make a smooth surface for the meal to fall on.[2]

The upper stones,[3] made of the same material as the lower, are always of the shape of a double cone or 'hour-glass'. Both halves of this double cone are hollow, and they are connected by a hole through the narrow part. This design seems to have had a double purpose: the upper 'funnel' could be employed as a hopper,[4] and the stones could be reversed at will, with the result that, at the cost of an initial outlay somewhat greater than if only the minimum hopper had been provided,[5] their life could be lengthened considerably. The extra weight thus given to the stone was probably also of value, but that it was not a primary consideration is shown by the fact that the stones could remain in use until they had lost much of their original weight. These upper stones were naturally much more fragile than the lower, and the surviving examples are often fragmentary and generally less well preserved. The letters appearing on some of these stones, e.g. that (from Ostia) shown in Plate 7, Fig. b, have been explained as makers' initials.[6]

The double cone is interrupted on these stones by two square pieces on opposite sides of the narrow part which are not cut away. These pieces always contain a square socket, leading towards the centre, but not penetrating into the central hole. At right angles to these sockets there is a much smaller round hole which could serve for the reception of pins to hold in place beams inserted into the square sockets. The stone on the left of Plate 5, Fig. a should help to make this description clear: the function of these sockets and holes is discussed later in this chapter.

For the reconstruction of the working parts of the Pompeian mill we have to rely largely upon the pictorial representations of it, which fortunately survive in comparative plenty.[7] They have all been known for many years and have often been discussed and

---

[1] Cf. also below, p. 94.

[2] For the pavements by which these mills are sometimes surrounded, cf. below, pp. 92, 99, and Plate 10, Fig. a.

[3] The name catillus is presumably a diminutive of catinus, 'a bowl'.

[4] But sometimes an additional wooden hopper was fitted; cf. Plate 5, Fig. b, and below, pp. 85–86.

[5] As on some hand-querns; cf. below, p. 112 and Plate 11, Fig. a.

[6] By de Rossi, Ann. d. Inst. 1857, pp. 277 ff.

[7] They were first assembled by Jahn, Ber. sächs. Ges. Wiss., 1861, pp. 340–8 with plate xii.

reproduced: the photographs contained in the present study are confined to the more important among them.

Best known among these monuments is the cenotaph of the baking contractor (*pistor redemptor*)[1] M. Vergilius Eurysaces, standing outside the Porta Maggiore at Rome, which was first described soon after its discovery in 1838[2] and has since figured in all discussions of our subject, though more because of its unusual character than because of anything which it contributes to our knowledge of ancient breadmaking techniques. The reliefs running along the top of it illustrate all phases of the bakery trade, but they are inaccessible and, according to published photographs,[3] crude and badly weather-beaten. Yet this monument, on which two donkey-mills can be clearly seen, would alone be sufficient to show that the Pompeian stones are correctly interpreted as grain-mills. In addition to the mills themselves, the reliefs show the donkeys behind the mills going round them in opposite directions, and two slaves, one of whom is bending down and apparently gathering up the meal from where the *meta* joins its base, while the other holds a whip. The workmanship is, however, too rough to show in detail how the donkeys were harnessed to the mills and how the harness was attached to the stones.

A sarcophagus in the garden of the Villa Medici at Rome[4] on one of its small sides shows a similar mill, this time with a horse harnessed to it and going round it in a clockwise direction. The harness is again very sketchy; but there is a raised ledge at the top of the *catillus* which seems to indicate that the latter was covered with a lid. Above the mill there is a funnel-like appliance which was probably a hopper.

A similar hopper is shown on a relief in the Museo Civico at Bologna.[5] This relief is very fragmentary, but the mill, with a channel for the meal running round it, can be clearly seen in the bottom left-hand corner. A horse is harnessed to the mill in an anti-clockwise direction, and a slave with a whip stands on the top of the mill-base. The hopper appears on a separate fragment, which, however, clearly belongs immediately above that

---

[1] For the inscription and its interpretation see *CIL*, i[2]. 1203–5.
[2] By Jahn in *Ann. d. Inst.* x. 231 ff. and *Mon. dell' Inst.* ii. 58.
[3] Cf. Blümner, fig. 14 and p. 40, where a full description is given.
[4] Jahn, *Ber. sächs. Ges. Wiss.*, 1861, pl. xii. 1; cf. Matz–v. Duhn, *Antike Bildwerke in Rom*, ii. 241, no. 2864, and Blümner, p. 40 and fig. 15.
[5] See Blümner, pp. 44–45 and fig. 19.

containing the mill. The detail of the harness is once again indistinguishable.

Mention has already been made of the channel which surrounds the mill on the tombstone of P. Nonius Zethus (Plate 7, Fig. *a*). Here the mill is driven by an ass, and the usual slave does not appear, though a whip above the head of the ass indicates that he must not be thought to be far away. Both this relief, moreover, and the fragment from the Vigna delle tre Madonne (Plate 5, Fig. *b*) show what appear to be grooves on the lower stones of their mills, and in doing so they provide the only known evidence for grooving on mills of the Pompeian type. After grooves first appeared on some saddle-stones, the Pompeian mill was, to judge by the evidence of extant stones, exceptional among stone mills of all ages in not having grooved stones.

There are, as we have seen, three reasons for the grooving of millstones. One of these is to regulate the flow of grain through and out of the mill: in this respect the steep conical slope of the Pompeian mill would do far more than grooves could do, and the effect of the latter in either retarding or accelerating the flow would be but slight.[1] If, on the other hand, the grooves were intended to give the stones a better grip on the grist, they would still be unnecessary on mills of the Pompeian type: the stone of which these mills are made is so porous that the grooves would have to be very deep in order to do more than is done by the natural surface of the stone.[2] The same would apply if the grooves were meant to ensure that the grain was cut rather than crushed at its first contact with the stones. On the relief shown in Plate 5, Fig. *b* the grooves may merely be meant to indicate that the grooved *meta* is a stone separate from the *catillus*, and the sculptor may also have intended to convey in this way an impression of turning and perhaps to suggest the meal flowing from the mill. Neither of these explanations, however, gives an adequate reason for the appearance of grooves on the Zethus relief, and indeed no likely explanation suggests itself: although grooves are never found on extant millstones of the Pompeian type, this relief must then be accepted as evidence that they were not unknown.

---

[1] Retardation, rather than acceleration, would probably be desirable; but, if so, the grooves on the relief in Plate 5, Fig. *b* run in the wrong direction.

[2] The porous lava of which these stones were made has the further advantage that it retains a rough surface even after wear.

The same two reliefs, unlike those mentioned before them, also show how these donkey-mills were fitted up for operation. Into the sockets on each side of the *catillus* beams were fitted which were held in position by pins going through them and through the stone sockets at right angles. These pins themselves appear to have been connected by an iron band surrounding the stone at its narrowest part. The purpose of this band is not obvious; but it can be clearly seen on the two reliefs, and many of the actual stones still show the groove into which it was fitted (cf. Plate 5, Fig. *a*).

Since the sockets could not penetrate through the centre of the stone, the two beams were connected over the top of the mill by three further beams, up the two sides and across the top of the upper half of the *catillus*. On some of the extant stones (e.g. the stone on the left of Plate 5, Fig. *a*) grooves can be seen where these beams passed the outer edges of the *catillus*.[1] The upper stone on the Zethus relief appears to be worn down considerably, and there is therefore a space between its top and the crossbeam. For the same reason the grinding half of the *catillus* only covers a small part of the cone of the *meta*.[2]

The driving animal was attached to the mill in one of two ways, depending quite probably on its height and on whether it was an ass or a horse: either a yoke was attached to one of the horizontal beams which projected from the centre of the stone,[3] or else the animal was harnessed by chains or ropes[4] to the centre of the mill on the inside and to the upper crossbeam on the outside. The former, imitated on one of the reconstructed mills at Naples (Plate 4, Fig. *b*), seems to be the method depicted—not very clearly—on the Zethus relief; the latter method is shown on the other Vatican relief[5] and on a further relief found in a baker's shop at Pompeii.

This Pompeian relief,[6] like some of the other pictorial monu-

---

[1] This is, however, by no means regular (*pace* Blümner, p. 28).

[2] If this explanation is correct the sculptor must have been mistaken in allowing the upright beams to come closer together near the top.

[3] On some of the reliefs the vertical and upper horizontal beams are absent, and the animal appears to have been fastened to a pole or yoke protruding from *one* of the square sockets in the *catillus*.

[4] Plate 5, Fig. *b* shows a chain; but a rope is mentioned in Apul. *Met.* ix. 11 and 12 (cf. also *Anth. Pal.* ix. 19. 7).

[5] Cf. here Lefebvre des Noëttes, *L'Attelage, le cheval de selle à travers les âges* (1931), p. 84.   [6] See Overbeck–Mau, p. 379, fig. 186; Blümner, fig. 20.

ments that remain to be described, shows an hour-glass mill in a highly stylized form. On it, as on a gem in the German Archaeological Institute at Rome,[1] which is remarkably similar to it, the mill is not even fixed to the ground, but the bottom of the *meta* is rounded off by a semicircle which, if it can be explained at all, must represent that part of the stone which was sunk into the ground and was therefore invisible once the mill was installed.[2] It would be as misleading to try to reconstruct a mill from these conventional representations as it would be to reconstruct the masts of a sailing ship from the 'tails' of a halfpenny. Both on the gem and on the Pompeian relief we can see the mill itself, the ass driving it, and some attempt to sketch the framework. In each case the mill is shown—presumably for reasons of symmetry—as raised higher than it can possibly have been in reality, and in each case there is quite clearly a central spindle round which the *catillus* revolved: to this spindle we shall return later in this chapter.

Another conventionalized mill dominates a Pompeian wall-painting depicting the feast of the Vestalia.[3] Once a year when this feast was celebrated[4] the mills stood idle and the garlanded asses were the heroes of the day. The only feature of the mill on this painting which deserves notice is a fitting which protrudes over the top of the *catillus* at its centre. Since the mill is shown without the usual framework, this would seem to indicate that some kind of central spindle was fixed to the top of the *meta*; but this again must await separate discussion.

The sarcophagus of L. Annius Octavius Valerianus in the Lateran Museum (see Plate 8)[5] shows the whole sequence of

[1] *Impronte Gemmarie*, iv. 79; Jahn, *Ber. sächs. Ges. Wiss.*, 1861, pl. xii. 5; Blümner, fig. 21.
[2] Jahn and Blümner must be wrong in describing it as a sack for the meal to fall into: a sack fixed in the way shown could not have collected the meal, and, since flour was always measured by volume, it is in any case probable that rigid receptacles rather than sacks were used for it.
[3] Blümner, fig. 23; Helbig, *Wandgemälde der vom Vesuv verschütteten Städte*, p. 154, no. 777; Gerhard, *Antike Bildwerke*, pl. 62. 3.
[4] On 9 June; cf. Blümner, pp. 35–36, n. 8 and references there (esp. Ov. *Fast.* vi. 311 ff.); also Wissowa, *Religion u. Kultus²*, p. 158; Mau, *Röm. Mitt.* xi. 80, *Pompeii, its Life and Art²*, p. 328; PW, ii. 2742, xx. 1826, 1832; and BE, i. 187–90.
[5] Cf. Blümner, pp. 25–26 with notes. The inscription (*CIL*, vi. 11743; 'Escaped am I. Bland hope, blind fate—away! To me you are nothing now: with others play.') is an imitation of a Greek epigram in *Anth. Pal.* ix. 49.

operations, from ploughing[1] to baking, which are needed to produce a loaf of bread. The last but one of these ought logically to be the grinding of the corn, as the major stage between the bringing-in of the harvest and the baking of the bread, and the apparatus, consisting of two disks, which the two men in the lower half immediately on the left of the central figure are operating may be intended to represent a mill. (If not a mill it must be a kneading-machine of a kind also familiar from Pompeii and Ostia,[2] but if so, there should be one stone and not two, one above the other.) Yet no extant mill designed for direct drive[3] by man or animal was, or is likely to have been, turned by means of a spindle attached to the centre of the upper stone. Such a spindle would make it extremely difficult to introduce the grist into the mill; the spindle would be weak at the point where it needs the greatest strength;[4] and all that could be achieved by it could be achieved more easily by attaching either one or two handles to the periphery of the upper stone where they are fixed on all extant hand- and animal-mills. The sculptor may have intended to depict a mill on the relief; but if so, he was mistaken in its construction,[5] perhaps because he confused mills with kneading-machines, which were turned in the way shown. Modern writers are not sure whether a mill or a kneading-machine is to be seen on the relief, and the sculptor himself, who was probably no expert, may well have confused the two.

On all the pictorial monuments the animals are harnessed very close to their mills. That this is a true picture of actual practice is shown by the fact that many of the mills at Pompeii are a mere 1 ft. 6 in. from the wall of the building, while the distance of mill bases from each other is often little more than 3 ft. Shortage of space was probably one reason for this, and the Romans—with little thought for the animal's feelings—may also have thought that greater efficiency would be the result of the shorter distance

---

[1] *Pace* Blümner, p. 26.

[2] See, e.g., Blümner, pp. 64–65.

[3] Geared mills (on which see below, pp. 122 ff.) are—and are bound to be—an exception to this rule.

[4] It would have to be attached to the stone by means of a 'rynd' (cf. below, p. 85), and it would also have to revolve in a socket in the lower stone for concentricity.

[5] The baking-oven which appears next to the mill was certainly not like those in use when the relief was cut: the date of the relief is shown by the formula *D(is) M(anibus) S(acrum)* to be Augustan at the earliest; cf. *PW*, xiv. 1058.

PLATE 8

SARCOPHAGUS OF L. ANNIUS OCTAVIUS VALERIANUS IN THE MUSEO LATERANO

covered by the horse or ass in its walk round the mill. A graffito
found in the *paedagogium* at the foot of the Palatine Hill at Rome
(Fig. 9)[1] at first sight presents an exception to this rule. This
graffito—'a rough, yet characteristic scrawl'[2]—shows an ass harnessed by means of a long halter round its neck to a mill which is
sketched behind and above the animal. The accompanying legend,

'work, little ass, as I have worked,
and you will profit by it',[3] provides
a good reason for placing the animal
rather than the mill in the foreground. (It was pointed out earlier[4]
that this is exceptional, and the only
other monument to which it applies
is the Pompeian wall-painting where
the asses are, as we have seen, the
heroes of the day.) Yet the animal
is not allowed to obscure the mill,
and if the halter is so long it is almost
certainly because the mill had to
be raised from its true position in
order that it might still remain fully
visible. The mill itself is too roughly

Fig. 9. Donkey with mill.
Graffito from the Palatine

sketched to help in the inquiry, except that once again a central
spindle is clearly shown.

The mill, finally, which appears on a fragmentary sarcophagus
relief from the *columbarium* of the freedmen of Octavia in the Vigna
Sassi near the Porta Latina at Rome[5] is also very rough and does
not show any new feature except that below the crossbeam there
is a bowl-shaped fitting similar to one which can be seen also on
the Zethus relief. On this mill again the top end of a central
spindle is visible, and it is to this and to the other internal fittings
of the Pompeian mill, for which the pictorial monuments cannot
provide more than an occasional clue, that we must now turn.[6]

---

[1] Garrucci, *Graffiti di Pompei*[2], pl. 25. 2, cf. 30. 19; Blümner, p. 45, fig. 22.
[2] Blümner, loc. cit.
[3] *Labora, aselle, quomodo ego laboravi et proderit tibi*; cf. Bücheler, *Carmina Epi-
graphica*, 1798.   [4] See above, p. 15.
[5] Blümner, fig. 18, after *Arch. Ztg.* xxxv, plate 7. 2 and p. 54; cf. Matz–v. Duhn,
Antike Bildwerke in Rom, no. 2863. The ass on this relief is wearing what may be a
muzzle (παυσικάπη; cf. below, p. 89): if so, this is the only pictorial evidence for a
muzzle in connexion with milling.
[6] No mention has here been made of a relief from Priolo in Lucania reported by

The two Vatican reliefs and several other monuments suggest
that some form of central rod or spindle was used in connexion
with the mounting of the hour-glass mill. Although the conical
shape of these mills might seem to make this unnecessary, the
pictorial evidence must be accepted, especially since it is confirmed by the remains of actual mills: some—though by no
means all—of the surviving *metae* bear traces of a spindle at the
top of their cone, and a spindle was one of two iron parts that
came to light during the excavation of a Pompeian mill.[1] This
extant spindle was very short, but since it was in a badly corroded
condition when found[2] part of it may have perished before it was
discovered: the monuments show a spindle reaching right up to
the crossbeam over the top of the *catillus*, and this is clearly the
spindle which connected *catillus* and *meta*.

Modern investigators, relying on the shortness of the spindle
actually discovered, have invariably taken it for granted that the
central spindle was firmly fixed in the top of the *meta*, as it is on
other types of contemporary mill.[3] This would necessitate a socket
in the top of the *meta*, and such a socket can in fact be seen on
a few of the extant stones (cf. Plate 9, Fig. *a*: the top of the *meta*
appears in the centre of the fragmentary *catillus*.). The Pompeian
wall-painting and the Palatine graffito also seem to show a
spindle fixed in the lower stone.

The Vatican reliefs, on the other hand, and the majority of
the stones found at Pompeii, suggest that the spindle was at least
sometimes attached firmly to the crossbeam and fitted with a
bowl-shaped end, which was placed on the top of the *meta* and
revolved round it. Some of the stones without socket (e.g. those
in Plate 6, Fig. *a*) show incised rings, presumably due to wear,
near the top of the *meta*, which agree well with such a hypo-

---

Orsi (*Notizie degli Scavi*, 1891, p. 359). The '*catillus*' on this relief is probably some
kind of capstan: the characteristic sockets are missing, and other implements on the
relief do not suggest any connexion with milling.

[1] Discovered by Mazois; cf. Overbeck–Mau, p. 387; Marquardt, *Röm. Privat-
leben*[2], p. 422, n. 1; Pasqué, *Mon. Ant.* vii. 499; Blümner, p. 27, n. 3. The reliefs
suggest that the spindle was sometimes made of wood, which may explain why
only one spindle has been found.

[2] Cf. Overbeck, loc. cit. If the iron parts did not belong to the donkey-mill
with which they were found (cf. below, p. 86), this is, of course, irrelevant.

[3] Notably the hand-querns described on pp. 103 ff., but not water-mills and the
like, where the spindle drove the upper stone (cf. below, pp. 122 ff.). But none
of these other mills are strictly comparable to the Pompeian donkey-mill.

thesis;[1] and if the bowl-shaped end of the spindle on the Zethus relief is of one piece with the spindle itself, the bowl at the upper end of the spindle, which appears on the relief, may provide a clue to the shape of the lower end, which unfortunately cannot be shown. Even a socket in the *meta*, moreover, does not make it certain that the spindle was fixed in it, since it may equally have revolved in the socket.

An arrangement of this kind may at first sight seem unreasonable, since a spindle attached to the crossbeam cannot be as effective in giving steadiness to the *catillus* as a spindle fixed in the lower stone. On the other hand it must have been very difficult, where the spindle was attached to the *meta*, to dismantle the mill: although the size of the mills on the relief from the Vigna delle tre Madonne appears exaggerated in relation to the mill slave, this relief, like the stones themselves, shows how hard it would be to lift the heavy *catillus* off the *meta* if a spindle nearly 2 ft. long had to be cleared above the top of the lower stone. This difficulty may well have made it seem advisable not to fix the spindle to the *meta*, but to attach it to the crossbeam.

Nor is it certain that to give steadiness to the *catillus* was in fact the main function of the central spindle; and this brings us to the other iron part which was found together with the single extant spindle. This was a disk, known in the technical language as rynd, which has a hole through its centre for the spindle, with four smaller holes near the periphery for the grain to flow through. The rynd is an integral part of rotary stone mills of all ages; for the upper stone has to be held in a position concentric with the lower, but it also needs a hole in its centre through which the grain can feed into the mill. The rynd bridges this hole without filling it completely, and thus provides a centre round which the stone can rotate, while allowing the grain to reach the stones in the right place.

Both the 'Olynthian' mill and some at least of the rotary hand-querns to be discussed presently had a hollow in the upper stone which could serve as a hopper. In the case of the 'Olynthian' mill no rynd was needed; but with rotary mills the necessary rynd is capable also of acting as feed control. Experiments with such a hand-quern[2] have shown that if the feed is too rapid

---

[1] The wear cannot have been caused by the *catillus*, which clears the *meta* altogether at that height; cf. Fig. 8.

[2] *Milling*, 24 June 1950; cf. below, pp. 152 ff.

(because the rynd does not block a sufficient part of the central hole) the hopper becomes useless and the grain has to be fed into the mill manually. The compact wheat grains tend to act as 'ball-bearings', causing the upper stone to 'ride' on them and passing through the mill unground.[1] This would be less likely to happen, owing to the greater weight of the *catillus*, with a large donkey-mill than with a hand-quern, but it must have been possible even with a large mill if the feed was sufficiently rapid.

The upper half of a Pompeian *catillus* is obviously capable of acting as a hopper, but it cannot do so as long as there is a possibility of too fast a feed from it into the mill proper. The separate funnel-shaped hopper with which the mills on some of the monuments are equipped[2] provided one possible method of controlling the feed, and the rynd may well have provided another. Only one rynd has been found, and we do not know whether rynds were at all common at Pompeii; nor is it even certain that the rynd which has been found was used with a large Pompeian mill, and not with one of the smaller hand-mills which are occasionally found there.[3] But it seems at least possible that rynd and hopper were in the case of the Pompeian donkey-mill alternative methods of controlling the feed. Of the two the rynd was clearly the more economical: it could be inserted into the *catillus* from below, and no further fixing would be required since the weight of the stone would suffice to keep it in place. Yet the rynd has one drawback: as the stones wear, the *catillus* drops lower and lower over the *meta*,[4] and there comes a time when the top of the *meta* protrudes above the centre of the *catillus* (see Plate 9, Fig. *b*). A rynd would become impossible long before this point is reached, and a hopper may well have been cheaper in the long run than the recutting or replacement of the stones which would be necessary if a rynd were used.[5]

---

[1] The critical point arrives when enough grain is under the stone to support its weight without being crushed.

[2] This applies to the relief from the Vigna delle tre Madonne, to the Bologna fragment, to the sarcophagus in the Villa Medici, and possibly to the Vigna Sassi relief.

[3] See Lindet, 1900, p. 23, and cf. below, p. 113.

[4] The drop would be much larger than the amount of wear—twice as large if the angle of the cone is 60 degrees, which is approximately the angle usual on the extant stones.

[5] If the rynd were inserted from above, it would be capable of acting as feed control, but it would not fulfil the main purpose of a rynd.

PLATE 9

a. Meta WITH SOCKET AT POMPEII

b. WORN *catillus* AT POMPEII

The other, and normally more important, purpose of a rynd—that of keeping the two stones concentric during grinding—was obviously less significant with mills of the Pompeian shape than with flat or nearly flat mills. On the other hand, it has often been pointed out[1] that it would be all but impossible to turn a mill of this type if the stones were allowed to come into contact with their entire grinding surfaces, and it has therefore been suggested that the spindle, either in connexion with a rynd, or in some other way, was used to keep the *catillus* suspended at a small distance above the *meta*.

The difficulty of turning the mill without such an arrangement has probably been exaggerated; for the Pompeian *meta* is, as we have seen, 'bell-shaped' rather than exactly conical. This shape was probably intended mainly to make the introduction of the grist gradual and to ensure a scissor-like cutting action on it as it approached the narrow part;[2] but it also meant that only a small part of the surface of the *meta* could come into contact with the interior of the *catillus*. This must have made the mill much easier to turn than if the two grinding surfaces had met over their whole area, and any difficulty there may have been was probably confined to times (especially just after restarting) when there was little grist between the stones. Even so, some form of suspension arrangement, to ensure a small but positive clearance between the stones, may have been necessary; and in view of the way in which the central spindle appears usually to have been fixed, this may well have been its main function. The weight of the upper stone could then be taken either by the rynd, if present, or else by the crossbeam and by the framework generally. In the former case the central spindle would almost inevitably have to be fixed in a socket in the *meta*, and since these sockets are rare on extant stones, it would seem that the alternative method was the more common. This is confirmed to some extent by the pictorial evidence (especially the Zethus relief), and if so, the rynd may well have been the exception rather than the rule at Pompeii.

In suspending the upper stone above the lower some provision must have been made for an adjustment of the distance between the stones, if only to keep this distance constant as the grinding

---

[1] See, e.g., Overbeck–Mau, p. 387; Blümner, p. 27.

[2] This would help to keep the bran particles large and to make subsequent sifting more effective.

surfaces became worn. Where a rynd was used this could be done only by washers inserted under the rynd: the mill would have had to be dismantled whenever an adjustment was needed, and the need for this may well have been a further reason for not using a rynd. Where the alternative method of suspension was used, a wedge could be inserted below the crossbeam without lifting off the upper stone, and it may be that the bowl-shaped fitting which can be seen on the Zethus relief was intended to facilitate adjustment made in this way. (There is even the suggestion of a wedge between the bowl and the crossbeam on this relief.)

It has been thought[1] that the purpose of such an adjustment was not only to ensure clearance between the stones but also to provide for different grades of grinding, to produce either coarse or fine meal. Provision for this was made on hand-querns of varying types perhaps as early as the first century A.D.,[2] and— probably even earlier—on olive-grinders.[3] On grain-mills the necessary adjustment would have to be very fine, but not impossibly so;[4] and although there is no positive evidence for graded grinding on the Pompeian mill, there is no certainty that it was not practised.[5]

The whole question of the internal fittings of these mills is so difficult, and there is so little evidence to go upon, that no certain conclusions can be reached, especially since it is doubtful whether the fittings used were as uniform as the uniformity of the stones themselves would suggest. A central spindle seems usually to have been present, but the purpose of this spindle and the method by which it was fixed must remain uncertain. Nor can we be sure whether a rynd was used in conjunction with, or as an alternative to, a separate hopper, or whether it was thought necessary to suspend the upper stone above the lower and to provide for an adjustment of the clearance. Without the pictorial monuments

---

[1] By, e.g., Blümner (pp. 27–28).

[2] Cf. Curwen, *Antiquity*, xi. 144–5, and below, pp. 118 ff.

[3] Cf. above, p. 58; Drachmann, *Ancient Oil Mills and Presses*, p. 9.

[4] An average grain of common wheat is about $\frac{1}{8}$ in. thick, and the adjustment would have to be much less than this. But the conical shape of the Pompeian mill means that the distance between the grinding surfaces would vary by only about half the amount of the vertical adjustment. (The 'bridge-tree' provided a similar, but much more effective, exaggeration of the adjustment on other mills; cf. below, p. 120.)

[5] Different grades of product will be discussed later; but they do not necessarily presuppose different grades of grinding.

(especially the two Vatican reliefs) we should know far less than
we do about these fittings, but even with their aid it is impossible
to be as certain about them as some previous discussions would
suggest. To end this chapter a word must be said about some of the
other implements shown on the Vatican reliefs. Some of these
will be discussed later;[1] others, though not immediately relevant
to our main subject, yet deserve some mention.

In the background of Plate 5, Fig. *b* a lamp can be seen on a
small shelf—and in the pseudo-Virgilian *Moretum* Simylus, the
'rustic tiller of a meagre farm', takes his place at the mill, 'and
on a little shelf, fixed to the wall for such a use, sets his trusty
light'.[2] It is a small detail, and interesting mainly because of the
Moretum passage: the lamp on the relief is probably meant to
indicate that, as we also know from literature,[3] the work was
never-ending and went on throughout the night.

For the blinkers worn by the horse on the same relief we also
have literary authority: Apuleius' 'Golden Ass'[4] mentions that
he had his eyes tied before being put to grind, and in a Greek
epigram[5] an ass complains that he has to do this work 'in dark-
ness'. For the muzzle, or projecting collar,[6] which as early as the
fifth century B.C. was worn by slaves and prevented them from
eating the product of their labour, these reliefs provide no evidence:[7] we know that it was used also for animals,[8] but probably
not when they were grinding, since the reliefs show that they
could be so harnessed to the mill that they could not bend down.
(The relevant passages may well refer to threshing animals, the
muzzling of which is expressly forbidden in the Bible.[9])

On the crossbeam on the Zethus relief there is a little bell,
which presumably indicated by its ringing that the mill was not

---

[1] Below, p. 167.
[2] *Mor.* 19 ff.:   'parvaque tabella,
    quam fixam paries illos servabat in usus,
    lumina fida locat.'
(But the mill in the *Moretum* is a hand-quern.)
[3] Ath. iv. 168b; *Anth. Pal.* xi. 251. 4; Babrius 29.2; Apul. *Met.* ix. 11; cf.
Blümner, p. 33.
[4] *Met.* ix. 11; cf. [Luc.] *Asin.* 42.   [5] *Anth. Pal.* ix. 301. 4.
[6] παυσικάπη; cf. Aristoph. *frag.* 302; Poll. vii. 20; Schol. Ven. Ar. *Pax* 14; and
Blümner, p. 33, n. 5.   [7] But cf. above, p. 83, n. 5.
[8] Eust. *ad Il.* xxii. 467, p. 1280. 37; Phot. 403. 6; Suid., s.v.
[9] Deut. xxv. 4; cf. 1 Cor. ix. 9, 1 Tim. v. 18.

idle: such bells used to be common with stone-mills of all kinds.[1]
For the hammer (?) below the bell no explanation can be suggested, and it is surely too far away from the bell to be connected
with it.[2]

Among the implements on the other side of the inscription on
this relief there are three corn-measures, the identification of
which is certain from similar measures on mosaics outside corn-
merchants' shops at Ostia.[3] The two larger measures are easily
identified as a *modius* and a *semodius*,[4] since these two measures
are prescribed by Cato for both his olive-yard and his vineyard;[5]
the smallest is probably a quarter-*modius*.[6] Ruler-like wooden
bars, like the two shown on the relief, were used for levelling off
the grain in the measure.[7] (They, too, appear regularly on the
Ostia mosaics.) The name *rutellum*, which is usually given to
these bars, is based solely, though with great probability, on an
early Latin fragment in which a corn-dealer is bringing with him
his *modius* and *rutellum*.[8]

These implements served the corn-merchant and miller of
antiquity in place of the sack and scales used nowadays. At a later
stage in this study we shall be much concerned with this difference
between measuring and weighing, which makes it peculiarly
difficult to assess in modern terms the quality of the products of
the ancient mill.

[1] Cf. Lindet, 1900, p. 25.
[2] *Pace* Blümner, p. 43.
[3] Cf. G. Calza, *Ostia, Nuovi Scavi* (Rome, 1947), pp. 10–11; Carcopino, *Ostie*
(Paris, 1929), p. 16.
[4] 1 *modius* = 2 *semodii* = 16 *sextarii* = 8·73 litres = 15·37 imperial pints (i.e. 1
sextarius = *c.* 1 pint).
[5] *Agr.* 10. 5 and 11. 3.
[6] One might expect a *sextarius*, but it is too large for this. In *Ed. Diocl.* xv. 48–51
wooden and iron-bound *modius* vessels are distinguished: those on the relief
appear to be iron-bound. (A *modius* and *semodius* are shown also on a sarcophagus
relief in the British Museum; *JRS*, viii. 180 and plate ii.)
[7] Cf. Jahn, *Ber. sächs. Ges. Wiss.*, 1861, p. 346.
[8] Lucilius, *frag.* 350 (Warmington).

XII

THE POMPEIAN MILL IN OTHER PARTS OF THE EMPIRE

So numerous are the finds of stones belonging to 'hour-glass' mills from the single site of Pompeii that they have largely overshadowed both the finds of other stones at Pompeii[1] and the finds of 'Pompeian' stones elsewhere. Writers who have described the Pompeian mill have little to say of the extent to which it was used in other parts of the Roman Empire,[2] and, since excavators are often not very interested in finds of this kind, it is difficult to know even now how widespread it was. Yet, although reported finds are for the most part confined to Italy, Roman Africa, and Gaul, there is some evidence to show that the Pompeian mill was also used in the Greek half of the Roman Empire.

On the basis of two literary passages[3] it has been thought that the little Aegean island of Nisyros, off the coast of Caria, was the most famous source of millstones of this kind. This may be so; but Nisyros was certainly not the only source, since the geographer Strabo,[4] who was an almost exact contemporary of Augustus, tells us that millstones were also made from the lava of Mt. Etna, and the 'grey, rough, porous tufa'[5] of which all the mills found at Pompeii are made is of a kind often found near volcanoes and probably local.[6] In general, volcanic lava was the most popular material because of its rough porous surface,[7] but other kinds of stone were also used, local stone being employed wherever a

---

[1] Cf. below, p. 113.
[2] See, e.g., Overbeck–Mau, p. 387; Blümner, p. 26.
[3] Strab. x. 488; *Anth. Pal.* ix. 21. 5. (Some would read the name also in *Anth. Pal.* ix. 418. 6; see below, p. 131 and n. 2.) Cf. Blümner, p. 29.
[4] vi. 269.
[5] Blümner, p. 29, n. 4.
[6] On the material of these mills cf. *PW*, xv. 2517; Blümner, p. 29 and notes; Mongez, *Mém. de l'Inst.*, N.S., iii. 480 ff.; Parsons, *Hesperia*, v, p. 86, n. 1; Jacobi, *Saalburg Jahrbuch*, iii. 83. (For a distinction between various types of millstone cf. Isid. *Orig.* xix. 10. 10.)
[7] Cf. Ov. *A.A.* iii. 290, *Med. Fac.* 58; Quint. ii. 19. 3; *Anth. Pal.* ix. 19. 8.

suitably hard and porous stone was available.¹ The export of
millstones on a large scale and over a wide area probably
developed only to districts where such stones were rare: the lava
of Andernach on the Rhine, which for centuries provided the
millstones for much of north-western Europe (including England),
seems largely to have gained its fame from the scarcity of suitable
material in the regions to which it was exported.

But even if Nisyros was not the centre of a millstone industry
of which the products reached most of the eastern Mediterranean,
there can be no doubt that animal-mills² were made of stone from
there, and that consequently animal-mills were in use in the
Greek part of the Mediterranean area. The French excavations
on Delos have in fact brought to light stones very similar to those
described in the last chapter,³ though much smaller and comparable rather to the small stones occasionally found at Pompeii⁴
than to the ordinary Pompeian donkey-mill. (Some of the mills
on Delos were surrounded by pavements resembling those which
at times surround the mills of Pompeii; cf. Plate 10, Fig. a.)

A variant form of segmentary lower stone has also been found
on Delos.⁵ But although it is probable, from their material and
location, that the lava segments found en grand nombre in the
houses there were combined to form the lower stones of animal-
mills, we cannot be certain of this; nor do we know, in the
absence of any parallel finds from elsewhere,⁶ how such a mill
looked when complete. A segmentary mill can have had no advantage except that segments are more easily transported than
complete stones: this supports the contention that local stone was
preferred wherever possible.⁷

¹ Lindet (1900, p. 29) draws attention to the local stone of which a mill found
at Amiens was made, and Strabo (x. 488) speaks of an abundance of millstones
among the people living near Nisyros.
² Anth. Pal. ix. 21 is spoken by an old horse.
³ Once it is recognized (pace Délos, xviii, p. 133 and n. 9) that the donkey-mill
on the Megarian bowl is doubtful, there appears to be nothing against assigning
these stones to the Roman era.
⁴ Cf. above, p. 64, and Plate 5, Fig. a. Two upper stones and one lower stone
are reported in Délos, xviii. 134 (cf. plates 391, 394, 396, and vol. viii, pt. 1, p. 229
fig. 108): their height (35 cm. for the upper, and 30 cm. for the lower stone) and
diameter (35–39 cm.) is approximately half that of 'normal' Pompeian stones.
⁵ Loc. cit. and fig. 158, plates 392–3, 397.
⁶ Except possibly at Ostia; cf. the stones in the foreground of Plate 10, Fig. b.
⁷ A third Delian type of stone has the top half of the catillus greatly reduced and
resembles a hand-quern rather than a Pompeian animal-mill.

PLATE 10

a. PAVEMENT SURROUNDING MILL AT POMPEII

b. GENERAL VIEW OF THE MILL AT OSTIA

An hour-glass mill found at Laurium was mentioned earlier, and we found reason to doubt the ascription of this mill to the great period of the Laurian mines in the fifth and fourth centuries B.C. It probably belongs to the first century A.D., when some parts of the mine were reworked and when Pompeii suffered the catastrophe which has preserved so many of these mills for us.[1] But whatever its date, and whether it was used for grinding grain or grinding ore,[2] this mill provides further evidence for the existence of Pompeian mills in the Greek half of the ancient world, this time on the mainland of Greece.

Pompeian mills, then, were in use both on the Greek mainland and on at least one of the Aegean islands; and Strabo's mention of a quarry for millstones on Melaena, a promontory opposite the island of Chios, suggests that this may have been true also of Asia Minor.[3] The evidence is small in bulk, but many stones may still be awaiting discovery, and others, already found, may have been omitted in the reports which are rarely as complete as that on Delos. The number of reported stones from sites, other than Pompeii, where the Pompeian mill is known to have existed is also very small, and here, too, much may still remain to be reported: mills of some kind must, after all, have been common wherever bread was eaten, as long as one mill could only serve a very few people.

Among the other sites where Pompeian mills have been found Ostia, the port of Rome, must take pride of place, not only because of its nearness to the capital, but also because it appears to be the only place outside Pompeii where a complete commercial mill has been discovered.[4] Part of this is shown in Plate 10, Fig. b; it contains ten mills of the usual type and size,[5] and is thus larger than any of the Pompeian establishments, where four or five is the usual number. It also gives an impression of much greater spaciousness both on account of its great height (as shown by an arch which must once have helped to support the

---

[1] But it may belong to the second century B.C., when the mines were also worked.
[2] The fact that both a Pompeian mill and 'Olynthian' stones were found at Laurium shows that the implements for grinding ore were like those used for grain at any given time.
[3] xiv. 645. But since Strabo says nothing about the type of mill made from Melaena stone, this must remain uncertain.
[4] See G. Calza, Ostia, Guida storico-monumentale², p. 130.
[5] But some of the metae at Ostia are hollow.

roof) and because the mills are not nearly so close to each other.[1] If it has received little attention this can be due only to the over-shadowing importance of Pompeii.

In the middle of the nineteenth century a number of millstones, all of lava and some with makers' initials[2] on them, were found lying about in the capital itself and in the countryside of Latium.[3] The report on them is concerned almost entirely with the lettering, and otherwise says merely that they 'are in every respect similar to those from Pompeii and do not offer any material for new observations': one could wish that a fuller description, or the preservation of the stones, had made a re-examination possible. In the same article the discovery of another stone in Sardinia is reported, but again no details are given except that it is *perfetta-mente simile ai pompejani*. A *meta* found at Vetulonia in Etruria, on the other hand, is described in a much later report[4] as made of granite with a terracotta base which provides a channel for the reception of the meal. This is similar to a stone at Naples men-tioned earlier,[5] except that in the case of the latter the channel is of one piece with the stone itself.

In North Africa, where a fair number of 'Pompeian' stones have been discovered, a *meta* with lava channel, rather smaller than the 'normal' Pompeian *meta* was found at Saint-Charles near Constantine,[6] and a complete mill, this time without a channel round the *meta*, is reported from Philippeville in Algeria.[7] The lower stone of this mill, like that of another found at Setif,[8] has sockets both in the top and in the flat lower face: the lower sockets must have been connected with the attachment of the mill to its base, but their precise purpose is uncertain. Another

---

[1] The distances between them vary from 4 ft. 8 in. to 7 ft., and no mill stands less than 2 ft. 9 in. from the wall: at Pompeii 3 ft. 6 in. from mill to mill is normal, and some mills are only 1 ft. 6 in. from the wall of the building.

[2] Cf. above, p. 77.

[3] de Rossi, *Ann. d. Inst.* xxix. 274 ff. and plate K.

[4] *Notizie degli Scavi*, 1894, pp. 356 ff.

[5] Above, p. 76.

[6] *Bull. Arch.* 1893, pp. 149–50, plate xv (found by L. Bertrand, reported by S. Reinach): diameter 55 cm.; height of *meta* 78 cm., of *catillus* 48 cm.; diameter of channel 115 cm.; depth of channel 15 cm.

[7] *Exploration scientifique de l'Algérie, Archéologie* (plates by M. Delamare, Paris, 1850; description by S. Gsell, Paris, 1912), plate 31, nos. 17 and 18; cf. Tissot, loc. cit. (above, p. 74, n. 4).

[8] Delamare and Gsell, plate 75, no. 1: the measurements show that this is a 'small Pompeian' mill.

catillus, found at Philippeville,[1] varies from the usual design in that protuberances for the reception of the beams cover the whole of one (presumably the lower) half of the stone.

A further Pompeian *catillus* is reported from Henchir el-Mzira in Tunisia,[2] and from Tunisia also comes the discovery of two stones which were interpreted as *metae* by the excavators.[3] The material of which these stones are made[4] supports this view, but their shape, as it appears on the diagrams, is such that, if they are *metae*, they are different from all others that we know.[5]

From the European part of the Roman Empire (apart from Greece) finds of Pompeian mills are, with one exception, reported only from the Gallic provinces, from Paris, Amiens, and Clermont-Ferrand.[6] That at least some of these mills were made in the neighbourhood where they were found is proved by the Amiens specimen which is made of a local sandstone; and the tombstone of one *M. Careieus, Marci libertus, Asisa, Pistor*, found in 1908 at Narbonne in the old Roman *provincia*,[7] shows that in Gaul Pompeian mills were worked in a way closely similar to that in vogue in Italy. On this relief there is a mill, driven by an ass with its eyes tied, complete with its framework and with a hopper above the centre of the crossbeam.[8]

Only one Pompeian stone has come to light in a European province other than Greece and Gaul: the Guildhall Museum in London possesses a Pompeian *catillus*, found on a site in Princes Street,[9] which shows that these mills were not entirely unknown elsewhere. It is hard to assess the significance of the fact that this

[1] Ibid., plate 160, nos. 11 and 12.
[2] Saladin, *Archives des missions scientifiques*, 3ᵉ sér. xiii. 141, fig. 247.
[3] Ibid., p. 48, fig. 74 (Henchir el-Heudba); p. 55, fig. 100 (Henchir Debdeba).
[4] *pierre dure* (p. 48); *pierre très poreuse et très dure* (p. 55).
[5] Their profile is curved inwards and they have a flat 'platform' (diameter 22 cm.) at the top; but the printed diagrams are very poor, and the main measurements of the stones (diameter 70 cm.; height 85 cm.) are close to those normal at Pompeii.
[6] Cf. Lindet, 1900, p. 29 and fig. 15.
[7] First published by H. de Villefosse, *Comptes rendus de l'Acad. des inscriptions et belles-lettres*, 1908, p. 498; cf. Espérandieu, *Bas-reliefs de la Gaule romaine*, ix. 190, no. 6903.
[8] A hopper in this position could hardly have worked: on other reliefs the hopper is off centre.
[9] *Antiq. Journ.* ix. 220. A mill found at Hamworthy (*Proc. Dorset Nat. Hist. and Arch. Soc.* lii. 124 and fig. 11) has an upper stone similar to the lower half of a Pompeian *catillus*, and may represent a British attempt to improve the Pompeian mill.

find is unparalleled; but it would be surprising if this were not due either to the accident of preservation or to faulty reporting, and if Pompeian mills had been as rare in Britain, Spain, Germany, and the Danube provinces, as the lack of extant stones suggests. Most of these territories had been occupied by Rome long before Pompeii was destroyed, and it is hard to think of any reason why the Roman occupation should not have brought the Pompeian mill in its train. Yet the available evidence does not allow us to say that mills of the Pompeian type were equally prominent in all parts of the Roman Empire.

XIII

ANIMAL-MILLS AND SLAVE-MILLS

LTHOUGH it has often been noticed that on all the monuments
that show the Pompeian mill at work the stones are turned
by animals,[1] the hour-glass grain-mill is commonly described as an 'animal- or slave-mill'.[2] In an earlier chapter
something was said about the distinction between slave- and
animal-mills in connexion with the name *mola trusatilis*, and the
conclusion was reached that no slave-mill that may have existed
when Pompeii was destroyed can have borne this name: we shall
now have to ask whether, apart from the name, it is right to say
that the Pompeian mill was worked by slaves as well as animals.

That some mills were still turned by hand after the animal-mill
had been invented is certain. In a Greek epigram, for instance,
the invention of the water-mill is said to relieve the mill-girls—
not asses or horses—of their weary task;[3] and in the pseudo-
Virgilian poem which has already been quoted the small-holder,
about to grind his corn, 'summons his two hands to the work,
dividing it between them: the left is bent on serving, the right on
the toil of the mill. This turns and drives the disk in constant
round; . . . and now and then the left takes over from her weary
sister and changes tasks with her.'[4] This mill, too, was worked by
man; nor can it have been of the usual Pompeian type,[5] since
even a small replica of the normal Pompeian mill could not be
turned with one hand.

But far more important than these few scraps of literary evidence are the many finds of rotary hand-mills on sites covering a
very wide area and a long period of time. Even in the Middle

[1] See, e.g., Reinach, *Bull. Arch.* 1893, p. 150.   [2] By, e.g., *BE*, i. 177 ff.
[3] *Anth. Pal.* ix. 418, quoted below, p. 131.
[4] *Moret.* 24 ff.:
> 'advocat inde manus operi, partitus utrimque:
> laeva ministerio, dextra est intenta labori.
> haec rotat adsiduum gyris et concitat orbem; . . .
> interdum fessae succedit laeva sorori
> alternatque vices.'

On the authorship of the *Moretum* see *Trans. Am. Phil. Ass.* 1930, pp. 195–216:
its date is almost certainly early imperial.
[5] *Pace* Fairclough (Loeb), ad loc.

Ages the feudal landlords had to take elaborate measures to pro-
tect their own large mills by the suppression of these 'querns',[1]
and in primitive societies they have survived to the present day:
they are frequently mentioned by modern travellers in the Middle
and Far East and in Africa, and they were in use even in the
Shetland islands at the beginning of the present century.[2] They
became finally obsolete only after the roller-mill with its large
capacity had made it possible to produce a better flour than any
of which the quern was capable[3] at so cheap a price that the labour
of grinding corn at home was no longer worth while. But granted
that these querns, to which we shall return presently, were still
worked by hand long after the animal-mill had become common,
it is still necessary to ask whether mills of the Pompeian type were
also driven by human as well as animal power, or whether, when
the fourth-century agriculturist Palladius[4] says that the water-
mill made both animal and human effort unnecessary, he has in
mind animals at the large mills and human beings at the quern.

If the Pompeian mill is called an 'animal- or slave-mill', and
if the examples of it actually found at Pompeii are often, and with
some confidence, described simply as slave-mills,[5] it is because
'it is evident from their close proximity to each other and to the
wall of the bakery that there was no room for them to be driven
by asses and none too much for the perambulations of slaves'.[6]
Now the measurements in question have already been quoted,[7]
and if a miller nowadays were to harness an animal to one of these
mills and to force it to walk round and round in such a narrow
circle, he would soon face a prosecution for cruelty: but the
monuments show clearly that animals were in antiquity harnessed so close to their mills that their use could only be ruled out
if the distance between wall and mill were smaller than the width
of the animal. This is nowhere the case.

In one Pompeian bakery, which has been fully reported as
typical of Pompeian bakeries generally,[8] the distance is in one

[1] Cf. BE, i. 210 ff.
[2] See Curwen, Antiquity, xi, plate iii.
[3] If whiteness is taken as the criterion, a flour of 85 per cent. extraction produced
by the roller-mill is still at least as good as a 35 per cent. flour from the quern; cf.
below, pp. 181–2.   [4] R.R. i. 41 (42).
[5] See, e.g., BE, i. 181; Jacobi, Saalburg Jahrbuch, iii. 84.
[6] BE, loc. cit.   [7] Above, p. 94, n. 1.
[8] By Overbeck–Mau, pp. 385 ff.

case just over 2 ft.[1] Yet it has been proved[2] that the mills in this bakery were animal-driven: the stones here (as elsewhere) are surrounded by pavements (cf. Plate 10, Fig. *a*) which probably indicate the presence of animals, since other parts of the bakery, where slaves must also have walked, are not paved; and, more conclusively, the mill-room is adjoined by a stable which, though badly ruined, could be identified as a stable by parts of the skeleton of an ass.[3] That asses were used to drive mills at Pompeii is, moreover, shown by the wall-painting of the feast of the Vestalia of which mention was made earlier. The greatest advantage of the rotary mill was, after all, that it made the employment of animals possible; and when, about forty years before the destruction of Pompeii, the emperor Caligula conscribed the mill-animals to carry his plunder, the result was a bread shortage at Rome:[4] this could hardly have occurred if it had been possible simply to substitute slaves for these animals.

In a seventeenth-century treatise on ancient mills[5] a distinction is made between the slave working in the mill (*serviens in pistrino*) on the one hand and the slave turning the mill (*molam circumagens*) on the other. This distinction, which has rarely been observed by later writers, is obviously valid: a mill-slave was not necessarily employed in the actual turning of the mill, and it will here be suggested that, once this is recognized, there is no evidence for the employment of slaves to turn mills of the Pompeian type.

The phrase *molam circumagens* in this treatise is clearly derived from the Gellius passage about the 'pushing-mill', which, as we saw earlier, provides little evidence for the employment of human beings on Pompeian mills. Similarly all the evidence for the employment of slaves to drive mills which is derived from the early comedies[6] must be discarded as probably referring to another kind of mill; and the fettered legs of mill-slaves,[7] though in no way remarkable for slaves working non-rotary mills[8] or for

---

[1] Measured by the present writer.
[2] By Mazois, *Ruines de Pompéi* (Paris, 1824), ii. 59.
[3] Ibid., fig. 528.   [4] Suet. *Calig.* 39.
[5] Heringius (cf. above, p. xxii, n. 1), p. 76.
[6] e.g. Ter. *Phorm.* 249. A pun in Cicero's *Letters to Atticus* (ii. 1. 9: 'ut Rhodi videretur molis potius quam Moloni operam dedisse') probably echoes similar conditions.   [7] Cf. above, p. 67 and n. 6.
[8] Or, for that matter, true that agricultural slaves were sometimes fettered (see, e.g., Cat. *Agr.* 56), but in their case considerations of security must have been very prominent.

those not actually working mills, could hardly be conducive to efficiency in an occupation which involved continuous walking.

There were, of course, at all times slaves in the *pistrinum*, and their plight was often little better than that of the animals that served there. But while Apuleius' 'Golden Ass', for instance, describes the fortunes of slave and animal as very similar,[1] it nowhere suggests that the two were put to the same employment—and surely a man transformed into an ass would mention it if his work had been the same as that of men not so transformed. Juvenal, moreover, for whom turning a mill is the lowest fate to which a horse can descend,[2] must have known of the famous examples of Plautus, Pittacus, and others,[3] who had demeaned themselves by doing similar work: yet when he comes to speak of the miserable lot of poets he says that they have come down to 'hiring bakehouses'.[4]

The use of animals in mills must have been economically advantageous, or animals would not have been used.[5] Nor is this surprising; for the mill appears to have been the place for the poorest sort of animal: Juvenal, about A.D. 100, speaks of the race-horse's 'slow-footed grandchildren, fit only to turn a mill';[6] a few decades later Apuleius' mill-donkeys are a sorry company;[7] and in the fourth century Ausonius mentions 'horses with but three feet and with their backs broken by the whip'.[8] The commonest mill-animal was undoubtedly the ass[9] which was notoriously cheap to keep,[10] and if horses were used they were horses unfit for any other purpose, their somewhat higher 'upkeep' costs being offset by their higher output and by the small initial outlay. In either case slaves must have tended to be more expensive, especially as a slave could not do as much work as even a donkey,[11]

---

[1] See *Note K*, p. 220. [2] *Sat.* 8. 67.
[3] Cf. above, p. 31, n. 2, and Heringius, p. 78.
[4] *Sat.* 7. 4.
[5] On this subject see N. Jasny, 'Wheat Prices and Milling Costs in Classical Rome', *Wheat Studies of the Food Research Institute, Stanford University, California*, vol. xx, no. 4, pp. 156 ff.
[6] *Sat.* 8. 67; cf. *Anth. Pal.* ix. 19–21, and, on mill-animals generally, Blümner, pp. 34–35 and notes.
[7] *Met.* ix. 13.
[8] *Epist.* 21. 35.
[9] See, e.g., Ov. *Fast.* vi. 318, Colum. vii. 1. 3.
[10] Cf. Plin. *N.H.* xviii. 44, Colum. vii. 1. 1, &c.
[11] Jasny (pp. 158–9) tentatively assesses the work done by a man and by a donkey at ¾ and 1¼ horsepower-hours per day respectively.

and if a slave would still be needed to drive the horse or ass, the same slave could supply the grist to the mill (cf. Plate 5, Fig. *b*) and perhaps sift the meal. (Even if slaves drove the mills, further human labour would still be needed both to keep the slaves at their task and to feed the mill and collect the meal.) If this difference in cost was at all considerable, the cheaper must, in commercial establishments, soon have ousted the more expensive; and all the evidence suggests that animal-power was considerably the cheaper.[1]

The word *pistor*, then, even when it does not refer to 'master bakers' like the Eurysaces of the monument, does not in classical Latin any longer denote the man who pounded grain: not only had pounding (*pinsere*) been superseded by grinding (*molere*), but human labour had almost certainly ceased to be employed on any but small hand-mills, and the *pistor* for whom, in A.D. 301, Diocletian's *Maximum-Price Edict* prescribes a daily wage which is twice the farm labourer's wage[2] must surely have been used for tasks other than actual grinding. In an epigram which may be contemporary with Diocletian the man who drives his own donkey-mill when he could at small expense obtain a donkey to do it for him is spoken of as a miser whose stinginess is almost beyond belief:[3] he might, perhaps, have used a slave instead of a donkey, but there is no evidence that it would have occurred to a Roman to do so. (One exception must perhaps be made: convicts may have been employed to drive mills, like those who worked the treadmill centuries later, and like the fettered criminals who pounded grain in mortars in Pliny's day.[4] But the evidence is not conclusive, and convicts are a special case in which the punitive

---

[1] See *Note L*, p. 220.
[2] vii. 1 and 12. The *pistor*'s wage of 50 *denarii* is the same as the price of half a *modius* [= *c.* ⅛ bushel] of wheat. (The *Edict* gives no other wage rates for occupations connected with milling or baking.) Cf. also *Note G*, p. 219.
[3] *Anth. Lat.* i. 103:
    'Cum possis parvo sumptu conducere asellum,
        qui soleat teretes volvere rite molas,
    cur nummi cupidus sic te contemnis, amice,
        ut cupias duro subdere colla iugo?'
The *Anthology* was first collected in A.D. 532–4, but this poem may well be earlier.
[4] *N.H.* xviii. 112. The *Theodosian Code* (ix. 40. 3, 5–7, 9; xiv. 3. 7, 17. 6) contains some orders of about A.D. 364, transferring to bakeries convicts who had earlier served in mines; but there is no proof that they were to turn mills. Cf. also Socrates, *Hist. Eccl.* v. 18. The only other evidence appears to be medieval; cf. Du Cange, *Gloss. med. et inf. Lat.*, s.vv. *molendinum de brachiis, molendinum sanguinis.*

element has often been thought more important than the economic use of labour.)

Diocletian's *Edict* also lists four kinds of mill—a horse-mill at 1,500 *denarii*, a donkey-mill at 1,250 *denarii*, a water-mill at 2,000 *denarii*, and a hand-mill at 250 *denarii* :[1] no slave-mill is mentioned, and the hand-mill must, from its low price, have been a small quern. Similarly Ofilius, a celebrated jurist of the first century B.C., distinguished between hand-mills and cattle-mills, assigning the former to *supellex* (household utensils) and the latter to *instrumentum* (stock-in-trade) ;[2] this distinction, too, surely indicates that even in Republican times there was a difference between large and small mills, and that only the small were commonly operated by hand.

The usual assumption, that rotary slave- and animal-mills existed side by side[3] (or that the same mills could be driven by either slaves or animals), ignores the most obvious benefit which rotary motion brought to milling by making the employment of animals possible. Our contempt for slave-owning societies tends to make us too eager to find some further hard and degrading work to which slaves have been put, and graphic descriptions are not lacking in modern literature of the sad plight of those who spent their days and nights walking round and round a Pompeian mill. The belief that slaves were used in mills of the Pompeian type is so well established that an uneasy suspicion must remain that it may after all rest on firmer foundations than appears to be the case : but until this belief has been justified on better grounds than it has yet been, the employment of slaves to drive the large Pompeian mill must be regarded as highly improbable.

---

[1] xv. 52 ff. The price for a *modius* [= *c*. ¼ bushel] of wheat is 100 *denarii* (i. 1).

[2] *Digest*, xxxiii. 7. 26.

[3] See, e.g., *BE*, i. 177, where the records of the two classes are said to be 'closely interwoven'. (*BE* further assume, without any evidence whatever, that among large rotary mills slave-mills preceded 'cattle-mills'.)

XIV

ROTARY HAND-MILLS

THE large hour-glass mill—whether driven by slaves and animals or only by animals—was undoubtedly not the only rotary mill of the Roman world, and smaller hand-querns are known to have been worked by human beings long after the Pompeian and other more advanced mills had been invented. Much of the detailed description of such querns that would have been in place in a study such as this has been made superfluous by two articles on querns in Britain by Dr. E. Cecil Curwen,[1] followed by a third, by Professor V. Gordon Childe, extending the area covered to the European continent and the Mediterranean basin.[2] The discussion in the present chapter will be concerned mainly with the developmental relationship between the two principal kinds of Roman mill; for the appearance of the quern is in most cases so different from that of the Pompeian mill that the development which led from one to the other presents a problem of special interest.

In the first of his articles Curwen put forward the novel hypothesis that the rotary principle first came to be applied to milling with the 'donkey and slave mills' which 'were a product of the increasing sophistication and complexity of town life', and that 'the rotary hand-mill was an adaptation of the new machine for the benefit of the peasants who lived far from the towns, and still had to grind their corn at home'.[3] At first sight this hypothesis has little to recommend it: it runs counter to one's instinctive expectation that the simple should have preceded the more complicated, and, as Childe has pointed out, 'such consideration for the . . . peasantry seems quite foreign to the spirit of bourgeois society in Hellenistic and Roman times'.[4] Childe considers that the soldiery, who also had to convert their grain into flour themselves, were more important in the townsman's eyes than the peasants, and in this connexion he draws attention to the

---

[1] *Antiquity*, xi (1937), 133–51; xv (1941), 15–32.
[2] Ibid. xvii (1943), 19–26.
[3] Curwen, 1937, p. 141.
[4] p. 24.

'hand-mills' which Xenophon mentions as part of the equipment of an army:[1] we saw earlier that these mills were probably not rotary, but they are a useful reminder that the supply of light portable mills for armies on the march must have been an important problem in antiquity,[2] and that the role of armies in the dissemination of new types of portable mill must not be underestimated.

Childe recognizes that Xenophon's 'hand-mills' need not have been rotary; but both he and Curwen believe that the donkey-mill goes back to at least 400 B.C., and Curwen's hypothesis rests largely on this belief. We saw earlier, however, that arguments based on the use of the name 'donkey' for the upper millstone—which Curwen thinks conclusive—must be discarded; and the archaeological indications, on the basis of which Childe considers Curwen's inferences from the literary evidence as established, have appeared on examination to be too tenuous to support this conclusion. Thus, while Curwen ascribes the invention of the rotary mill to a 'forgotten forerunner of Archimedes' (c. 287–212 B.C.),[3] the inventor may, on present evidence, equally well have been contemporary with, or even somewhat later than, Archimedes; nor can we be certain that the revolving grain-mill was 'with the possible exception of the potter's wheel . . . the earliest piece of machinery to replace an oscillating movement by a continuous rotary one':[4] the rotary olive-grinder may well be older than the rotary grain-mill.

But if neither the large nor the small rotary mill can be shown to have existed as early as Curwen and Childe believed, it is not as easy as Curwen thought to decide which is the older. The first literary mention of the donkey-mill is to be found either in Cato or in Plautus; and if, as we shall find reason to suspect, Cato's 'Spanish' mill (*mola hispaniensis*)[5] was a rotary hand-mill, the time-lag between the first mention of the donkey-mill and the first mention of the rotary quern is cut down to a few decades or disappears altogether.[6]

The next reference to a rotary hand-mill comes from the

---

[1] Cf. above, p. 17.
[2] Vegetius (*Mulomed.* iii. 49. 2 Gesner) mentions a weight of 5 Roman pounds = c. 3·6 lb.], but extant stones are usually heavier; cf. Schulten, *Numantia*, iv. 227.
[3] 1937. p. 138.   [4] Ibid. pp. 137–8.   [5] *Agr.* 10. 4.
[6] The survival of the mortar to the first century A.D. (Plin. *N.H.* xviii. 112) does not, as we have seen, prove a late origin for the quern (*pace* Curwen, 1941, p. 16).

pseudo-Virgilian *Moretum*, which was written about a century
and a half after Cato's book. But even if this were the earliest
mention of a quern, it would be impossible to argue that the
donkey-mill must have been invented before the quern because
its name occurs in literature some 150 years earlier. Not only is
the number of passages involved too small for such an argument,
but archaeologically the hand-mill precedes the donkey-mill by
at least the same interval of time.[1] The first finds of rotary hand-
mills dated with any degree of certainty come from the besiegers'
camp at Numantia in Spain[2] and belong to the early second
half of the second century B.C.: this date is so close to the first
certain occurrence of the donkey-mill in literature that it is impossible to decide which was prior on what would be the most
satisfactory basis.[3]

Yet, if we remember that the main advantage of the rotary
grain-mill[4] was that it made the employment of animals (and
other motive powers) possible, and that a desire to use animals
may well have provided the economic impetus for the new invention, Curwen's hypothesis loses much of its initial improbability.
The studies by Curwen and Childe of the development of the
quern after its first invention may, moreover, themselves provide
a basis for testing Curwen's hypothesis, if they can show whether
the donkey-mill is likely to have been derived from the quern or
the quern from the donkey-mill.

The available material is still very incomplete; but by using
two criteria suggested by Curwen, Childe felt able to distinguish
two coexisting families of rotary querns in the Mediterranean
basin and in the 'La Tène province' in the rest of Europe. (Outside the La Tène province—in 'Free Germany' and Scandinavia
—no rotary querns were current till the third century A.D.,[5] and
we may therefore confine our attention to the 'Roman' world,
though we may in some cases have to go back to before the
Roman era.) One of these criteria is concerned with the shape of
the stones, and more particularly with the slope of the grinding
surfaces; the other with the direction—vertical or horizontal—of

---

[1] The quern found by Orsi at Syracuse (above, p. 55) is here ignored.

[2] Schulten, *Numantia*, iii. 265 and plate 29. 3; iv. 73, 130, 227, and plate 50.

[3] All the datable archaeological evidence for the donkey-mill is considerably later.

[4] Unlike other rotary appliances, such as the potter's wheel or the olive-grinder.

[5] Cf. Childe, p. 19, and below, p. 113.

the handle-socket which every rotary quern must have in its upper stone.[1]

In the case of the donkey-mill a horizontal socket, with a horizontal attachment protruding from this socket, is the obvious way of turning the *catillus*, while on the quern a vertical handle is far more convenient: a horizontal handle on a quern, therefore, may seem to indicate the derivation of the quern from the donkey-mill. But although this criterion is valuable in that it helps to group the extant examples, it is not as reliable as it has been thought to be; for a horizontal socket does not necessarily presuppose a horizontal handle. None of the wooden handles have come down to us, and a reconstructed hand-mill in the Naples Museum (Plate 11, Fig. *a*) shows that it is a simple matter to fix a vertical handle even where the socket is horizontal. The additional leverage obtained by making the handle travel round a larger circle than if it were fixed vertically in the stone may have been quite important; and if so, it is no accident that the steeper and smaller querns show the horizontal socket more often than the flatter and larger stones.[2]

The slope of the stones is a less definite means of grouping extant stones, since practically all of them are sloped to some extent: but, if less definite, it is more important and more interesting a criterion than the direction of the handle-socket. The early saddle-stone was, as we have seen, always set at an angle so that the grain could feed through the mill by gravity; and the Pompeian mill in a rather different way followed the same pattern. With the Olynthian mill, on the other hand, which was set horizontally level, the grain was pushed towards the outer edges by the rubbing action of the upper stone, and the flow was regulated also by the herring-bone striations, which at the same time helped in the actual grinding. The effect of the rubbing action disappears when the stones move concentrically with one another; but on a rotary mill turned at any considerable speed it is replaced by centrifugal force which, in combination with an effective system of striations, was, by practical experience extending over several centuries, found sufficient in medieval and modern

---

[1] Sometimes the upper stone has a radial groove in its upper surface instead of a socket; but this may here be classed together with horizontal sockets.

[2] Cf. especially the late Roman, or post-Roman, disk type discussed by Curwen, 1937, p. 146.

PLATE 11

a. RECONSTRUCTED HAND-MILL AT NAPLES

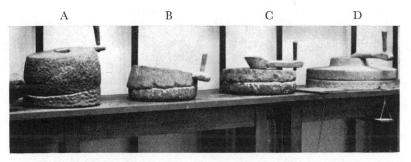

b. SERIES OF RECONSTRUCTED QUERNS IN THE MUSEUM OF THE SUSSEX
ARCHAEOLOGICAL SOCIETY AT LEWES

stone-mills to ensure a steady feed through the mill without the
assistance of gravity. Ancient mills never quite reached the point
where the stones became flat, but a tendency in this direction can
be observed, and prima facie the flatter of any two pairs of stones
is the more highly developed.

At first sight a conical mill has many advantages over the flat
mills to which we are so accustomed that they appear normal to
us: not only could the meal flow outwards naturally, but the
stones offered a larger grinding surface than flat stones of the
same diameter, and the problem of keeping the stones concentric
while allowing for the continuous feed of grain into the mill at
the centre was minimized. Yet these advantages are outweighed
by those of the flat mill: the conical shape was unnecessary after
all to ensure the outward flow of the grist, and might even cause
the grain to be hurried prematurely out of the mill;[1] a rynd-and-
spindle arrangement is more efficient in keeping the stones concentric than a conical slope; flat stones were easier to prepare and
to 'dress'; and although flattening might necessitate an enlargement of the diameter, this did not mean an increase in the volume
of the stones, which might even be considerably decreased,[2] with
a corresponding decrease in the weight of the stones, their cost,
and the cost of their transport. Hence it is not surprising that
querns should have become flatter as time went on; and for more
advanced systems of milling, in which the upper stone was rotated
from below by a spindle penetrating through a hole in the lower,[3]
flat (or nearly flat) grinding surfaces were a necessity.

Curwen's analysis of rotary querns in Britain, from the pre-
Roman La Tène culture onwards, shows a great variety of types
in use within a relatively short period. (Some details are given
in Table I.) A developmental grouping of these presents considerable difficulties: a single quern might well have a life long enough
to outlast considerable innovations,[4] and, since Britain was almost
certainly far distant from the place where the invention originated,
British querns probably show greater variety than that which

---

[1] Cf. Curwen, 1941, p. 29.
[2] Especially that of the upper stone: the lower stone of a conical mill could be
hollowed out below at the same angle as the grinding surface, but this could not
be done with the upper stone, if it was to have a 'hopper' in it.
[3] Cf. below, pp. 122 ff.
[4] Curwen (1937, p. 144, n. 13), from modern Scottish evidence, gives it 70–80
years, cf. *BE*, i. 159, 170.

TABLE I

Development of the Rotary Quern in Britain

Based on Curwen, Antiquity, xi. 133 ff.; xv. 15 ff.

Type and date	Diameter	Thickness of upper stone	Angle of grinding surface	Handle socket	Hole in upper stone	Remarks
PRE-ROMAN from c. 100 B.C.	12–14 in.	6–8 in.	c. 20° or segment of sphere	horizontal	oval or circular with slots	'beehive' shaped externally; three sub-groups distinguished with minor differences.
ROMANO-BRITISH DOMESTIC (a) Early: flat-topped	increased c. 15 in.	decreased c. 2½ in.	decreased 15° or less	radial groove or absent	oval, later rectangular	sometimes grooved. lower stone also c. 2¼ in. thick with spindle socket which later becomes hole right through stone.
(b) Later: with hopper projecting upwards from upper stone	20 in. or more*	2–2½ in.	10° or less	absent	rectangular	hole right through lower stone; under side of this stone is concave.
FLAT TYPES (a) Flat 'Beehive' Iron Age AB (Hunsbury)	tapering from 12 to 7–8 in.	6–10 in.	3° or less flat or nearly flat	horizontal leading into central hole	round with hopper	usually grooved. rynd problem unsolved (grain cannot pass spindle); 'beehive'-shaped externally.
(b) Roman legionary (?) late first–early second century A.D.†	similar to (a)	similar to (a)	3° or less	horizontal	similar to (a)	grooving rare; 'beehives' externally; rare in agricultural settlements.
(c) Disk type late Roman or post-Roman	variable	thin	3° or less	vertical	round	hole through lower stone; under side of lower stone slightly concave.

* The fragment of a stone 3 ft. 7 in. in diameter reported from Selsey seems reminiscent of the 'Saalburg' stones; cf. below, pp. 123 ff.

† The querns from the Scottish brochs (first to fifth century A.D.) are explained by Curwen as barbaric derivatives from the legionary type. Their thickness progressively decreases and the handle-socket travels upwards to become nearly vertical. They are distinct from the southern domestic querns in having flat grinding faces.

ROTARY HAND-MILLS

109

would be met with nearer the original home. Yet Curwen finds that such a grouping is possible, mainly on the basis of increasing diameters combined with the introduction of grooved grinding surfaces[1] and with a decrease in the thickness of the upper stone and a lessening of the slope.[2] The general line of development is well illustrated by a series of querns in the Museum of the Sussex Archaeological Society at Lewes (see Plate 11, Fig. *b*) which, though it does not show all, or nearly all, the local varieties found, leaves little doubt about the tendencies that were at work.[3]

The probable coexistence of two families of querns in Europe, suggested by Childe, may well have been one of the factors contributing to the great variety that prevails in Britain. Throughout the La Tène province, and in Algeria and on Delos, the existence of a quern with a thick upper stone of small diameter and a horizontal socket (cf. quern *A* in Plate 11, Fig. *b*), externally like the British 'beehive' (see Table I) but often rather flatter, is well established. From the examples found on Delos[4] it is probable that this type of quern goes back to the second century B.C., and, on present evidence, this must be regarded as the time when querns of Childe's first family probably originated in the Graeco-Roman world.[5]

The querns from the besiegers' camp at Numantia of the mid-second century B.C., to which reference has been made already, belong to Childe's second group, of which the most pronounced characteristic is a vertical handle (not, of course, extant) set in a vertically slotted lateral projection in the upper stone (see Fig. 10). Querns of this group are apparently found only in the Spanish peninsula, where they probably go back to pre-Roman days,[6] and

---

[1] Grooving is an unsatisfactory criterion, since its absence may be due not only to bad imitation of a grooved type but also to wear coupled with bad maintenance.
[2] But there are some exceptions, the most important of which is the small angle on some early specimens (Curwen's 'Hunsbury type'; 1937, p. 142; 1941, pp. 16 ff.); cf. Table I and below, p. 114.
[3] Cf. Curwen, 1941, pp. 24 ff. (The querns were restored by Curwen.) The quern marked *B* was used in the grinding experiments described below, pp. 152 ff.: it is said to come from Iver in Buckinghamshire, and is assigned by Curwen to the first century A.D.
[4] *Délos*, xviii. 131; cf. Childe, p. 20. (The same dating may apply also to the donkey-mills found on Delos.)
[5] They must then have spread fairly rapidly to reach Britain between 100 and 50 B.C. (cf. below, p. 110), but this is not improbable.
[6] 'In the Celtiberic west of the Peninsula', Childe, p. 20; cf. Schulten, *Numantia*, ii. 244.

their presence in the Roman camp at Numantia suggests that they entered the Roman area from Spain: when Cato, writing only a few years before the siege of Numantia, includes a 'Spanish

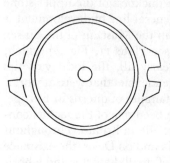

mill' in one of his lists, he may, therefore, well have had this kind of quern in mind.[1] (That a small quern should have been considered advisable in addition to the large donkey-mill need cause no surprise: a motorist may also own a bicycle.) By the projections for handles on stones of this group Childe is reminded of similar projections 'that are found, unslotted, on the rubbers of saddle-querns of the preceding first phase of Iberic Iron Age Culture in Catalonia':[2] if so, the handle fittings on these Spanish querns may indicate that this family at least was derived direct from a developed form of saddle-quern, similar perhaps to that shown in Fig. 2, without the intervention of the donkey-mill.

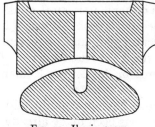

Fig. 10. Iberic quern

The case of the 'La Tène family' is rather different, although here too the earliest extant stones belong to the period for which the donkey-mill is first attested. The La Tène culture, which, probably in the early first century B.C., brought these querns to Britain, owed much to Graeco-Roman sources, and the quern, too, must have come from Greece or Rome since it did not reach the Scandinavian countries (which did not receive La Tène or Roman invasions) until the third century A.D. Yet the quern did not come to Britain with the first La Tène invaders in the third century B.C., but with a later wave, which probably means that the rotary hand-mill, if not the rotary mill generally, was still unknown in the Graeco-Roman world at the earlier time.

Curwen, in support of his contention that the rotary quern

---

[1] This was first suggested by Childe, loc. cit.

[2] Ibid.; cf. *Anuari d'Estudis Catalans* vi (1915–20), 647, fig. 469. These stones are themselves reminiscent of those from Priene and Delos discussed above, p. 43.

was derived from the animal-mill, points out certain similarities between the animal-mill and the earliest British querns. Among these the direction of the handle-socket is, as we have seen, not conclusive; nor does the slope of the grinding surfaces do much to support Curwen's view, since some of the earliest querns found in Britain are, like those from Spain, comparatively flat:[1] yet there is an unmistakable similarity between the donkey-mill and some of the earlier querns found in the Roman world, and Curwen has rendered a great service by drawing attention to it.

Something was said earlier about mills occasionally found at Pompeii which are exactly like the common animal-mills, but much smaller. It may be that these mills were designed to be worked by animals too young or too small to work a mill of the normal size, but they may also have been intended for operation by a human being: if the 'normal' Pompeian mill was worked only by animals, the small replica of it is then the closest relative among man-operated mills to the animal-mill, and on Curwen's hypothesis it should be the prototype of the quern. It is true that, since a mill of this kind must have been worked by walking round it and not by a mere movement of the arms of an otherwise stationary worker, it might more aptly be described as a slave-mill than as a hand-quern: but the transition from the one class to the other is easier than has often been thought. Some of the mills usually classed among hand-querns (e.g. that in Plate 11, Fig. a) cannot have been easy to work from a stationary position, and some large modern querns have, for the same reason, had two handles and been worked by two women facing each other.[2] The real difficulty in accepting the small Pompeian mill as the prototype of the quern is the good state of preservation in which its stones are often found: this suggests that they can hardly have belonged to the very early days of the rotary quern, since many of the more highly developed querns go back to a time considerably earlier than the destruction of Pompeii.

But even if these obvious replicas of the animal-mill are ignored

[1] An animal-mill of the Pompeian type moves so slowly that steeply sloping stones are needed to ensure the flow of grain through the mill: this is unnecessary with the much faster moving quern.

[2] Cf. Curwen, 1941, p. 30, and *BE*, i. 168 (with illustrations). Querns of this type usually have vertical handles; but even with the small Pompeian mill, which must have had horizontal handles, this would have been possible, though it is perhaps not probable.

there remains a similarity between the animal-mill and many of the earlier querns. Some British examples are quoted by Curwen;[1] and further evidence comes from the reconstructed quern at Naples mentioned earlier (Plate 11, Fig. *a*) and from stones found on Delos,[2] in Algeria,[3] and at various places in the La Tène province.[4] Some of these querns have the characteristic symmetrical upper stone of which the upper half is capable of acting as a hopper. But even these early examples are not as steeply sloped as the normal animal-mills, and as time went on querns tended to become flatter. A comparison between the relevant measurements of the three reconstructed mills at Naples (see Table II) shows that the decrease in the thickness of the

TABLE II

Comparison between three Reconstructed Mills at Naples

	Large Pompeian (Plate 4, Fig. b)	Small Pompeian (Plate 4, Fig. a)	Quern (Plate 11, Fig. a)
Height of *catillus*	2 ft. 1 in.	1 ft. 2 in.	7 in.
Diameter of *catillus* at widest point .	2 ft. 4 in.	1 ft. 3 in.	1 ft. 1 in.
at narrowest point . . .	1 ft. 2 in.	8 in.	11 in.
Depth of hollows in *catillus* (approx. = depth of sloping part of *meta*)*.	11 in.	6 in.	3 in.
Distance of *catillus* from mill-base when in position on *meta* . .	1 ft. 2 in.	9 in.	5¾ in.

* Since both the hopper and the grinding faces became flatter the stone remained symmetrical and the depth of the hollows on either side of it equal.

upper stone was brought about both by a flattening of the grinding surfaces[5] and by a gradual lessening of the hopper part of the *catillus*. But the grinding surfaces never in antiquity became quite flat, and traces of a hopper can be seen even on late querns.

To the published examples already mentioned, which, though similar in other respects to the animal-mill, show this flattening, there should be added an example from the Villa Boscoreale on

[1] 1937, p. 140 ff.
[2] *Délos*, xviii. 131.
[3] Delamare and Gsell, op. cit. (above, p. 94, nn. 7–8), plate 75. 1 (a 'small Pompeian' mill).
[4] Cf. Childe, p. 19 and n. 7 (with references).
[5] On the Naples quern the slope is rounded.

PLATE 12

b. SMALL MILLSTONE AT POMPEII

a. SMALL *meta* FROM THE CASA DI SALLUSTIO
AT POMPEII

PLATE 13

a. SMALL MILLSTONE AT NAPLES

b. PAIR OF 'LARGE SAALBURG' MILLSTONES

the slopes of Mt. Vesuvius[1] and some further instances from
Pompeii itself. Some stones can be seen lying about there—
utterly neglected for the many 'bigger and better' mills—which
must surely have been the *metae* of rotary querns of the type just
described: they are made of the same lava as the large animal-
mills, and on two such stones at least (Plate 12, Figs. *a* and *b*)
a central spindle-socket can be clearly seen.[2] All these stones support Curwen's hypothesis by showing that there was a similarity
between the animal-mill and at least some of the earlier hand-
querns.

But the problem may be rather more complicated than Curwen
thought. Childe,[3] pointing out that a 'Nordic' origin for the
rotary quern is ruled out by its late appearance in 'Free' Germany and Scandinavia, suspects that it came into being in a more
westerly region than has usually been considered likely—i.e. in
the Spanish peninsula: yet he feels reluctant to accept this, both
because he shares the belief that the donkey-mill must have
existed in Greece by the fourth century B.C., and for another
reason which suggests 'that the home of the invention should be
sought even further *east* than the regions hitherto surveyed'.[4]

Pairs of stones, not unlike querns but considerably smaller,
have been found on some very early sites in Palestine. They are
'4–6 inches in diameter, with their plain faces in contact and a
raised collar round the nether stone into which the upper fits;
a tenon in the middle of the nether fits into a mortise in the upper'.[5]
These stones, which are usually interpreted as 'paint-grinders',
are much too small for grain-mills; but they might seem to point
to the simultaneous existence of the rotary corn-grinder which in
appearance closely resembles them. Yet, in spite of the fact that
the mills of the Old Testament are, like Homeric and other
early mills, commonly thought of as rotary,[6] no finds of rotary

[1] *Mon. Ant.* vii. 493–4 and fig. 65.
[2] A less heavy type of stone can also sometimes be seen in the forgotten corners
of both Pompeii and Ostia. (Plate 13, Fig. *a* shows one such stone—almost certainly from Pompeii—in the Naples museum.) These small stones (12–14 in.
in diameter) probably belonged to a rotary grinder, but they cannot have been very
satisfactory since they are made of a conglomerate much softer and grittier than the
normal lava.
[3] p. 19.   [4] Ibid., p. 23.
[5] Macalister, *Gezer* (London, 1912), ii. 35 ff., quoted by Childe, pp. 23–24.
[6] See, e.g., Benzinger, *Hebräische Archäologie* (Freiburg, 1894), pp. 84–85; also
above, p. 8.

grain-mills are reported from Palestine from before the hellenistic period, which in Palestine extends well into the first century B.C.; and the earliest rotary grinders with a completely per-forated upper stone that have been found there belong to the early Arab age.[1] This suggests that the 'paint-grinder' did not develop into a quern in Palestine, and there is one important difference between the two which may account for this apparent paradox.

Some early British querns[2] had a hopper in the upper stone, but the hole leading from this hopper to the top of the lower stone was, as is shown by remains of iron fittings, too narrow to allow the grain to pass the spindle. The hopper, which thus could not serve as a hopper, seems to indicate that this type of quern was a bad imitation of something more advanced: it clearly did not function properly, and it is archaeologically established that it was soon abandoned. Once the 'Olynthian' mill had provided for a continuous feed of grist into the mill, a similar arrangement was evidently considered essential on grain-mills of all kinds, and henceforth no mill that failed to contain it was considered satis-factory. With small quantities, as in the case of paint, it matters little how the mill is fed, especially if the substance to be ground is one that needs fairly long grinding before the required particle size can be obtained: with corn the individual grains are quickly reduced to meal, but comparatively large quantities are involved even in small-scale milling, and the absence of a continuous feed becomes a serious inconvenience: it may well have been the difficulty of keeping the stones concentric while allowing for the continuous passage of grain into, and meal out of, the mill that prevented the Palestinian 'paint-grinder' from becoming a corn-mill.[3]

It may seem improbable that a small problem of this kind, which could be solved simply by introducing a rynd, should have held up the development of the rotary quern for any length of time; but the chief advantage of the rotary mill over earlier corn-grinders was, after all, not that it brought revolving hand-mills, but that it made possible the employment of motive powers other than human labour. With the hand-mill the advantage of rotary

---

[1] Some 'round millstones', found together with saddle-querns and Olynthian mills, are reported from Tell Halaf (von Oppenheim, *Tell Halaf*, Eng. trans., p. 206); but they cannot be accurately dated and may well be hellenistic.
[2] Notably Curwen's 'Hunsbury type' (1941, p. 18); cf. above, p. 109, n. 2.
[3] See *Note M*, p. 220.

over oscillatory motion is slight, and Curwen[1] even relates that some of the larger modern Scottish querns, though rotary, were worked by a backward-and-forward movement by two workers: here the advantage of rotary motion was evidently not considered sufficient to compensate for the continual changing of hands which it would have involved.

The 'rynd problem', then, was probably not solved early in Palestine,[2] and, since the donkey-mill had probably not come into being in the fourth century B.C., Childe's suspicion that the quern may have originated in the eastern part of the Mediterranean basin must, at least for the present, be discounted. It still appears likely that both the quern and the rotary mill generally were invented in a more westerly part of the area, and the Spanish querns to which Childe was the first to draw attention are still the earliest rotary mills of which examples are extant. These querns, it will be remembered, were probably derived direct from the saddle-stones.

If the Spanish quern is indeed the *mola hispaniensis* mentioned by Cato, it would appear that in Italy by about 160 B.C. the donkey-mill was quite well established while the hand-quern was a newcomer which still retained a name that connected it with its country of origin. If so, the rotary mill must have been invented twice over in two different places and in two different forms: the large, steeply conical animal-mill is first found in Italy, while the quern, flatter and more portable, seems to derive from Spain and to have come to Rome with the conquest of that country. Yet Curwen is undoubtedly right to insist that in Italy, in the Graeco-Roman world generally, and throughout the La Tène province, the early quern shows features which can only be explained by the influence of the animal-mill upon it; and in some respects—e.g. the steeper slope of the grinding surfaces—these features are retrograde in comparison with the Spanish quern: this makes it difficult to assume that the La Tène family of querns is directly descended from the Spanish family, although the Spanish family is probably the older of the two.

[1] 1941, p. 30.
[2] It is not clear whether the querns from Tell Halaf in North Syria (cf. above, p. 114, n. 1) had a perforated upper stone or not. But if they are hellenistic this does not affect the present argument, since they may be either imports from further west (if perforated) or else further examples of the 'unsuccessful' type found at Gezer by Macalister.

It may be that the Romans received from Spain the bare idea that the rotary principle, which they knew in connexion with the donkey-mill, could be adapted to the hand-mill, and that they then invented their own version of the hand-mill. But this is mere conjecture, and not very probable conjecture at that; for at whatever time the rotary mill was invented, the invention must have been so epoch-making that it is unlikely to have been made independently in two different places. A suspicion must therefore remain that there was a common origin about which we still know nothing. On the available evidence it is probable that the place of this common origin was somewhere in the western part of the Mediterranean basin, the part round which the distribution of the Pompeian mill is also centred. The time of the invention may well have been the period when Rome was struggling with Carthage for the supremacy over that part of the world. Further research there may yet find the answers to many of the questions that have had to be left unanswered in this chapter.

Once invented the rotary mill spread very quickly throughout the Roman world. In some places—e.g. Britain—it even preceded the Roman conquest; but it remained confined in antiquity to those parts of the world which were at some time under Roman domination,[1] and the part played by the Roman armies in promoting the rapid diffusion of the new invention must have been very great indeed.

Julius Caesar[2] tells us that when the Helvetians in 58 B.C. set out for their migration they took with them 'food ready ground' (*molita cibaria*) for three months, and it seems safe to infer that this 'food' was ground on mills—whether rotary or non-rotary— of a size large enough to prevent them from being easily transported. Now for short marches Roman armies, too, may have ground their grain before setting out; but we know from inscriptions on some extant millstones that in the second and third centuries A.D. the hand-quern was part of the equipment of the *contubernium* of ten men, while the *centuria*, of approximately a hundred men, had a larger mill, at least in the more permanent camps.[3] A similar arrangement appears to have been in force at

---

[1] The only possible exception is the Far East, which cannot here be considered.
[2] *B.G.* i. 5. 3.
[3] Cf. H. Jacobi, *Saalburg Jahrbuch*, iii. 85 and references there (esp. [Front.] *Strat.* iv. 1. 6); also Veg. *Mil.* ii. 8, 13.

the siege of Numantia in the middle of the second century B.C.,[1] and by the middle of the first century B.C. provision difficulties could be caused to an army on the march if it lost the mills that it carried,—even though sufficient corn was available.[2] It was clearly the quern, rather than the donkey-mill, that was spread by Roman armies in this way, and if the quern thus achieved a much wider diffusion than the donkey-mill it must have been because it was both more portable and much cheaper: the progressive flattening of the stones, which formed a prominent feature of its development, helped further to lessen both its weight and its cost.

Even with a steeply conical mill a rynd-and-spindle arrangement was, as we have seen, desirable: with flatter stones it became indispensable, and it has remained so to the present day. Grooving, too, became more necessary—and is in fact more frequent—as the grinding surfaces became flatter, and when at last they became quite flat, grooving too had become indispensable. The upper stone meanwhile remained solid and heavy for some time: its weight was needed as long as the grist passed fairly rapidly through a sloping mill whose diameter had to remain small if the whole appliance was not to grow too cumbersome. Once flattening had retarded the passage of the grain the upper stones could be made less thick, and thinner upper stones are a marked feature of the more advanced querns. The thickness of the lower stones remained approximately what it had been earlier near the periphery, but the effect of the flattening was to make the stones thinner near the centre, until a stage was reached when they had become too light to remain stationary during grinding unless they were held by hand or securely anchored to a table or to the floor.[3] How this was done when the quern was moved about from place to place we do not know: perhaps the soldier working it squatted on the floor, in the way familiar from photographs of modern querns in use,[4] with the quern itself embedded in the soil; or it may be that a different arrangement, to be described presently,[5] was sometimes employed.

---

[1] Cf. above, p. 105 and n. 2.

[2] Plut. *Anton.* 45: the mills in this case appear to have been carried by animals, but even so portability must have been important.

[3] During the experiments at Lewes (cf. above, p. 109, n. 3) the stone was not anchored, and it was found more strenuous to keep the lower stone from turning than to do the actual grinding.

[4] e.g. *BE*, i. 135, 165, 168.   [5] Below, p. 120.

The quern, then, was used wherever a portable mill was needed, and considerations of portability almost certainly influenced its development. But although it was as the portable mill that the quern achieved its great territorial diffusion, it was also used by soldiers in permanent stations, and it was above all the domestic mill of the small household. This was its main function for many centuries, and it must have been the function of many of the querns that have been found. In the household also we meet the quern in the Augustan poem mentioned earlier, where it is worked by a man who 'goes away and *stands* at the mill':[1] these words appear to refer to a mill which had its fixed place on some kind of understructure[2] to which the lower stone was probably anchored in some way.

It must have been on querns of this type that a further development first took place, a development that can be seen also on some modern Scottish querns in connexion with which it has been described as follows:[3]

The quern usually stands in a niche of the porch of the cottage upon a bench constructed for the purpose. The lower stone, left very much in the rough underneath, is bedded in clay so that a level grinding surface may be obtained;[4] and the hole for the spindle, no longer a mere socket but a perforation passing entirely through the stone, is tightly fitted with a block of wood, also perforated, serving for a bearing for the spindle which passes through it and below the stone and rests on a narrow board beneath. The top stone, as usual, rests by means of its wooden rynd upon the top of the spindle. The adjustment for coarse or fine grinding is secured by raising or depressing the spindle (and so the top stone) from below. . . . The spindle stands upon the narrow board, or bridge tree, one end of which rests loosely on a recess in the wall behind the table; the other end being held up by a string doubly twisted, which passes through a hole in the front of the table, and is secured by an oblong wooden button. . . . By turning the oblong button the string is either twisted and shortened, or untwisted and lengthened; the bridge tree being thus raised or lowered and with it of course the upper stone: any degree of grading being

---

[1] [Virg.] *Moret.* 19: 'abit adsistitque molae.'
[2] Perhaps the *molile* (?); cf. *Note E*, p. 219.
[3] *BE*, i. 173–4, after A. Mitchell, *The Past in the Present* (1880), pp. 33 ff.
[4] —and so that it may be firmly held: the clay would grip a rough surface better than a smooth one, which is an advantage additional to the smaller cost of a rough surface. (L. A. M.)

thus easily obtainable without the ancient trouble of lifting off from time to time the upper stone.

An arrangement of this type, illustrated in Fig. 11, requires (in addition to an efficient rynd fixed in the upper stone) a lower stone that is completely perforated, and such lower stones are

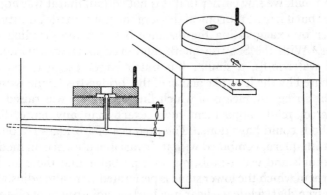

FIG. 11. Diagram showing view of and section through adjustable Scottish quern (cf. quern *D* in Plate 11, Fig. *b*)

found among Romano-British querns. At least one of these, from Glastonbury,[1] must date from before A.D. 70, and in view of the modern parallels it has been inferred that the perforation of the lower stone means that these querns, too, were adjustable.

This question was touched on in connexion with the Pompeian mill.[2] The importance of adjustment in the case of oil-mills is beyond doubt,[3] and it is well known that flours of different grades could be produced in antiquity. Since, moreover, Columella prefers the oil-mill to the *trapetum* just because it was adjustable,[4] it has been thought either that Columella's *mola* was used for both oil and corn, or that it was at least of a construction similar to that of the corn-mill, so that what applied to one must have applied to the other.[5] But it has now been shown[6] that the *mola olearia* was quite different from the grain-mill; the argument that the grade of flour produced depended solely, or mainly,

---

[1] Curwen, 1937, p. 145. [2] Above, pp. 87–88.

[3] Cf. above, p. 58, and Drachmann, op. cit., pp. 41–44. The secret of how to avoid crushing the kernels by adjusting the mill to the size of the olives was lost for a time later. [4] xii. 52. 6.

[5] See, e.g., Jacobi, *ibid.*, p. 87.

[6] By Drachmann, loc. cit., following Brøndsted, *Recherches à Salone*, i. 112.

upon the setting of the stones is fallacious;[1] and the adjustment for olives was far less fine than that which would be required for grain.

Yet, as the Scottish quern shows, some provision for adjustment has at times been made even on small mills. As regards the Pompeian mill, we saw earlier that it is not certain that it was adjustable; but if it was, the conical shape of the stones made adjustment easier by exaggerating the distance between the grinding surfaces.[2] With the Scottish quern, and even more with windmills and water-mills, a similar but much larger exaggeration was procured by the leverlike action of the 'bridge-tree':[3] the twisting of the string, by means of which the bridge-tree was raised and lowered, made adjustment more exact than any more direct methods could have done.[4] The presence of a bridge-tree on the Scottish quern, combined with its invariable presence on modern windmills and water-mills, makes it probable that those ancient querns of which the lower stone is perforated were also adjustable. It is true that, while we hear much of the adjustment of oil-mills, there is no mention in ancient writings of a similar arrangement for the grain-mill[5]—and we saw earlier that the difference in this respect between the two may well be more important than has commonly been thought: but the argument from silence cannot be pressed, and we are left with the mute witness of some completely perforated lower stones which suggest that there were in antiquity at least some grain-mills capable of adjustment.

If this cannot be regarded as certain it is because there are at least two other possible explanations for the complete perforation of the lower stone. The first of these must apply to some querns found at La Tène[6] which appear to have consisted of three distinct stones: the upper stone is of the normal 'beehive' type with hopper and handle-socket; but the lower stone is divided into a disk, a mere $2\frac{1}{2}$–3 in. thick and pierced right through, and a base

---

[1] It will be shown later that sifting and perhaps repeated grinding must at least have been important factors.

[2] Cf. above, p. 88, n. 4.

[3] See, e.g., *BE*, ii. 311. On some windmills a complicated system of levers was used to achieve the same result.

[4] Its effect resembles that of the thread on a screw, and screws have in fact been used instead of string; cf. *BE*, loc. cit.

[5] The 'difference in the mill' (*molae discrimen*) in Plin. *N.H.* xviii. 87 does not imply that the mill was adjustable; cf. below, p. 156.

[6] Vouga, *La Tène*, pp. 77–80 and plate xxvi; cf. Childe, pp. 19–20.

with a gently tilted surface containing a blind socket for the spindle. The spindle here seems to have been used not only to keep the stones concentric, but also to keep the whole mill in position on its base. Since the socket in the base is blind this quern cannot have been adjustable, and the main function of the hole in the lower stone must have been to keep the mill steady during grinding.[1] This was essential where the lower stone was light enough to be easily transported, and it may be that this explanation for the hole in it applies to other querns besides those from La Tène. The other explanation, which again must apply to at least some stones, is connected with a new way of driving the mill, and this must next be discussed in some detail.

[1] It can only have helped to do so, and other methods must have been used to prevent the lower stone from revolving.

XV

THE GEARED MILL

THE Augustan architect and engineer Vitruvius in the tenth book of his work *On Architecture*, after discussing some water-driven machines for raising water from one level to another, goes on to describe a machine for grinding corn, thus:[1]

Water grinders are turned on the same principle and have the same construction, except that at one end of the axle [of the water-wheel] a toothed drum is fixed. This is placed vertically on its edge and turns with the wheel. Adjoining this, there is a second and larger drum, also toothed and placed horizontally, by which it is gripped. [Or, with the text of one Renaissance edition,[2] '. . . placed horizontally, which holds an axle that at its extreme upper end has an iron dovetail by which the mill is held'.] Thus the teeth of the drum which is on the axle, by driving the teeth of the horizontal drum, cause the grindstones to revolve. In the machine a hopper is suspended and supplies the grain to the mill, and by the same revolution the flour is kneaded.[3]

This passage contains the only description of a grain-mill of any kind that has come down to us from antiquity, and the essentials of the construction are clear: a vertical water-wheel is used to drive a gear-wheel which meshes into a second and horizontal gear-wheel whose revolution turns the mill (see Fig. 12).[4]

The relevance of this passage to the question of the perforated lower stone, mentioned at the end of the last chapter, becomes obvious when it is realized that the axle which is attached to the horizontal 'drum' must at its other end be attached to the

---

[1] See *Note N*, p. 220.

[2] By Fra Giocondo, whose reading ('. . . quo continetur axis habens in summo capite subscudem ferream, qua mola continetur') may be what Vitruvius actually wrote; cf. *CR*, N.S., vi. 193 ff.

[3] The last few words seem to refer to a kneading-machine driven by the same water-wheel as the mill. At Pompeii and Ostia kneading-machines driven by men or animals are frequent (cf. Blümner, pp. 64–65); but this is the only Roman evidence for water-driven kneading-machines.

[4] In the diagram, which is based on Jacobi's reconstruction, the horizontal 'drum' is smaller than its vertical counterpart, and not larger as prescribed by Vitruvius. This is due to some uncertainty concerning the Vitruvius text, on which see *CR*, loc. cit.: the gearing ratio probably depended on the current (speed and volume of water) of the mill-race or stream by which the mill was driven.

movable—i.e. the upper[1]—millstone, and that to reach the upper
stone it must penetrate through a hole in the lower. (The text of
Fra Giocondo's Renaissance edition makes this explicit, but it is
clear also from the generally accepted text.) From Augustan
times onwards, therefore, the perforation of a lower millstone

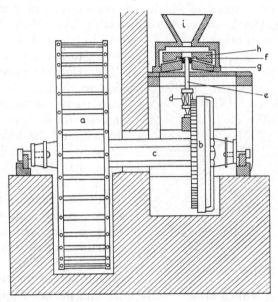

FIG. 12. Roman water-mill according to Vitruvius
a—water-wheel; *b*—vertical 'drum'; *c*—axle of *a* and *b*; *d*—horizontal 'drum';
e—axle of *d*; *f*—iron dovetail; *g* and *h*—millstones; *i*—hopper.

may mean that the mill was driven from below: in Vitruvius this
principle is confined to water-mills, on which more will be said
in Chapter XVI; but there is good evidence to show that it was
employed also, certainly by the third century A.D., to drive mills
for which no water power was available. Some of the forts on the
Roman frontier fortifications in Germany—notably the Saalburg
on the Taunus range[2]—have yielded a great number of millstones

---

[1] Mills with movable *lower* stones have been known very occasionally, but the
extant stones here to be discussed show that mills modelled on Vitruvius were of
the normal kind with movable upper stones.

[2] The Saalburg was abandoned between A.D. 260 and 270, and objects found
there must normally date from before then; cf. Jacobi, *Der obergermanisch-raetische
Limes des Römerreiches*, Abt. B, Bd. ii. 1, no. 11 (Lief. 56), pp. 70 ff.; Fabricius, ibid.,
Abt. A, Bd. ii, Strecke 3 (Lief. 52), pp. 126 ff.

which are unlike any that have been discussed so far, though their similarity to some of the more developed querns is unmistakable. These stones fall into two classes, large and small; and inscriptions on some of them show that the large belonged to the *centuria* and the small to the *contubernium*.[1]

The larger stones, of which a representative pair is shown in Plate 13, Fig. *b,* are made of a basaltic lava,[2] their diameter varying from 66 to 81 cm. [= 26–32 in.] and their thickness from 7 to 20 cm. [=$2\frac{3}{4}$–8 in.].

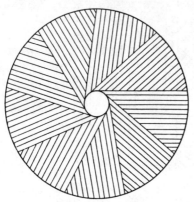

FIG. 13. Grooving pattern on Saalburg millstones

(The relatively great variation in thickness is due at least partly to wear.) Both stones are completely perforated, and the hole in the upper stone is usually much larger than that in the lower. In the grinding surface of the upper stone there are dovetail-shaped recesses on opposite sides of the central hole: sometimes there is a double dovetail (see Plate, 14 Fig. *a*), but one of the two pairs of recesses is then always badly worn and the other appears to be a recut. The grinding surfaces are normally grooved in the pattern shown in Fig. 13,[3] and slope at an angle of approximately 10 degrees. The lower face of the lower stone usually slopes at a similar angle, but the upper face of the upper stone —i.e. the top face of the assembled mill—is flat, sometimes with a slightly raised rim near the periphery. In this face there are sometimes two blind holes on opposite sides of the centre, which were probably sockets for rings by which the stone could be lifted.

The shape of these stones is alone enough to show how the mills to which they belonged were set up for operation: the dovetailed stone must have gone on top; the spindle, with an attachment to fit into the recesses, must have come to it from below

---

[1] See *Saalburg Jahrbuch*, iii. 21 and 85, n. 1; also above, p. 116.
[2] From Niedermendig; ibid. 83. (The ruler in the photograph is 40 cm. [= 16 in.] long.)
[3] Absence of such grooving appears always to be due to wear.

PLATE 14

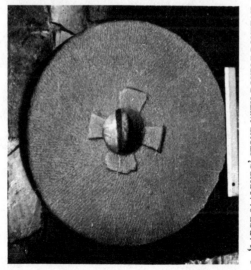

b. PAIR OF 'SMALL SAALBURG' STONES

c. WORKING PARTS OF 'LARGE SAALBURG' MILL

a. 'LARGE SAALBURG' STONE WITH DOUBLE DOVETAIL

(or the hole in the lower stone would have been useless) ; and the Vitruvius passage makes it at least probable that the lower end of the spindle was geared to another wheel. These inferences received striking confirmation when, in 1912, two of the working parts of a mill of this type were discovered in a well dating from the early third century A.D.: they are shown, fitted into each other, in Plate 14, Fig. c.

One of these parts is an iron spindle, 80 cm. [= 31½ in.] long and fitted at one end with iron dovetails which fit accurately enough into the recesses in the upper stones. (This, incidentally, is exactly described by Fra Giocondo's text of Vitruvius.) Near its other end the spindle is of a square section, fitting into the central hole of the other part discovered, which consists of two strong oak disks, 20 cm. [= 8 in.] in diameter by 4 cm. [= 1⅝ in.] thick, bound by iron rings and held apart by six forged iron bars, 3 cm. [= 1¼ in.] in diameter and 16 cm. [= 6¼ in.] long.[1] Probably these working parts were thrown into the well in order that the mill might be useless to an enemy.

It is hard not to see in the oak disks with the iron bars between them one of Vitruvius' 'drums', and if so, its evident connexion, via the spindle, with the upper millstone shows that it must have been the second 'drum' which was 'placed horizontally': the vertical 'drum' must then have been considerably larger, so that the mill revolved faster than the wheel by which it was driven. (This is the gearing ratio shown in Fig. 12.) But although, with this one exception, everything thus argues for a mill of the Vitruvian pattern, the stones and other parts found in Germany cannot have belonged to a water-mill. At the Saalburg, and at some of the other sites where these stones are plentiful, the frontier fortifications ran along the top of the Taunus range, where deep wells had to be sunk even for drinking and washing water: no water-mill could possibly have been used there, and while a windmill working on the same principles would have been possible there is no evidence at all for the use of windmills in antiquity.

Yet the resemblance to the Vitruvian water-mill is too close to be accidental, and Jacobi therefore reconstructed a 'slave'-mill

[1] The disks actually have twelve holes (plus the central hole) each; but this again is probably due to reuse after one set of holes was worn out. For details see *Saalburg Jahrbuch*, iii, plate 17. (A second and similar spindle was found soon afterwards in another well.)

(shown diagrammatically in the right-hand half of Fig. 14) which works on the same principle except that the water-wheel is replaced by a cranked handle, to be turned in a vertically rotary direction by slaves or soldiers.[1] (He found in practice that a long handle was needed at which four to six men could work, who

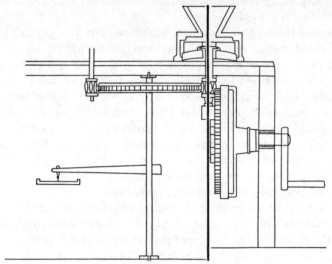

FIG. 14. Reconstruction of Saalburg Mill

could then grind 100 kg. [= 220 lb.] of grain in an hour—no mean achievement for a mill of this type: by adjusting the gearing ratio he could presumably have varied the number of men needed on the one hand, and the capacity of the mill on the other.) An alternative method of reconstruction, shown in the left-hand half of Fig. 14, is, however, also possible: if both 'drums' are made horizontal an animal can drive the mill, or even several mills. The practical advantages of this alternative are obvious, and Jacobi adopted the other method only because it preserves the power transmission prescribed by Vitruvius. In doing so he could rely, among other parallels, on two medieval mills of which photographs appear in Bennett and Elton's *History of Corn Milling*.[2]

[1] The reconstructed mill is now in the Saalburg Museum; for a photograph of it see *Saalburg Jahrbuch*, iii. 92, fig. 46.
[2] i. 222–3; Jacobi (p. 90) quotes Kammerer, *Die Entwicklung der Zahnräder* (1912), figs. 4, 6, 7, 8.

But there are parallels also for the alternative reconstruction. Few medieval milling establishments of any consequence, according to Bennett and Elton, were without a horse- or ass-mill of this type, which 'was greatly esteemed by mill-owners, being free from the frequent inconveniences attending windmills during calms, and water-mills during droughts, floods and frosts'.[1] Sometimes several mills were attached to the same driving-wheel; but even if the animal only drove one mill this mill would still be cheaper to run than that envisaged by Jacobi, and cheaper also (owing to the better design, which allowed the animal to develop its full power) than the Pompeian animal-mill—and even on the latter the use of slaves was, as we have seen, uneconomical.[2]

Yet, although animal-mills of the Pompeian type existed in antiquity, there is no ancient evidence for the reconstruction of the 'large Saalburg' mill here suggested, whereas Jacobi's reconstruction is supported by the text of Vitruvius. On the other hand, as Jacobi himself admits, the Vitruvian system of power transmission is 'theoretically more complicated', and Vitruvius' mill does not prove that the transmission of power through a right angle was earlier than the transmission used in the alternative reconstruction of the Saalburg mill: horizontal water-wheels— necessary if this alternative were to be applied to the water-mill— have been known;[3] but they are most inefficient when compared with their vertical counterparts; and Vitruvius in the context of the present passage is clearly concerned to show that even a vertical wheel can be used to drive a horizontal engine. He is describing an advance over a simpler system which, however, was preferable in the conditions prevailing at the Saalburg: the one consideration, therefore, that made Jacobi adopt the vertical driving-wheel does not contradict the alternative view, which is preferable on all other counts and is presupposed by Vitruvius himself.

Millstones of the 'large Saalburg' type are not confined to that site: Jacobi[4] mentions finds in other forts of the Roman *limes* in Germany and in Britain,[5] and several are to be seen in one of the

---

[1] i. 196–7.
[2] On the other hand it might be argued that soldiers, who might otherwise be idle, would be very cheap labour.
[3] See below, p. 132 and Fig. 15.   [4] p. 83.
[5] Cf. J. Curle, *A Roman Frontier Post and its People, The Fort of Newstead in the Parish of Melrose*, pp. 145–6, plate xvii; but the stones there shown are of the 'small Saalburg' type.

courtyards of the Naples Museum. Some of these stones may well
have belonged to water-mills of the Vitruvian pattern, but the
existence of a water-mill must not, as we have seen, be inferred
automatically from the presence of such stones.[1] Yet the existence
of the Saalburg mill itself provides some evidence for the practical
application of Vitruvius' design, even if it does not prove the
employment in practice of a vertical water-wheel to drive a mill.
(The tone of the Vitruvius passage, however, suggests not a new
invention, but rather something already in existence.)

The primary function of the hole in the lower stone was in all
these cases connected with the actual driving of the mill: we do
not know whether on the large Saalburg mill provision was
made for an adjustment of the distance between the stones, as
later practice might suggest. Such an adjustment could easily
have been arranged by raising or lowering the bearing in which
the lower end of the spindle revolved, and its existence is perhaps
made more probable than it would otherwise be by certain considerations that concern the smaller of the two types of mill found
at the Saalburg. These mills, too, normally have perforated lower
stones; but the difference between the two types was in all
probability not merely one of size.

On the large Saalburg mills the central hole in the upper stone
is, as we have seen, invariably provided with a dovetail-shaped
recess in the grinding surface, so that the stone could be driven
by an iron dovetail fitting into this recess and firmly attached to
the spindle: in the smaller stones the dovetailed recess goes right
through the stone, and the rynd, which here takes the place of the
iron dovetail, is firmly fixed in it. (Plate 14, Fig. *b* shows a representative pair of these stones with the iron rynd, which has
survived in several instances.) Where the recess does not go right
through the stone it is usually let into the *upper* face, and in these
cases also the rynd must have been fixed in the stone. A fitting of
this kind rules out the possibility that these mills were, like the
larger ones, driven from below, especially since the hole in the
rynd is always round, so that the mill cannot have been driven by
a square spindle fitting into a square hole in the rynd. Although
small mills with a mechanical drive are known from later times,[2]

[1] Parsons' account of the Athens water-mill (*Hesperia*, v. 70 ff.) unfortunately
ignores the Saalburg mill altogether.
[2] Cf. *BE*, i. 223.

PLATE 15

a

b

TWO VIEWS OF RECONSTRUCTED 'SMALL SAALBURG' MILL IN THE
SAALBURG MUSEUM

the smaller mills found at the Saalburg must, then, have been
turned by hand, and this is confirmed by the handle-socket in
their upper stones which usually takes the form of a hole going at
an angle through the edge of the stone (see Plate 16, Fig. *a*).

But if so, what of the hole in the lower stone? It may still mean
only that the spindle was fixed to a base below the mill in order
to keep the stones steady during grinding[1]—or, perhaps, that the
spindle, instead of being permanently fixed, was inserted loosely
in the lower stone when the mill was assembled, in order to avoid
bulkiness and damage during transport. On the other hand it
may mean, as both Curwen and Jacobi thought, that these mills
were adjustable; and this view is supported, in addition to the
modern parallels discussed earlier,[2] by the direction of the handle-
socket in the stones here under discussion. It will be shown in a
moment that this may indicate that the mill was stationary rather
than portable, and the construction of an adjustable mill is
necessarily such as to make the mill difficult to transport, though
the converse need not be the case.

Yet, if these mills were adjustable, and therefore fixtures, it is
not easy to see why they should have been used side by side with
efficient large mills: portability must surely have been the main
advantage which the small possessed over the large, and there
seems to be no good reason why the small should have survived
without it in circumstances like those prevailing in the Roman
frontier forts.[3] The rynd, moreover, must, if the upper stone was
held suspended above the lower, have had to support the entire
weight of the upper stone by means of the lead by which it was
fixed in the stone; and if this was the case it would surely have
been better to have the recess for the rynd in the *lower* face of the
upper stone, as in the larger mills. The way in which the rynd was
fixed in the stones, therefore, provides a further argument against
the view that these mills were adjustable.

Jacobi's final reconstruction of a mill of this type (see Plate 15,
Figs. *a*, *b*)[4] is based on the belief that it was both adjustable and a

---

[1] Cf. above, pp. 120–1.

[2] pp. 118–20. The Saalburg Museum contains a modern Polish quern of a
similar construction.

[3] This, of course, applies only where—as in a military camp—large numbers had
to be catered for: that a small household should have a quern even when large
commercial mills were at work need cause no surprise.

[4] *Saalburg Jahrbuch*, vi. 60, fig. 24. (For a similar reconstructed mill at Nuremberg

fixture. The adjustment works on a principle similar to that of the modern Scottish quern (Fig. 11), and the provision of a box in which meal could be collected, and a spout through which it could be extracted, are common-sense additions if the mill is to be regarded as a fixture. For the handle-fitting—self-explanatory on the photographs—Jacobi could rely on some medieval querns[1] and perhaps also on the slanting handle-socket on some of the stones, although the latter might equally well have served for an ordinary quern-handle or strap. The angle of these sockets is such that a handle of the kind suggested by Jacobi would have had to be very short if fixed in the actual socket: if it is fixed externally (as in Plate 15, Fig. b)[2] the socket provides no indication of how the handle was fitted, and much of the reconstruction becomes entirely conjectural. If the small Saalburg mill was adjustable—and if it was not a mere portable quern, as had at first been thought—it seems unlikely that the larger, and mechanically more advanced, mills did not provide for different grades of grinding.[3]

But adjustable or not, the quern had by then reached a degree of perfection which has not been materially exceeded since, though it survived for many centuries in Europe and still survives elsewhere. The large Saalburg mill, meanwhile, incorporated all the principles of the mill driven by wind or water (except that the stones did not become quite flat until later), with the result that it was not radically superseded until the modern steel-rollers took the place of the stone-mill.

cf. ibid. iii. 87, fig. 40.) This supersedes a simpler reconstruction by L. Jacobi (*Das Römerkastell Saalburg*, plate xxvii. 4).

[1] *Saalburg Jahrbuch*, iii, figs. 41–42 = *BE*, i. 163–4.
[2] That it was fixed externally is suggested by some remaining traces of metal.
[3] Saddle-querns, incidentally, were found in the pre-Roman sites near the Saalburg.

XVI

WATER-MILLS

Ἴσχετε χεῖρα μυλαῖον, ἀλετρίδες· εὕδετε μακρά,
κἢν ὄρθρον προλέγῃ γῆρυς ἀλεκτρυόνων·
Δηὼ γὰρ Νύμφαισι χερῶν ἐπετείλατο μόχθους·
αἱ δὲ κατ᾽ ἀκροτάτην ἁλλόμεναι τροχιὴν
ἄξονα δινεύουσιν· ὁ δ᾽ ἀκτίνεσσιν ἑλικταῖς
στρωφᾷ Νισυρίων κοῖλα βάρη μυλάκων.
γενόμεθ᾽ ἀρχαίου βιότου πάλιν, εἰ δίχα μόχθου
δαίνυσθαι Δηοῦς ἔργα διδασκόμεθα.

Oh stay your busy hands, ye girls that grind at the mill;
Let not the cock that heralds dawn disturb your sleep.
The river-nymphs are bidden by Demeter's will
To do your work; and on the topmost wheel they leap
And turn the axle's winding spokes, upon whose coil
Concave Nisyrian millstone's weight revolves anon.
A golden age has come again; for free from toil
We learn to taste what fruits from Mother Earth are won.

VITRUVIUS probably wrote between 25 and 23 B.C.;[1] the epigram that heads this chapter dates from about the same time,[2] and shows that in Vitruvius' day the water-driven grain-mill was no longer a mere theoretical possibility. This poem would presumably not have been written then if the water-mill had not been introduced very recently : yet the geographer Strabo, again at about the same time,[3] mentions a water-mill at Cabira in Pontus (some way inland from the southern shore of the Black Sea), a district with which he himself was very familiar. The apparent association of this mill with a palace of Mithridates probably means that it belonged to the early first century B.C., and if so, it is the earliest water-mill of which evidence survives.[4]

[1] Cf. Schanz–Hosius, *Gesch. d. röm. Lit.*[4] (Munich, 1935), ii. 387.
[2] *Anth. Pal.* ix. 418 (cf. *Oxford Book of Greek Verse*, no. 592). It is probably by Antipater of Thessalonica, though it has been thought that Antiphilus of Byzantium, a contemporary of Antipater, was the author. (The mention of Nisyros in the poem rests on an emendation, which makes it inadvisable to use it as evidence for a millstone industry on Nisyros; cf. above, p. 91.)
[3] xii. 556. Strabo lived from 64/63 B.C. to A.D. 21 at least; cf. *Oxf. Class. Dict.*, s.v.
[4] A verse in Lucretius' [94–55 B.C. (?)] *De Rerum Natura* (v. 516), in which some —cf. Blümner, p. 47, n. 4—have seen an allusion to a water-mill, refers merely to a wheel for raising water, as described by Vitruvius, x. 5. 1.

The various types of water-mill are discussed in an article by Curwen in which he follows up his earlier treatment of rotary querns.[1] In this article Curwen distinguishes the primitive 'vertical' mill, with a vertical shaft carrying at its lower end a horizontal water-wheel (Fig. 15), from the geared Vitruvian type, with

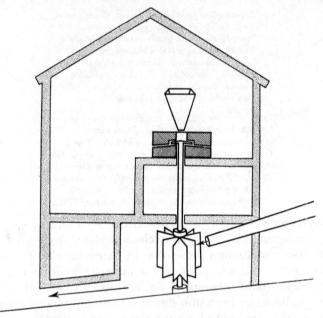

FIG. 15. Vertical water-mill

vertical water-wheels which may be either undershot or overshot or breast-wheels (see Fig. 16). The 'vertical' mill with its direct drive[2] and small water-wheel (usually consisting of about eight vanes or paddles fitted immediately to the shaft) is considered by Curwen to be a direct descendant of the quern and prior to the more developed Vitruvian mill; and he thinks that both Strabo's mill and the mill described in the epigram were of the more primitive kind. But the evidence for this is far from conclusive: about Strabo's mill we have no information whatever, and the information contained in the epigram must be treated

[1] *Antiquity*, xviii. 130 ff.
[2] i.e. the axle of the water-wheel is also the axle round which the upper stone revolves.

with some reserve, as a poetic description of an otherwise unknown piece of machinery always must.

Curwen relies on the address to the grinding maids and on the
mention of the crowing cocks when he supposes the mill of the
epigram to have been a replacement of the quern in the peasant
households of the countryside : but the maids make a much better

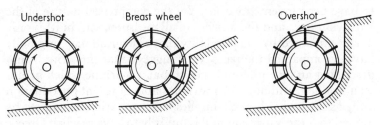

Fig. 16. Three types of vertical water-wheel

contrast to the water-nymphs than would a donkey or a horse,
and the crowing of the cock is surely no more than a poetic
description of early morning and one of the most commonplace
at that. Nor is it possible to elicit from the epigram the structural
information that Curwen finds in it. It is true that the 'nymphs
leaping down upon the top of the wheel' can hardly be leaping on
a Vitruvian water-wheel which in all probability was undershot ;[1]
but the description fits an overshot wheel much better than it
fits the 'water pouring down the chute from a mill-race on to the
horizontal[2] floats or vanes of the wheel of the primitive vertical
mill'. There is no direct evidence for the existence of overshot
wheels when the epigram was written, but traces of such a wheel,
belonging to a later period, have been found in Greece,[3] and the
evidence is so scanty that its earlier existence cannot be ruled out.
The fact, moreover, that only the wheel, one shaft, the spokes (on
Curwen's interpretation the iron dovetail), and the stones are
mentioned in the epigram does not prove that the mill was not of
the Vitruvian pattern, with two shafts and a gearing mechanism :
the 'winding spokes' are surely a more natural description of the
latter than of an iron dovetail.

[1] Cf. Vitr. x. 5. 1.
[2] This is Curwen's description (p. 135), but the floats must surely have been tilted.
[3] Cf. below, p. 137 : it belongs to the fifth century A.D.

On the other hand, the fact that the water-mill must have been a recent invention when the epigram was written gives some support to Curwen's theory, as does the evidence, assembled by Curwen, for the existence and long survival of the vertical mill,[1] since this evidence has its distributional centre in the Mediterranean basin and especially its eastern part: the vertical mill is, after all, simpler than the Vitruvian, and therefore likely *a priori* to have been invented earlier. Yet the compressed nature of the Vitruvian text (and the absence of all measurements in it) is only partly explained by the possibility that a diagram may originally have accompanied the passage: it suggests that the writer is not describing an invention of his own, but a machine which he has seen working. Although this was probably of recent introduction and, as Vitruvius himself implies,[2] still a rarity, it cannot be argued that the Vitruvian mill is unlikely to have reached Greece by the time when the epigram was composed.

It is a little surprising to find that Curwen, who advocates the theory that the commercial donkey-mill preceded the small household-quern, should take the opposite view in the case of water-mills[3] by supposing that the vertical type was directly derived from the quern, and that the larger Vitruvian mill was an elaboration of it: we still do not know in which order the two were invented, but it is at least possible that the small vertical mill was an adaptation for household use of the more complicated design described by Vitruvius. The idea that water-power could be used to drive a grain-mill must originally have come to a man who was no mean engineer: such a man may well have been capable of designing the Vitruvian gearing mechanism as well.

Whatever the answer to this problem, the water-mill must have existed by Augustus' time, and probably half a century earlier. The time of its first invention can therefore not be very far removed from that of the earliest authentic evidence for the existence of rotary mills of any kind, at least outside Spain; and this may suggest that the rotary mill must after all have appeared on the scene earlier than the second century B.C. Yet while this possibility cannot, as we have seen, be ruled out, technical progress is often less a matter of continuous development than of rapid advance after centuries of inaction. It is, after all, not so very long ago

[1] Cf. also *BE*, ii. 10–30.
[2] x. 1. 6.
[3] In this he follows *BE*, ii. 9 ff.

PLATE 16

a. VIEW OF UPPER STONE OF 'SMALL SAALBURG' MILL SHOWING
HANDLE SOCKET

b. LOAVES OF BREAD FOUND AT POMPEII

that, after a long era without change, the steam-engine first made
self-propelled vehicles possible; but once the principle of self-
propulsion was established, the electric and internal combustion
motor, and even the aeroplane, followed in swift succession. And
the aeroplane itself has gone a long way since the underlying
principle was mastered only a few decades ago. The introduction
of rotary motion into milling also represents the solution of a
fundamental problem, and the very rapidity of the subsequent
development may merely show once again how important a step
the invention of the rotary mill was.

The period of the first introduction of the water-mill is, unlike
that of the rotary mill generally, quite well defined; but it is less
easy to be certain about the speed with which the water-mill
replaced other types of mill. The Italian humanist Pomponius
Laetus (1487), in a most confused comment on the pseudo-
Virgilian *Moretum*, says that 'water-mills were installed in the
Tiber at Rome a little before Augustus',[1] and this date may come
from a fuller edition than that which has come down to us of
Virgil's commentator Servius, whose information is often reliable.
The date is intrinsically not unlikely, and though it has been
thought[2] that it is derived merely from the 'frequent' occurrence
of water-mills in Augustan writers, this can hardly be so, since
the only relevant passages are the three mentioned at the beginning of this chapter.

Even if water-mills were first installed at Rome 'a little before
Augustus', they cannot have replaced animal-mills very rapidly.
In A.D. 39 or 40 Caligula could still endanger the city's bread
supply by commandeering the mill-animals;[3] and Suetonius, reporting this early in the second century, does not mention any
change during the intervening period, as he surely would have
done if the water-mill had found universal acceptance by his time.
The only literary reference to a water-mill in the latter part of the
first century comes from a very corrupt passage in Pliny,[4] which,

[1] '—at the time of the Greeks when they had destroyed the (?) vaults' ('Paulo ante
Augustum molae aquis actae Romae in Tiberi factae, tempore Graecorum cum
fornices diruissent')—whatever the end of this sentence may mean; cf. Blümner,
pp. 46–47 and 47, n. 1. (*BE*, ii. 3–4, think *Paulo* refers to L. Aemilius Paulus; but
this does not merit serious discussion.)
[2] By Blümner, loc. cit.
[3] Suet. *Calig.* 39; cf. above, p. 99.
[4] *N.H.* xviii. 97: 'maior pars Italiae ruido utitur pilo, rotis etiam quas aqua
verset obiter et molat' (ed. Sillig). Much of this is untranslatable, but there seems

whatever its exact meaning, seems to show that the writer had heard of some kind of water-driven grinding appliance, but knew little about it and took no interest in it: this again suggests that the water-mill cannot have been at all common in the first century.

The Saalburg mill, on the other hand, though itself not a water-mill, was almost certainly developed from one, and thus presupposes the fairly common practical application of the Vitruvian principle by the early third century; and traces of water-mills have been found on Hadrian's wall in Britain.[1] The first discovery here was made at Haltwhistle Burn,[2] where the presence of a mill, dating probably from the second half of the third century, is proved by millstones and parts of a water-wheel, which was undershot as Vitruvius prescribes. This discovery drew attention to the possibility that there might be other water-mills elsewhere along the wall, which had been overlooked earlier.

Thus Professor I. A. Richmond now feels able to say that a construction at Chollerford Bridge near Chesters[3] is so obviously a water-mill that the truth of this explanation leaps to the eye once the possibility of it is taken into account. Yet this construction was once explained as a lift-and-swing bridge,[4] because a stone with eight slots in it was found there, which must in fact have been the core of a composite hub of wood, stone, and iron. The mill-race at Chollerford Bridge is associated with an alteration of the narrow first bridge, and this suggests a third-century date for it.[5] The remnants of a third water-mill were found where the wall crossed the old bed of the river Irthing at Willowford

to be a reference to water-wheels in connexion with milling; cf. Blümner, p. 46, n. 8.

[1] My thanks are due to Dr. M. V. Taylor, who drew my attention to these finds, and to Professor I. A. Richmond, who in a letter has added to the published information on the Chesters mill.

[2] In 1908; *Proc. Soc. Ant. Newcastle-upon-Tyne*, 3rd ser., iv. 167. (Cf. Bruce–Richmond, *Handbook to the Roman Wall*[10], p. 147.) The millstones are 30 in. in diameter and 12 in. thick for a complete mill, i.e. very similar to the 'large Saalburg' stones. Some hand-mills were also found there.

[3] *Handbook*, p. 80. The information in the text is based on Professor Richmond's letter.

[4] By Sheriton Holmes, *Proc. Soc. Ant. Newcastle-upon-Tyne*, 2nd ser., ii. 178 ff.; but cf. also ibid., 3rd ser., ii. 283.

[5] See *Handbook*, p. 166. But the mill is, according to Professor Richmond, an integral part of the tower and abutment, and not the later insertion which it was once thought to be.

Bridge:[1] here again the water-wheel was undershot; again the mill is associated with an enlargement of the bridge; and again some objects (a stone spindle-bearing and some fragments of millstones) have been found, to confirm the mill interpretation which was first put forward in 1924.

These mills on Hadrian's wall prove what the large Saalburg mills had suggested—that water-mills were becoming increasingly common during the third and perhaps the late second century A.D.: the earliest water-mill known in detail, however, belongs to the fifth century. It came to light during the American excavations in the Athenian agora,[2] and exactly followed the Vitruvian pattern, even to the point of having the horizontal gear-wheel larger than the vertical.[3] (This arrangement was unusual,[4] but it was suitable enough for a stream or mill-race in which, as was probably the case at Athens, a small volume of water flows fairly rapidly.) The only difference between this mill and that of Vitruvius was that the water-wheel at Athens was overshot.[5]

Like other ancient mills, the water-mill has in the past received little attention, and much of the evidence that has here been quoted has not long been available. This evidence has already made it possible to put back by at least a century and a half the date which Bennett and Elton in 1898 gave for the first proved use of the Vitruvian mill:[6] it can now be regarded as certain that an edict of the emperors Honorius and Arcadius of A.D. 398,[7] which according to Bennett and Elton laid down regulations for the recently introduced water-mills, was in fact designed to put an end to an abuse that had arisen in connexion with these mills, which were by then well established.

Other ancient water-mills of which traces have been found[8]

[1] Ibid., pp. 165–6; cf. *Trans. Cumberland and Westmorland Antiq. and Arch. Soc.*, N.S., xxvi. 429 ff. The date of this mill is uncertain.
[2] See Parsons, *Hesperia* v. 70 ff.
[3] Ibid., p. 83: the respective diameters are 1·11 m. [= 43·7 in.] and 1·36 m. [=53·5 in.].
[4] Cf. above, p. 122, n. 4, and *CR*, N.S., vi. 193–4.
[5] Water-wheels are discussed by Parsons on pp. 80 ff. (The reconstructed wheel in the Naples Museum, quoted by Parsons, can be seen in the background of Plate 4, Fig. *a*.)
[6] ii. 36.
[7] *Cod. Theod.* xiv. 15. 4, quoted by *BE*, ii. 41.
[8] The Naples water-wheel was found at Venafrum and shows that there was a water-mill there; cf. Parsons, p. 76, n. 1.

cannot be dated at all accurately; but the mention of a price for one in Diocletian's *Edict* of A.D. 301[1] confirms that by the end of the third century the water-mill had begun to supersede earlier mills, though it had by no means ousted them yet: in the *Edict* it still takes third place after the horse- and donkey-mill, and it is followed only by the hand-mill. In the fourth century also Palladius,[2] advocating the introduction of water-mills on country estates in connexion with the baths, shows both that it was well enough known not to need detailed description and that it was still uncommon enough not to be installed as a matter of course. A contemporary poem[3] tells of a water-mill on a tributary of the Moselle.

At least two centuries, then, seem to have elapsed after the invention of the water-mill before it began to be generally adopted. This is surprising; but perhaps the geographical limitations which the new mill imposed upon the mill-owner, particularly in cities, can to some extent account for it: an animal-mill could be placed anywhere, but a water-mill had to be near some running water or a substantial aqueduct. Such an aqueduct, issuing from the Lacus Sabatinus (Lago Bracciano), supplied the mills on the Janiculum, where water-mills at Rome appear to have been concentrated,[4] and where scanty traces of such mills have been found.[5] Both the poet Prudentius[6] and the regional lists of the city[7] mention them there in the fourth century; an edict against the millers of A.D. 488 in the fifth;[8] and Procopius, the historian of the Gothic War, in the sixth.[9]

All this time the hand-mill had survived: it was to survive for many more centuries, and the energy needed to suppress it in the Middle Ages bears witness to the vigour of its survival. Animal-mills, too, survived as a stand-by until modern times;[10] but in

---

[1] xv. 54; cf. above, p. 102.
[2] *R.R.* i. 41 (42).
[3] Auson. *Mos.* 362. On the spread of the water-mill cf. M. Bloch, *Ann. d'hist. écon. et sociale*, vii. 538 ff.
[4] Cf., in addition to the references in the next few notes, the edict of Honorius and Arcadius just mentioned.
[5] van Buren and Stevens, *Mem. Amer. Acad. in Rome*, 1915–16, pp. 59 ff.; 1933, pp. 69 ff.
[6] *C. Symm.* ii. 950.
[7] In *Regio XIV*; cf. Richter, *Topographie d. Stadt Rom* (Munich, 1901), p. 281; Platner–Ashby, *Topographical Dict. of Ancient Rome* (Oxford, 1929), s.v. *Molinae*.
[8] *CIL*, vi. 1711.
[9] *Bell. Goth.* i. 19. 8, 19 ff.   [10] Cf. above, p. 127.

Rome at least there were by the sixth century not enough of them
to fulfil the needs of the population when the water-supply of the
Janiculum was cut by the Goths. Then it was the shortage of
water, and no longer (as in Caligula's day) the shortage of
animals, that caused a crisis and led to the introduction of floating
mills which were to some extent independent of the supply in the
aqueducts.[1] But by then the Middle Ages had started.[2]

[1] On these 'ship-mills' cf. Blümner, p. 49, and Procop., loc. cit.: they were
ordinary water-mills mounted on anchored boats which could rise and fall with the
level of the water.

[2] Some further examples of 'large Saalburg' upper stones have been found
in Romano-British villas at Woolaston, Gloucestershire (*Arch. Cambr.* xciii. 109,
122, and plate iiB) and at Chew Park, North Somerset (information kindly
supplied by Mr. P. A. Rahtz). Here the dovetail-shaped recess penetrates right
through the stones, and the mills in question can therefore not have been
adjustable. In both cases water-mills would have been possible, though no
evidence for them has been discovered, and at Woolaston it is even conceivable
that a water-mill may have been connected with the bath installations, as
Palladius advises.

CONCLUSION

THE problem to which an answer was sought in this review of ancient grain-mills was how the windmills and water-mills which were the predecessors of the modern roller-mills came into being. At the outset we saw that the windmill was a medieval invention and thus outside the scope of this inquiry: but the origin of the windmill has almost been found once the origin of the water-mill has been traced, since the technique of milling is the same for wind- and water-driven mills.

That the water-mill is a Roman invention has long been known, and it has long been admitted that it originated late in classical antiquity. The water-mill, however, is the only invention in the realm of milling with which Greece and Rome are commonly credited, and the belief is still widely held that, with this one exception, grain-milling remained essentially unchanged from the time of Homer to that of the decline of the Roman Empire: this belief is true to the extent that throughout this period—and for fifteen centuries thereafter—corn was ground by being rubbed between two stones. But when it is said that mills remained unchanged during this long period, more is usually meant than that two stones, one fixed and one movable, were invariably present: it is implied rather that all the essentials of those mills which preceded the modern roller-mill were known at the beginning of the classical era. It was in this sense that the common belief was questioned at the beginning of this inquiry, and as soon as it was questioned it was seen to rest on very flimsy foundations.

Rotary motion is the prerequisite of any mechanical mill; for no non-rotary mill can be worked either by an animal or by inanimate power: on this basis our search has shown that the period under review may be divided into two parts which roughly coincide with what may be called the Greek and Roman eras. In the 'Greek era' we have failed to find any compelling evidence for the existence of the rotary mill: the mortar, we saw, must be left out of the discussion of grinding implements proper; but the simple saddle-quern—probably the first advance over the original rock-crushers and the first movable mill of any kind—was for a long time the grain-mill of Greece as of other parts of the world. When it was finally superseded it was not by the rotary mill, but by the lever-operated hopper-rubber, which was in all probability both the peculiar contribution made by Greece to the history of milling and the mill most used in hellenistic times. If the saddle-quern had been the first mill properly described as such, this development gave rise to the first mill that was mechanical, in however limited a sense: here for the first time some of the work was taken away from the operator and transferred to a mechanical contrivance. But the operator had still to be a human being, and the work was still hard and dreary: relief from it could come only with rotary motion.

When it was adopted for the grain-mill, rotary motion was no longer a novelty: not only had the potter's wheel long been known, but revolving oil-mills may have preceded revolving grain-mills by a considerable time. One reason for this was probably that with the oil-mill it was desirable to keep the upper stone suspended during grinding to avoid crushing the kernels. Since this could most easily be achieved by making the mill rotary, it provided a motive for the introduction of rotary motion into the oil industry other than that of making the employment of animals possible —and a motive not applicable to the grain-mill.

But the grain-mill also presented a special technical problem which had not been encountered elsewhere: a way had to be found of keeping the two stones concentric while allowing for a continuous feed into and out of the mill. It is always tempting to think that the solution to a problem of this kind was found by the 'practical Romans'; and it is in fact from Roman Italy that the earliest clear evidence for the donkey-mill, which must have been rotary, comes in the second century B.C. The evidence is, however, still so scanty that a second-century origin for the rotary mill cannot be regarded as proved, though it is suggested as a working hypothesis for the present: the possibility of an earlier origin, and one in a different part of the world, cannot be discounted, especially since the rotary hand-mill may well have found its way to Italy from farther west.

Whether the animal-mill or the hand-quern was the earlier is still not clear. The almost instinctive assumption that the small must have preceded the large is offset by the consideration that rotary motion alone could make animal traction practicable. This

may well have given the impetus to the development; for technical innovations often occur when the circumstances of the times
make them desirable. Nor can the possibility that animal-mill
and quern were invented independently be ruled out: even if the
primary advantage of the rotary mill was that it could be driven
by animals, the quern had advantages of its own in that it was
much easier to work than the earlier hand-mills. It was because of
this that it soon replaced the earlier hand-mills for the needs of
soldiers and small households, especially in the countryside and
where a portable mill was needed. For the same reason it may
have been independently invented in the first place.

The animal-mill (and we found reason to doubt its description
as a 'slave-and-animal' mill) is the mill best attested for Rome
and a large part of her empire during the first centuries B.C. and
A.D.; but the hand-quern, too, became increasingly common
from the second century B.C. onwards, and it survived for centuries after the 'Pompeian' mill had been forgotten. The development of the two proceeded along similar lines: the steep conical
slope, which had at first been thought necessary, became progressively less steep, and this meant that stones became less bulky,
cheaper, and easier to transport. Two factors must have con-
tributed to this development: the 'rynd problem' was finally
solved, and an effective system of striations—originally invented
before the rotary mill—was applied to the new mills. The point
where stones became quite flat was, however, not reached in
antiquity.

Flatter stones in turn made it possible to perforate the lower
stone, and thus to provide for an easy adjustment of the distance
between the stones. If we found it hard to decide how many
ancient mills were in fact adjustable, it was because the hole in
the lower stone may also have been put to a different and more
important use. It meant that the mill could now be driven from
below, and it thus opened the way for the introduction of the
water-mill and for that of a much more efficient (slave-and-)
animal mill than the Pompeian where water-power was not
available. At first the simple direct drive, with a horizontal
water-wheel, may have been used for such mills; but the invention of the Vitruvian system of power transmission soon super-
vened. Yet even after Vitruvius the water-mill did not replace the
animal-mill for a considerable time, but by the end of the Roman

era the water-mill was becoming increasingly common; and although the windmill (which was to make it possible to use inanimate power even where there was no water) still remained to be invented, the grain-mill had reached a degree of perfection which allowed it to remain essentially unchanged for well over a thousand years.

One great puzzle remains: how was it that techniques of grain-milling that are rightly associated nowadays with the most primitive stages of civilization remained in use for so long in an area which in other respects was highly civilized at the time? Technical problems undoubtedly had to be overcome before any important advance could be made; but in view of what happened in other fields it is hard to believe that they could not have been overcome much earlier if a serious attempt had been made, and if the need to make the grinding of corn less of a drudgery had been acutely felt.

In our own day the demand for labour-saving appliances in the home—and consequently a rapid development of such appliances —became noticeable as domestic help became more expensive and less readily available. Although it may be invidious to compare the maid of not so long ago with the slave of ancient Greece, it may well be that the cheapness of human labour, and the wide social gulf between those who had work done for them and those who did it, meant that there were few incentives for finding methods of easing such work or of making it unnecessary for human beings to do it at all; and there may after all be a parallel between the emergence of the rotary mill and that of the washing-machine. It may be argued that the same influences—notably the existence of slavery—were still at work when the improvements which they are said to have retarded did finally take place: yet we found that for grinding corn animals largely took the place of slaves either when the rotary mill first appeared or very soon afterwards. The reason for this was undoubtedly economic: the employment of animals must have been an advantage at the time, though perhaps a smaller advantage than it would have been at a later period. It is at least tempting to suppose that the introduction of animals into milling coincided with a period when the relative prices of slave and animal labour made the employment of animals more attractive than it had been earlier; and it may well have been an economic variation of this kind that led to the invention of the rotary mill. Once this invention had been made, the way was clear for many further developments; and other motive powers, cheaper than both the animal and the slave, could now be employed. At the same time the initial outlay, and the amount of capital needed, increased with each improvement; and it may well have been this increase, together with the fact that not every site is suitable for a water-mill, that delayed the widespread adoption of the latter.

In addition to these economic factors, which cannot here be discussed in detail,[1] the grain-mill was probably subject also to those conservative influences which always tend to delay innovations in everyday occupations: a certain way of doing the work is often firmly engrained, and the habit of long ages has to be broken before something new can be introduced. But once the habit is broken, improvements may follow each other in quick succession.

Thus the development of the corn-mill was not a continuous one, with all important advances separated by approximately equal intervals of time—and indeed technical progress never takes place in that way. Instead, long periods with little or no advance are followed by comparatively brief spurts of energy, as it were, which may revolutionize a whole industry. The history of the corn-mill after the original invention—which was the greatest innovation of all—contains two such periods: one of these falls in the last century or so; the other falls in the period of classical antiquity, and especially in the last two centuries of the pre-Christian era, when new inventions followed each other so rapidly that it is difficult now to be sure of their exact sequence. It has become unfashionable of late to regard the period between the classical and the modern as the Dark Ages; but in corn-milling at any rate the light provided by classical antiquity was strong enough to cast its shadow over many centuries.

---

[1] On them cf. Bloch's article, cited a little earlier (p. 138, n. 3).

PART II · FLOUR

I

GRAIN PRODUCTS OTHER THAN FINE MEAL AND FLOUR

BEFORE we began to trace the development of the grain-mill in antiquity we saw what place the reduction of grain in the mill holds among the processes by which cereals are prepared for human consumption. Man's digestive organs—unlike those of other grain-eating animals—compel him to cook grain in some way before he eats it; but grinding before cooking is not indispensable, and is in fact often either omitted altogether or replaced by a mere rough crushing. For baked grain-products, on the other hand, grinding is necessary; and the special position which 'naked' wheat occupies among the grains because of its peculiar suitability for bread also means that fine meal and flour are far more often made from naked wheat than from any other cereal.[1]

But the actual grinding is only one part of what the modern miller has to do in order to produce flour from wheat. This is not the place for a description of the intricate processes to which grain is subjected in the modern mill before it is ready for the baker; but we have seen already that it is comparatively rare nowadays for the whole of the grain to be used for 'wholemeal' bread, and that it is usual to eliminate the indigestible outer coat or 'bran' (or at least the greater part of it) from the meal. This is a task which has to be undertaken by the miller in addition to, or rather in combination with, the reduction of the grain to the particle size required for satisfactory baking, and the commercial quality of a flour largely depends upon the degree of success with which this task is accomplished. There is evidence that a similar practice was in existence during the period here

[1] Except perhaps rye; but rye can be left out of consideration for classical antiquity.

under review, and the succeeding chapters are devoted to an examination of this evidence. This is necessary if we wish to know anything about the meal or flour from which bread was made in antiquity; but it involves very considerable difficulties. It is possible, admittedly, to discuss the terminology of our ancient authorities by itself, and to rest content with the conclusion that different grades of meal and flour were prepared and that one was less coarse, or more expensive, than another. Such a discussion can be conducted within the confines of classical scholarship, and this is the way in which the ancient evidence has been dealt with in the past by the few scholars who have addressed themselves to it[1]—with one exception, to which we shall return in a moment. But this approach cannot take us far: it can tell us nothing about the quality of the meal, flour, or bread, of antiquity in relation to our own. If we wish to glean information of this kind from the ancient evidence we must relate it to what modern experience shows to be practicable, and this means that classical studies must be brought into contact with modern science. The difficulties of this are obvious.

An attempt to surmount these difficulties has been made in an article by N. Jasny on 'Wheat Prices and Milling Costs in Classical Rome'.[2] This article, which constitutes the first attempt to solve the real problem, on the basis of practical experience brings into the discussion a number of important points that had previously been left out of account; but it suffers from certain defects in its handling of the ancient evidence which make a re-examination of the latter worth while. The present writer cannot hope to rival Jasny's practical experience, but he has been fortunate enough to have the opportunity of acquiring some familiarity with the processes here in question, and he hopes that this has enabled him to take Jasny's work a step farther. Before we turn to these problems, however, it may not be out of place to say something about a few of the grain products not ordinarily used for bread; for these, too, have been of great importance in human nutrition.

We saw earlier that the long survival of the mortar is to be

[1] Notably Voigt, *Rhein. Mus.*, N.F., xxxi (1876), 105 ff. Neither Blümner (pp. 49 ff.) nor *PW* (ii. 2734 ff.) had much to add to what Voigt had written several decades earlier.

[2] *Wheat Studies of the Food Research Institute, Stanford University, California*, vol. xx, no. 4 (March 1944).

explained by its use for the hulling of husked grain. All cereals other than the bread grains (naked wheat and rye) and some exceptional barleys have normally to be subjected to this process, and it is often the only process to which grain is subjected between threshing and cooking. Today this applies especially to most of the forms in which rice is eaten and to the 'pearl' barley from which a porridge is made: for ancient times the Greek name πτισάνη, derived from πτίσσειν, 'to pound', and transliterated into Latin as (p)tisana, provides a good example of it.[1] Although this name often denotes a gruel made from grain after hulling,[2] it is sometimes used for the peeled (and perhaps roughly crushed) grain itself,[3] and originally it was probably the generic name for husked grain freed from its hulls. (But since barley was in classical Greece the husked grain par excellence, πτισάνη soon became associated with barley, from which it is normally made when we meet it in ancient literature.[4]) The word πιστίκιον, which occurs in Diocletian's Edict as the Greek for 'clean' spelta,[5] is evidently another name for husked grain without the hulls, and κάχρυς is almost certainly a third.[6] Similarly χῖδρα were probably roasted whole grains of unripe barley[7] or wheat.[8]

Even where grain was not used whole it was not always reduced to a very fine particle size. This applies particularly to those cereals which, for the reasons mentioned earlier, were not suitable for bread: the final products made from these cereals often demanded a material less fine than flour. Just as there is a place in modern times—and especially in modern Italy—both for the fine flour from which bread is made and for the semolina which is used for 'pasta', so some of the less fine materials, like χόνδρος and alica, maintained their place side by side with bread flour in

[1] Cf. also the ancient names for starch (ἄμυλον, amylum = that which is unmilled); see Blümner, pp. 95–96; PW, i. 2001–2.
[2] e.g. Hipp. Acut. 7, 10; Gal. vi. 502 K.
[3] Cf. Nicopho 15 and perhaps Hipp. Acut. 6 (also the 'song of the pounding women' quoted by Athenaeus xiv. 619a from Aristophanes). In Latin, too, the word appears to have had both meanings.
[4] For exceptions see Diosc. M.M. ii. 86 W.; Gal. vi. 496 K.; Plin. N.H. xviii. 71.
[5] i. 7. It is probably a transliteration of a Latin word *pisticium, derived from pinsere as πτισάνη is from πτίσσειν.
[6] Cf. Cratin. ap. Plut. Sol. 25; Ar. Nub. 1358, Vesp. 1306; &c.
[7] See, e.g., Schol. Ar. Eq. 806, Pax 595.
[8] Cf. Hesych., s.v.; also Ar. frag. 889; Poll. vi. 62. The emphasis on 'unripe' in all our authorities suggests that 'unripe grains' was the proper meaning of the word.

ancient times,[1] and for their preparation, too, the mortar may well have been employed.[2]

Alica, according to Pliny,[3] was prepared from emmer by a process of repeated pounding, accompanied by sifting, which yielded various grades of groats, three being apparently the usual number.[4] The manufacture of χόνδρος is described in very similar terms in the tenth-century *Geoponica*,[5] where it, too, is made of emmer. Originally, however, χόνδρος[6] appears to have been a 'product name', like 'groats', not associated with any particular cereal,[7] and its association with the husked wheats probably does not go back beyond the Roman period.

Cato[8] tells us that *alica* was used for *puls*, which, as we saw earlier, was for a long time the staple food of Latium—and the interest which Pliny[9] takes in it shows that in the first century A.D. it still retained much of its importance. Bread from these groats was not entirely unknown,[10] but it was unusual, and bread and groats are opposed to each other as early as the fourth century B.C.[11] The fact that groats were, at least sometimes, prepared in a place different from the mill[12] confirms the conclusion that their purpose, too, was different from that of the flour that came from the mill; which is, of course, still true today.

Another product, no less coarse than χόνδρος and *alica*, was known by the name of κρίμνα, the only difference being that this product was usually associated with barley,[13] and especially so in

---

[1] But they were thought less nourishing; Cels. ii. 18.

[2] Cf. Poll. iii. 78, vii. 19 (misinterpreted by Blümner, p. 57, n. 3); Hesych., s.v. χονδροκοπεῖον; and Blümner, p. 57 with n. 4.

[3] *N.H.* xviii. 109 ff. The name is connected with (*h*)*alicastrum* (one of the words for emmer), and appears in Greek as ἄλιξ.

[4] *Minima* or *cribraria, secundaria*, and *excepticia* or ἀφαίρεμα, the last-named being the coarsest.

[5] iii. 7. 1–2; cf. Diosc. *M.M.* ii. 96 W., Trypho *ap.* Athen. iii. 109c.

[6] And perhaps also *alica*; cf. Plin. *N.H.* xviii. 71.

[7] Cf. especially Theophr. *H.P.* iv. 4. 9. [Arist.] *Probl.* 929ᵇ 1, and perhaps Stesich. 2; also the adjective χόνδρος, 'coarse'.

[8] *Agr.* 85.

[9] *N.H.* xviii. 83–84. His statements that *puls* (loc. cit.) and *alica* (xxii. 128) were unknown to Greece, where *tisana* and *polenta*—both usually made from barley— were used instead, supports the contention that the husked wheats were unimportant in Greece.

[10] Trypho, loc. cit.; cf. Mnesith., ibid. 115 f.

[11] Theophr., loc. cit.

[12] Cf. Blümner, p. 57.

[13] Gal. xix. 115 K.; cf. Arist. *Hist. An.* 501ᵇ 31, Ath. iii. 126c–d. (The word may even be cognate with the Greek name for barley.)

all probability after χόνδρος had become associated with the husked wheats. Galen,[1] however, in contrasting κρίμνα with two other products, ἄλφιτα and ἄλευρα, points out that strictly all three are the names of different grades of material from *any* grain, κρίμνα being the coarsest and ἄλευρα the finest, with ἄλφιτα lying between the two.

Ἄλφιτα and ἄλευρα[2] were by the fourth century B.C. firmly associated with barley and naked wheat respectively,[3] and in view of the real difference between the two names this must mean that by the fourth century, and perhaps earlier, barley was not normally ground into a meal as fine as that which was made from wheat. This is again confirmed by a suggestion in our evidence that ἄλφιτα, as well as χόνδρος, were made in a place different from the ordinary flour-mill, and presumably with different implements.[4] (The difference between the implements, as opposed to the difference between the products themselves, may have come into play only when technical advances brought increasing specialization with them: in Homer[5] the same mill produces both ἄλφιτα and ἀλείατα, but by the fifth century the 'making of ἄλφιτα' is a trade distinct from breadmaking.[6])

The Latin *polenta*—again usually made from barley[7]—was almost certainly the equivalent of the Greek ἄλφιτα.[8] Pliny expressly associates *polenta* with Greece,[9] and its occurrence in Plautus[10] also suggests that *polenta* (ἄλφιτα) from barley was the equivalent in the diet of Greece of the Italian *far*. *Far*, moreover, was itself the name of a ground product as well as that of the husked wheat from which this product was normally prepared.[11]

The old Italian *far*, pounded in their mortars by the original *pistores*, was, as we saw earlier,[12] eaten in the form of *puls*, which

[1] xix. 76 K.; cf. xii. 45, Diosc. *M.M.* ii. 90 W., Blümner, p. 55, notes 10–11.
[2] Or ἀλείατα (in Homer) or ἄλητα. [3] See *CQ*, xliii. 113 ff.
[4] Poll. iii. 78, vii. 19; cf. below, p. 151.
[5] *Od.* xx. 106–8; cf. ii. 355.
[6] Xen. *Mem.* ii. 7. 6.
[7] Cf. Plin. *N.H.* xviii. 72 ff.
[8] Cf. especially Ov. *Met.* v. 450, 454 with Hom. *Hymn to Demeter* 208, and see *Thes. Ling. Lat.* s.v. *alphitum*. (The contrast in Pliny, loc. cit., between *polenta* and *farina subtilis* seems analogous to that between ἄλφιτα and ἄλευρα; and *pollen polentae* in Cat. *Agr.* 156. 5 was probably identical with (παι)πάλη; cf. below, p. 162, n. 1.)
[9] *N.H.* xviii. 72 ff. (where he deals for the most part with Greece); cf. also above, p. 148, n. 9. [10] *Note I*, p. 219.
[11] See *Note O*, p. 221. [12] Above, p. xviii.

was the staple diet of Rome before the bread (and naked-wheat) age began. A similar clear distinction can be traced in Greek between the products made from ἄλφιτα and those from ἄλευρα:[1] the former were used for 'kneaded things' (μᾶζαι),[2] while the latter were baked into bread. (Bread was, of course, also kneaded; but it was distinguished from the μᾶζα by being baked afterwards.) If a Greek wanted to express the thought of our 'half a loaf is better than no bread', he said, 'even a μᾶζα is good as a makeshift for bread';[3] and where Shakespeare speaks of 'the bitter bread of banishment',[4] Aeschylus has 'the μᾶζα of slavery'.[5] This μᾶζα was the everyday food of the greater part of the Greek population for as long as barley retained its importance in human nutrition—just as the Romans could be dubbed 'porridge-munchers'[6] before the naked wheats replaced the husked in Italy.

The difference between μᾶζα and *puls* on the one hand and bread on the other was not merely a difference between final products and between the grains from which these products were made: it also involved a difference between a coarse and a fine grade of meal. Both naked wheat and the fine flour made from it were considered unsuitable for μᾶζα and *puls*,[7] but suitable for bread, while the opposite is true of barley and emmer and the less fine meal made from these grains. Bread from husked wheat and barley was made and eaten occasionally,[8] but such bread cannot have been either very common[9] or very satisfactory. When bread was made from these husked grains they too may at times have been ground into fine flour;[10] but on the whole the distinction between the fine material and the less fine coincides with that between the raw grains on the one hand and that between the finished products on the other.

[1] See, e.g., Plat. *Rep.* ii. 372a–b. In almost every early passage where μᾶζα is found, ἄλφιτα occurs in the immediate context.

[2] The word is connected with μάσσειν, 'to knead', and the Greeks were very conscious of this; cf. Plat. loc. cit., Hdt. i. 200, Ar. *Eq.* 55, 57, 1105, *Pax*, 1 ff., &c.

[3] Ἀγαθὴ καὶ μᾶζα μετ᾽ ἄρτον, Zen. i. 12.

[4] *Richard II*, iii. i. 21.

[5] δουλία μᾶζα, *Ag.* 1041 (cf. Fraenkel, ad loc.).

[6] Plaut. *Poen.* 54, *Most.* 828; cf. above, p. 71, n. 3.

[7] Cf. Ath. iii. 114e–f, and above, p. xxi.

[8] Cf. Xen. *An.* iv. 5. 31, Plin. *N.H.* xviii. 74, Cels. ii. 18, 25, &c.

[9] Bread without epithet was made from naked wheat, and bread from other grains had to have the name of the grain added; cf. Poll. vi. 72 and *CQ*, xliii. 113.

[10] See, e.g., Plut. *Pyth. Or.* 397a; Gal. vi. 474, 504 K.; Diosc. *M.M.* i. 72. 2 W.

THE PRODUCTION OF DIFFERENT
GRADES OF MEAL

THE distinction between the various products discussed in the last chapter was primarily one of particle size, and the question now arises how meals of different particle size were produced in antiquity. We saw that if it was desired to produce πτισάνη and the like by merely freeing husked grains from their hulls the mortar was used from the earliest times and throughout our period: on the other hand, while in Homeric times the same 'mill', normally in the household, was used for both coarse and fine meal, the production of ἄλφιτα had in classical Greece become a trade separate from the milling of flour. What does this imply about the implements used to produce these different grades of meal?

It is difficult to know when the separate trades came into existence, but it is tempting to think that it happened at the time when the mill itself began to develop: it is at least possible that the new and more advanced mills (i.e. the 'Olynthian' grain-rubber in the first instance) were reserved for naked wheat, from which a fine flour was to be produced, while the old saddle-stone and the mortar remained satisfactory for the more superficial grinding of ἄλφιτα, *polenta*, and χόνδρος, *alica*. The mortar was certainly used for hulling, and since all these products were made from husked grains it would be natural to reduce the grain in the implement in which it was hulled, with perhaps a change of pestle. This procedure is, moreover, expressly attested by Pliny for both husked wheat and barley.[1]

Special names for producers of and dealers in ἄλφιτα first appear in literature in the late fifth and early fourth century B.C.[2] This may be accident, but it coincides with the time when in all probability the first major development of the grain-mill took place. With the new mills that were then introduced the weight

---

[1] See *Note P*, p. 221.
[2] See especially Xen. *Mem.* ii. 7. 6, and cf. Ar. *Av.* 491, Hyp. *frag.* 224–5, Nicopho 19, and *Note D*, p. 218.

of the upper stone came to rest 'automatically' on the grist, and the grooves in the stone surfaces determined the length of its journey through the mill. Consequently a tendency towards a standard particle size must soon have shown itself, and this particle size may well have been too fine for ἄλφιτα and more suitable for a meal destined for baking.

Yet even with these new mills the operator was still reasonably free to grind either more or less finely, and we cannot be certain that they were not used for ἄλφιτα as well as ἄλευρα: of the later rotary mills, on the other hand, some at least could not have been used for coarse meal. During some experiments made with quite a small rotary hand-mill at Lewes in connexion with this study[1] it became evident that a considerable part of the grist would be reduced to fine flour by one journey through the mill, and there was nothing the operator could do to avoid this. Once these mills had come into use for fine flour, it seems probable that where a coarse product was desired preference was given to the mortar, and perhaps the saddle-quern. (The evidence for the survival of the saddle-quern after the introduction of rotary mills cannot here be discussed). When, however, the rotary mill became adjustable it may again have been used, as the roller-mill is nowadays, for the production of both fine and coarse meal. But this is not likely to have happened before the late part of the classical period.[2]

But, although the question how coarse meal was produced cannot be ignored altogether, it is with the fine meal known as ἄλευρα in Greek and as *farina* in Latin that we are here mainly concerned. Fine meal and flour are preferred for baking because they produce a loaf that is better cooked, better risen, and of better texture than that made from coarser grades: all our evidence suggests that this fact was discovered early, and, although there were some exceptions,[3] fine meal and flour were throughout our period thought desirable for breadmaking. Since for this purpose grain was undoubtedly ground on the mills discussed in the first part

[1] Cf. above, p. 109, n. 3. In what follows the name 'Lewes experiments' is used.

[2] Perhaps the mysterious water-mill in Plin. *N.H.* xviii. 97 (on which see above, p. 135, n. 4) was adjustable, in which case it may have been used for hulling and coarse grinding. But the text is so corrupt that it would be unwise to infer too much from the sentence in question.

[3] Especially the existence of bread from groats (above, pp. 148, 150) on the one hand, and the low reputation of bread from *pollen tritici* (below, p. 174) on the other.

of this study, the preference for bread, for which reasons were given at the outset, has meant not only a development towards the growing of naked wheat at the expense of other cereals, but also a continuous effort to produce fine flour with the least possible amount of labour and at the lowest possible cost.

But the story does not end there. Good flour tends to be judged not only by the quality of the grain from which it is made, nor yet only—or chiefly—by its fineness. White bread has, as we saw earlier, long been in greater demand than dark bread, and for white bread a flour is needed from which as much as possible of the dark and fibrous bran coat of the grain has been eliminated.

Bran—and especially its outer layer, the pericarp—is for the most part indigestible and passes through the human body substantially unchanged. Its presence, therefore, adds little to the nutrient value of a flour, and means only that a greater amount of bread has to be eaten for the same amount of nourishment to be obtained from it.[1] It is probably this fact which, long before the reasons for it were known, caused a general preference for white bread to establish itself, with the result that white bread has long been regarded as a mark of superior civilization or of superior social standing. For the existence of this preference, whatever its cause, there is ample testimony not only in our own day, but also both in medieval and earlier modern times[2] and in the Roman period. 'To know the colour of one's bread'[3] was a Roman equivalent of knowing one's place—and the lowlier the place the darker was the colour of the bread: several imperial writers describe the prevalent custom of giving dark bread to a socially inferior guest,[4] and Suetonius merely provides the exception to prove the rule when he tells us that Julius Caesar had his baker thrown into chains for giving 'different' bread to his guests.[5] It was mentioned earlier that the difference in question might be

[1] For figures see Moran and Pace, quoted by Lockwood, *Flour Milling*[2], pp. 284 ff. ('Long extraction' also impairs the keeping qualities of flour, but this need not concern us here.)

[2] Cf. Ashley, *Bread of our Forefathers, passim.*

[3] Juv. *Sat.* 5. 74–75.

[4] See ibid. 67 ff. (cf. above, pp. xx–xxi); Mart. ix. 2. 4; Petron. 64. 8; Fronto *ad Anton.* i. 3 (p. 101 Naber; vol. ii, p. 120 in the Loeb edition); and perhaps Quint. *Inst.* vi. 3. 60. [On different fare for guests cf. also Mart. iii. 60; Pliny (the Younger), *Epp.* ii. 6; Luc. *de Merc. Cond.* 26.]

[5] *Div. Iul.* 48.

one between kinds of wheat;[1] but the chapters that follow will show that it might also be, and often was, a difference between grades of flour from the same wheat.

This preference for white bread has for some time[2] encountered a certain amount of opposition both among ordinary consumers, some of whom have found 'wholemeal' bread more palatable, and—more recently—among some medical men and experts in nutrition, who have argued that the elimination of the bran leads to the loss of some valuable vitamins,[3] and that a diet that leaves too little to the digestive system may itself have harmful results. (There is nothing new in this: in Petronius' *Feast of Trimalchio* one of the speakers asks for wholemeal bread, saying, 'I prefer it to white; it gives me strength and it helps with the digestion'.[4]) But this opposition has never been strong enough to influence the main development, and it has long been the miller's aim to produce as white a flour as possible by eliminating the bran without rejecting part of the endosperm at the same time.

Unlike the husk of the husked grains, the bran proper cannot be removed by a hulling operation, since it forms part of the actual grain; but the modern miller, by a large number of operations, tries first to split the grain open without crushing it, and then to peel or shave the endosperm as completely as he can from its bran coat. Only then does he set out to reduce the endosperm to flour. In practice, however, he cannot reach this ideal even with the most modern implements: some endosperm always adheres to the bran, and if an attempt is made to use all the endosperm, some of the bran is crushed during the later stages of the 'shaving' process and finds its way into the flour. Since the bran content of the grain rarely exceeds 12–14 per cent.,[5] a flour of 85 per cent. extraction should theoretically be quite white: in fact a flour of 85 or even 80 per cent. extraction is much less white than one of 75 per cent.[6]

---

[1] Cf. above, pp. xix–xx. (Or it might, in later times, be the difference between rye and wheat, which Goethe called the 'shibboleth, or *Feldgeschrei*, between Germans and Frenchmen'.)

[2] Especially after modern milling methods had begun to make really white flour possible.

[3] Particularly vitamin B1: in recent years, however, millers have tried to avoid this loss or to make it good in other ways.

[4] 66. 2: 'et panem autopyrum (cf. below, p. 160) de suo sibi, quem ego malo quam candidum; et vires facit, et cum mea re [causa] facio, non ploro.'

[5] See *Note Q*, p. 221.

[6] Flours of up to 75 per cent. extraction can now be produced without any noticeable admixture of bran.

The modern miller employs various complicated operations in producing his flour; but essentially he still relies, as his predecessors have done for many centuries, on the fact that bran offers more resistance to the action of the mill than endosperm. Provided that grinding does not continue until the bran, too, is crushed to powder, a white flour can be obtained by sifting the meal through a sieve which allows the powdery endosperm to pass while retaining the larger bran particles.[1] It is for this reason that the sieve has long been an adjunct of the mill.

Stone-milling cannot produce a flour as white as that to which we are accustomed; for even in its most perfect form, and even when accompanied by the most up-to-date sieves, it inevitably involves greater pulverization of the bran. So-called 'long-extraction' flours—i.e. those containing more than 75 per cent. of the total grain weight—are affected more than those in which less of the grain is utilized;[2] but the Lewes experiments have shown that even a 35 per cent. flour from a Romano-British quern, sifted by modern methods, has a fibre (bran) content at least as high as a good 85 per cent. roller-milled flour.[3] All comparisons between ancient and modern flour, therefore, must recognize that the best flour that could be produced in antiquity would not be rated very highly today.

In modern mills the use of the sieve is accompanied by repeated grinding—or rather 'cutting', since care is taken with the roller-mill to avoid crushing the grain between two flat surfaces. The rollers themselves are appropriately 'dressed' (i.e. grooved) and 'set' (i.e. moved closer together or farther apart) for each successive operation; the sieves that intervene between the various operations are of the aperture and material (wire, grit gauze, or silk) most suitable for each stage; and two or more sieves can be used in combination to yield three or more intermediate or final

[1] Air currents can also be used at some stages of the process, since the bran is much lighter than the endosperm and can therefore be 'blown away'—but this is once again a modern refinement.

[2] Lockwood (p. 285) estimates the fibre content of an 85 per cent. stone-milled flour as three times that of a similar flour produced by efficient roller-milling.

[3] Admittedly the Lewes quern was not the best possible stone-mill, especially since its stones were not grooved. Yet the experiments showed that the best flour that could have been produced on a quern was no whiter than a good 85 per cent. roller-milled flour, although on a good stone-mill it is possible to produce a flour of an extraction rather higher than 35 per cent. which is still as white as a modern 85 per cent. flour.

products. And even before the grain reaches the mill proper, it often has its moisture content adjusted by a process of 'conditioning', whose main purpose is to make the bran more resistant to the action of the mill. Among all these operations it is important to distinguish those which effect the actual separation of bran and endosperm from those designed to keep the bran particles as large as possible: sifting cannot produce white flour unless the particle size of the endosperm when it reaches the sieve is smaller than that of the bran, while conditioning, coarse grinding, or repeated grinding, are not ends in themselves, but serve to make the grist suitable for the most effective sifting.

It has often been thought[1] that ancient distinctions between grades of flour from the same grain depended on whether the mill was made to grind coarsely or finely; whether the meal was sent through the mill once or more often; and whether sifting was used after grinding. But this view is almost certainly mistaken. We have seen that the object of grinding grain for bread cannot have been the production of coarse flour *per se*: coarse grinding, where bread flour is concerned, if employed at all, can have been employed only to avoid bran pulverization. But if this was its purpose, there would have been no point in performing this operation at all except as a preliminary to a second and finer grinding, and meal ground coarsely must have been sent through the mill a second time. Both coarse and repeated grinding, moreover, must be regarded as subordinate to sifting; for the sieve alone can effect the grading of flour.

If we go on to ask which of the subsidiary processes now in use had their parallels in antiquity, we find immediately that this is true of conditioning. Not only were the husked grains moistened and roasted before hulling,[2] but Pliny tells us that *siligo* moistened with salt water produced a whiter flour, but less of it, than the same grain milled dry:[3] this is exactly the effect to be expected if the bran is kept large without adequate facilities for 'shaving' it.

The setting of the mill for coarse or fine grinding, on the other hand, may probably be ignored, at least for the greater part of the classical period, since it is unlikely that the mills used were

---

[1] See, e.g., Blümner, p. 49.
[2] For moistening cf. Plin. *N.H.* xviii. 72 ff. and 98; for roasting above, p. xvii.
[3] Ibid. 87 (quoted below, p. 170). The phrase *molae discrimine* in this passage need not, and probably does not, imply adjustable mills: it may well refer merely to differences in milling method. Cf. also Jasny, *Wheat Prices*, pp. 149–50.

adjustable. It is true that with the saddle-quern and the 'Olynthian' mill the operator had some control over the particle size of the meal, but this control was very incomplete, and rotary mills probably did not become adjustable until fairly late. Coarse grinding, therefore, can hardly have been used in antiquity, as its equivalent is nowadays, to split open the grain before it was crushed: stone-mills are in any case less suitable for such a process than the modern rollers.

The case for repeated grinding is different. When Seneca compares the action of the mill to that of the teeth, he mentions, as one of the points of resemblance, that 'that which falls out'—i.e. passes through unground (or unchewed)—'is brought back several times until frequent grinding reduces it to minuteness':[1] if the analogy holds, the main aim of the later grindings was to reduce that which escaped during the earlier stages. The Lewes experiments have shown that even with a rotary quern (and a fortiori with a saddle-quern or 'Olynthian' grain-rubber) a considerable part of the grist passed through the mill unground or partly ground on its first passage.[2] This part of the material could profit by further grinding, especially if the flour from the first grinding could first be drawn off through a sieve.

Sifting between successive grindings is convenient for several reasons: it makes it unnecessary to regrind what is already sufficiently ground (and, since excessive friction impairs the baking qualities of flour, regrinding of fine flour is undesirable as well as unnecessary); fine flour, especially from the softer wheats, tends to clog the stone surfaces and to make grinding difficult;[3] and later grindings are apt to pulverize more of the bran than the first, so that it is useful to sift off the flour from the first operation—the whitest flour possible—before giving further treatment to the 'overtails' that remain on top of the sieve. If more than two grinding operations are employed it is natural, for the same reasons, to repeat the sifting after each grinding.

The only evidence for the use of the sieve between grindings, and the main evidence for repeated grinding, is that derived from practical experiment; but it seems reasonable to suppose that

[1] *Ep.* 90. 22–23, quoted above, p. 7, n. 3.
[2] The amount of this might have been smaller had the quern been effectively grooved, but even then it would certainly have been far from negligible.
[3] This again became very clear at Lewes, especially with the softer of the two wheats used in the experiments.

practical experience must have led ancient millers to the same conclusions. We shall have occasion to return to this problem, and at this point no final conclusion need be reached: even if the grist only passed through the mill once, the sieve still had to be used if it was desired to produce anything other than wholemeal, since it provides the only means of effecting a separation among ground products. Sieves might be made of various materials and might have widely differing mesh apertures; they might succeed only in drawing off the very coarsest bran, or they might only allow the finest flour to pass: but a sieve must be used if anything worthy to be called flour, rather than meal, is to result, and we are entitled to infer that a sieve was used wherever we hear of a contrast between flour, and bread made from flour, on the one side, and wholemeal, and wholemeal bread, on the other—even though we may find it difficult to assess the qualities of either.

III

SIEVES AND SIFTED FLOUR IN CLASSICAL GREECE

IN a poem of the seventh or sixth century B.C. Semonides of Amorgos complains of the woman 'who will not touch the mill, nor lift the sieve, nor throw the refuse out of the house, nor sit by the oven, afraid of the soot'.[1] At first sight this passage, with its mention of the mill, the sieve, and the baking-oven, in the right order, seems to provide convincing evidence for the practice of flour-sifting at this early period, especially since the 'refuse' to which it refers may itself be that which is left on the sieve after sifting.[2] But although this may be the right interpretation, it would be unwise to accept this evidence too readily, since sieves and strainers still have a great variety of uses and were used just as extensively in ancient times.[3]

Even if, as the run of the passage suggests, the use which Semonides had in mind for the sieve was in some way connected with grain, it does not necessarily follow that the sieve was employed for the division of meal into flour and bran: Aristophanes shows by an epithet that a sieve which he mentions was used for separating the grain—*before* grinding—from weed seeds contained in it,[4] and the mesh aperture of such a sieve can have been little smaller than the thickness of the grain (i.e. about 0·1 in.). It is probably the same sieve that is referred to in the first century A.D. as *cribrum viciarium vel loliarium*,[5] and the 'sieve made of hide

---

[1] *Frag.* 7. 59 ff. (for the date cf. *Oxford Class. Dict.*):

οὔτ' ἂν μύλης ψαύσειεν οὔτε κόσκινον
ἄρειεν οὔτε κόπρον ἐξ οἴκου βάλοι
οὔτε πρὸς ἱπνὸν ἀσβόλην ἀλευμένη
ἵζοιτ'.

[2] This is suggested by LXX *Ecclus.* xxvii. 4; but Semonides may, of course, be referring to ordinary cleaning. (The Latin *sordes*, too, may mean either 'filth' or, as in Non. 445. 14, the refuse in the meal.)

[3] See, e.g., Plat. *Gorg.* 493b, *Rep.* ii. 363d; Ar. *Nub.* 373; Ath. xiv. 647 f; Cat. *Agr.* 18. 7, 25, 48. 2, 107. 1; Col. v. 6. 6, vii. 8. 7; Plin. *N.H.* xvi. 54, xvii. 73, xxviii. 145.

[4] κόσκινον αἰρόπινον, *frag.* 480 (*ap.* Poll. x. 114, q.v.).

[5] Col. viii. 5. 16.

160 FLOUR

for use on the threshing-floor', which appears in a list of sieves in Diocletian's *Edict*,[1] must have been used immediately after threshing and before the grain reached the mill.

But even where sifting is mentioned as following after some kind of milling operation, it is still not certain that it was to separate the bran proper from the flour. Husked grains (especially barley) were also eaten in classical Greece, and the sieve may have been employed merely to separate the husks from the grain after hulling. The verb βράττειν, which occurs among the miller's and baker's activities in an Aristophanic fragment,[2] may well describe such a process: it is preceded by πτίττειν, 'to pound'— and pounding was the prerogative of husked grains.[3]

When all this is borne in mind, it is not easy to find any direct evidence from classical Greece for the use of the sieve to separate bran from endosperm after milling. The words which by themselves must denote flour-sieves, rather than sieves generally,[4] are all late Greek; sieves mentioned in classical literature may in every instance have been used for some other purpose; nor is such pictorial evidence as survives more helpful.[5] Yet there are a few indirect indications: Athenaeus[6] quotes Phrynichus,[7] a contemporary and rival of Aristophanes, and Alexis,[8] a comic poet of the fourth to third century B.C., as referring somewhere in their plays to ἄρτοι αὐτόπυροι or αὐτοπυρῖται. These words are usually taken to denote wholemeal bread;[9] and if wholemeal bread had a special name to distinguish it from other kinds, bread from sifted flour must have been known.

But even this indirect evidence is not free from difficulty. Although 'wholemeal' was certainly the meaning of the words in

---

[1] κόσκινον ἁλωνικὸν ἀπὸ βύρσης, xv. 56a. (On the cleaning of grain before grinding cf. Jasny, *Wheat Prices*, p. 150.)
[2] *Frag.* 271. LS translate 'to winnow', and this may be the meaning in some passages; but see Hesych. s.v. ἀποβράσαι, *E.M.* 125. 43, and Blümner, p. 11, n. 1.
[3] The same sequence occurs in Eust. *ad Il.* x. 249, p. 801. 63, and *Geopon.* iii. 7. 1.
[4] Especially ἀλευρόττησις and γυριστήριον; cf. below, p. 166.
[5] See Blümner, p. 62, fig. 24 (an undoubted sieve, but not necessarily being used for flour-sifting); p. 69, fig. 29 (not necessarily a sieve); cf. also p. 69, n. 1, and *Ἀρχ. Ἐφ.* 1896, pp. 201 ff.
[6] iii. 110e.
[7] *Frag.* 38.
[8] *Frag.* 121.
[9] See, e.g., LS, s.vv.; and on the whole question cf. Blümner, pp. 75-76 and notes.

question in later Greek,[1] their derivation suggests that it was not their original meaning, and that they at one time denoted either 'bread made from wheat (πυρός) proper' (as opposed to σιτάνιος)[2] or 'bread made wholly from wheat' (and not from a mixture of, for instance, wheat and barley) :[3] this was probably still their meaning in the period with which we are here concerned. A similar change can be observed in the case of the word πύρνον, which originally must have included all wheaten bread, though it later came to denote wholemeal bread only.[4] (The change in the meaning of αὐτόπυρος may have taken place when a branny πιτυρίας loaf came to be made from the overtails of the sieve *only* : compared with this, wholemeal bread must have been a delicacy, and Galen[5] considers the wholemeal loaf—αὐτόπυρος—to be intermediate in quality between the πιτυρίας and bread made from sifted flour.)

Fortunately we can go a step farther than this; for wholemeal bread did, after all, have a special name as early as the fifth century B.C. Galen, after expressly saying that αὐτόπυρος in his day meant wholemeal bread, adds that the older physicians had a different name—συγκομιστός—for this.[6] This name occurs in the Hippocratic writings, and at least once in the oldest part of them, which was probably written about 430 B.C.:[7] it provides the earliest clear reference to wholemeal bread and—by implication—the first definite evidence for the use of sifted flour. We cannot be certain that flour-sifting was practised in Greece before the fifth century; but the name συγκομιστός would hardly have

---

[1] Cf. Cels. ii. 18, Petron. 66. 2, Non. p. 445. 14. In Plin. *N.H.* xxii. 138 αὐτόπυρος means 'well-leavened', and in Ath. iii. 111e ἀποπυρίας—from πῦρ, 'fire'—probably has the same meaning : Pliny may have confused two words, but it is interesting to compare Gal. vi. 482 K., where the presence of bran is said to lessen the need for leavening.

[2] Cf. above, pp. xix–xx and especially Plut. *de Tranq. An.* 466d.

[3] i.e. κριθόπυρον; cf. *Arch. Pap.* i. 174. In Phrynichus the αὐτοπυρίτης is clearly a delicacy, and not something inferior. On the analogy of other αὐτός compounds a word like *αὐτοπιτύριος, 'bran and all', would be needed to denote wholemeal bread.

[4] Philem. *ap.* Ath. iii. 114d. (The word first occurs in Hom. *Od.* xv. 312, xvii. 12, 362.)

[5] vi. 483 K.   [6] Ibid.

[7] *Vet. Med.* 14; cf. *Acut.* 37, and, on the much-debated date of these writings, W. H. S. Jones, ' "Hippocrates" and the *Corpus Hippocraticum*', *Proc. Brit. Acad.* xxi. 103 ff. In *Aff.* 52 the name ἀνερεικτός, 'unsifted' (lit. 'unpounded') is used in the same sense. (Αὐτοπυρίτης in *Int.* 20, 22 may well be connected with πῦρ, 'fire', like διπυρίτης, 'twice-baked', ibid. 25.)

been used in the fifth century if sifted flour had not been known then. Nor need it be thought, because the evidence for it is indirect and uncorroborated, that the practice was not widespread: any reference to flour-sifting in the literature of this period could only be incidental, and the relevant monuments are not numerous enough for the absence of pictorial representations of it to be significant.

Apart from actual evidence, moreover, it is intrinsically probable that flour-sifting was practised, and practised on a fairly large scale, even at this comparatively early time. If the word ἄλευρα denoted a meal or flour finer than ἄλφιτα, and if this fine meal was of a reasonably uniform particle size and free from large pieces of bran, either special efforts must have been made to reduce all the bran to a fine powder, which is not at all easy, or else the bran must have been separated from the meal by sifting.[1] It is hard to believe that all the bran was, or could have been, pulverized; and if the bran was drawn off, this could have been done only by sieves, which, after all, were in existence for many other purposes.

By 330 B.C., when the word for bran (πίτυρον) occurs in Demosthenes' speech On the Crown,[2] sifted flour must certainly have been known—and since bran here features in religious ritual, it is unlikely that its production had only been introduced recently. During the intervening eighty years or so barley had probably become far less important in the human diet than formerly,[3] and new mills may have been invented: but the sifting of flour was almost certainly not one of the great innovations in the field of cereal nutrition which the fourth century had brought.

In view of the lack of evidence with which we have had to contend in this chapter, it is not surprising that little can be said about the nature of the sieves that were used. The κόσκινον, mentioned by Aristophanes and Semonides, was, according to a much later definition,[4] made of reeds, and it may have been made of reeds from the outset. But while the κόσκινον was certainly a

---

[1] The words παιπάλη, πασπάλη, and παλημάτιον, in Aristophanes (Nub. 260, 262; Vesp. 91; frag. 682) probably denoted the finest part of ἄλφιτα, separated out by sifting. Unfortunately the definitions of these words are late (for references see Blümner, p. 54, notes 10–13): otherwise it could reliably be argued that if sieves were used for ἄλφιτα, they must certainly have been used for ἄλευρα.

[2] Section 259.   [3] Cf. CQ, N.S., v. 136 ff.

[4] Poll. vi. 74; cf. Blümner, p. 50, notes 6, 8, 9.

sieve,[1] the names of other implements which later also denoted sieves may not have done so when they were used by Aristophanes;[2] and neither Aristophanes nor any other classical Greek writer gives us any detailed information, although there is a suggestion in Herodotus[3] that linen sieves, too, may have been used. In some cases, moreover, flour-sieves were not woven at all, but made from a solid sheet or board with holes punched in it.[4]

It is unlikely that these flour-sieves were either very regular in their aperture or very fine. Such sieves would suffice to eliminate large pieces of bran and unground or half-ground grains from the flour; but they could hardly do more than that, and even purified flour in classical Greece must have been very dark indeed by our standards.[5]

---

[1] See especially Ar. *Nub.* 373. (The sieve of the Danaids and the sieve of Eratosthenes for finding prime numbers were also κόσκινα.)

[2] Especially κρησέρα (*Eccl.* 991; later a flour-sieve of wool or linen, but in Aristophanes perhaps a pack-cloth) and τηλία (*Plut.* 1037; in Aristophanes a large ring, such as the *rim* of a sieve would be).

[3] i. 200.

[4] See Blümner, fig. 24, and *Ed. Diocl.* xv. 57.

[5] The use of the word συγκομιστός (= 'brought together') for wholemeal bread suggests, incidentally, that the grain was ground more than once, the meal being sifted between grindings and all products being 'brought together' for wholemeal; cf. Gal. vi. 483, xix. 142 K. (Diphilus *ap.* Ath. iii. 115c, however, explains συγκομιστός as = ἄσηστος, 'unsifted'.)

IV

ROMAN FLOUR-SIEVES

THE last chapter has shown that for the existence of the flour-sieve in classical Greece there are rather stronger indications than there were for the rotary mill. The 'Homeric' bowl, moreover, on which the Olynthian mill is shown in operation, also shows a sieve; and although here again it may be the cleaning of grain rather than the sifting of flour that is depicted, this bowl may well provide a link in time between the Greek and the Roman parts of our period. Yet, as was the case with the rotary mill, the first explicit mention of a flour-sieve comes from the Latin writers, where, like the rotary mill, the flour-sieve makes its appearance in some of the earliest extant works.

In his recipe for a kind of cake (*placenta*), Cato prescribes the straining of cottage cheese through a *cribrum farinarium*:[1] the name of this sieve shows that its primary function was to sift meal or flour, and although Cato does not mention its use for either *farina* or *alica*, both of which are also ingredients of the *placenta*, the connexion between *cribrum farinarium* and *farina* is obvious. The word *farina*[2] was probably associated originally with *far* (emmer), but this association soon became obsolete,[3] and in classical Latin it denotes—like ἄλευρα in Greek—meal from all kinds of grain, though wheat is in the nature of the case the most frequent raw material. But whereas it is usually thought that *farina* was wholemeal and identical with the Greek ἄλευρον αὐτόπυρον,[4] it appears probable that it was rather a 'flour' from which some of the

---

[1] *Agr.* 76. 3. The *incerniculum* of chap. 13 may not have been a sieve, as is commonly thought: an *incerniculum* in Plin. *N.H.* viii. 175 is certainly not a sieve, and in a third passage (Lucil. *frag.* 638 Warm.) the reading is doubtful; cf. Blümner, p. 51, n. 2, and *LSh*, s.v.

[2] Cf. here Jasny, *Wheat Prices*, p. 151; Blümner, p. 53 and n. 14; Voigt, *Rhein. Mus.* xxxi. 114 and n. 22.

[3] Cf. Plin. *N.H.* xviii. 88; Isid. *Orig.* xx. 2. 18.

[4] The argument to this end (cf. Voigt, loc. cit.) is based on the omission of *farina* in a list of ground products in Cels. ii. 18. This is taken to mean that *farina* was identical with αὐτόπυρον in the list. But this need not be so, since Celsus' list may, as we shall see, imply a method of milling in which *farina* was not one of the products.

coarse bran had been removed, and there are several indications
that this was at any rate its normal meaning. (There may have
been some exceptions: *farina* serving as food for pheasants,[1] for
instance, was probably not a sifted product.)

The most striking indication is that whenever Latin writers
wish to refer to wholemeal they have to use Greek names for it:[2]
Greek distinguished between wholemeal (ἄλευρον αὐτόπυρον, συγ-
κομιστόν, or ἀνερεικτόν) and the 'clean' ἄλευρον καθαρόν,[3] but this
distinction has no parallel in Latin. Isidore of Seville[4] suggests
that both *farina* and *furfures* (bran) normally resulted from milling,
and Pliny, too, in at least one passage[5] contrasts *farina* and *furfur*:
such a contrast would not make sense if *farina* was wholemeal.
And the name of the *cribrum farinarium* itself suggests that some of
the bran must have been removed by sifting; for if the name of
this sieve is parallel to that of the *cribrum pollinarium*, of which
more will be said presently, *farina* must denote the 'throughs'
of a sieve, and not an unsifted meal.[6] It is true that a sieve which
was capable of being used also for cheese cannot have produced
a very fine flour,[7] and we shall see later that there are other
grounds for believing *farina* to have been a meal of very high
extraction; but it is unlikely that it contained all the grain as
it came from the millstones.

Yet it would be rash to infer that nothing finer than the meal
suggested by Cato's *cribrum farinarium* was produced in the second
century B.C. Several decades before Cato, Plautus mentions a
cribrum pollinarium,[8] and although he has nothing to tell us about
the use of this implement, the name itself shows what it must have
been: *pollen* (or later *pollis*) was, and remained, the finest flour
that could be produced,[9] and a *cribrum pollinarium* must have been
a sieve of separating such a flour from the coarser stock. The
mention of such a sieve by Plautus—like the mention of *pollen* by

---

[1] Pallad. *R.R.* i. 29. 4.
[2] For references see above, p. 161, n. 1.
[3] e.g. Hipp. *Aff.* 52; Gal. xv. 577 K.　　　　　　[4] *Orig.* xx. 2. 18.
[5] *N.H.* xviii. 87 *fin.*, quoted below, p. 170.
[6] The difference between *farina bona* and *far subtile* (see *Note O*, p. 221) may
be relevant here: this difference may have consisted not only in the finer particle
size of *farina* but also in its (relative) freedom from bran.
[7] Cf. Jasny, p. 150.
[8] *Poen.* 513: the context shows that the finest possible sieve is meant.
[9] See *Corp. Gl.* ii. 589. 66, and cf. ibid. 551. 28 and below, p. 172. The word
may be cognate with Greek (παι)πάλη, on which see above, p. 162, n. 1.

FLOUR

Cato[1] and Terence[2]—shows that it must have been possible by the second century B.C. to produce a flour of this type, and that a sieve substantially finer than the ordinary *cribrum farinarium* must have been known by then.

Two centuries later Pliny in one place distinguishes between *cribra pollinaria* and *cribra excussoria*, both made of linen,[3] while in another he contrasts a *cribrum farinarium* with two narrower sieves.[4] The *cribrum farinarium* of the one passage and the *cribrum excussorium* of the other were probably identical,[5] and if so, these passages show that two main types of sieve were in use in Pliny's day: one of these must have served to separate the coarser bran from the meal, while the other separated a finer flour from the 'throughs' of the first sieve. It is interesting, moreover, that Pliny should ascribe the invention of the linen sieve to Spain, where, as we saw earlier, other advances in the realm of milling may well have taken place; and the rhetorician Pollux[6] suggests that it was the replacement of reeds by linen that first produced a sieve really suitable for flour.

Pollux distinguishes the linen sieve (ἀλευρόττησις[7]) from the coarser reed sieve (κόσκινον) and stresses its greater suitability for the sifting of flour.[8] Although flour-sieves, too, could probably be referred to by the generic name κόσκινον (just as we call them sieves, or the Romans called them *cribra* without epithet), this passage suggests that the name ἀλευρόττησις was the Greek equivalent of the Latin *cribrum farinarium* or *excussorium*, and that it was of the same character and grade. But if so, we should expect to find a Greek equivalent also for the sieve by which finer flour was produced: the Greek name for this flour was γῦρις,[9] and the name γυριστήριον for a sieve is in fact found in late

---

[1] *Agr.* 89, 156. 5, 157. 9.   [2] *Ad.* 846.   [3] *N.H.* xviii. 108.

[4] In the preparation of 'impure' *alica*, ibid. 115. The narrowest of these three sieves still allowed sand to pass through, and Jasny (pp. 150–1) infers from this that *pollen* cannot have been very fine by modern standards. But the *cribrum angustissimum* of this passage need not have been either the finest sieve procurable or similar to the *cribrum pollinarium*.

[5] Cf. Voigt, p. 118.   [6] vi. 74.

[7] Cf. also ὀθόνη in Hesych., s.v. ἀποβράσαι. (For the spelling see Zonar. 125.)

[8] The κρησέρα (cf. above, p. 163, n. 2), mentioned by Pollux as a woollen alternative to the ἀλευρόττησις, was, according to Gal. xix. 115 K. and Phot. 177. 26, made of either wool or linen. Cf. also Scribon. *Comp.* 6; *E.M.* 60. 25; *Anecd. Bekk.* 382. 24; Fest. *ap.* Paul., s.v. *Ignis Vestae*; *PW*, xi. 1483–4; *DS*, i. 1568.

[9] See *Corp. Gl.* vii. 102 and references there; and cf. Diosc. *M.M.* ii. 85. 2 W. with Plin. *N.H.* xxii. 127.

Greek.[1] If both these Greek names are less common than their Latin counterparts, it may be merely because the passages dealing with the subject are fewer in Greek than in Latin; but it is also possible that the distinction between two types of flour-sieve is hard to trace in Greek because one of the two—and obviously the finer— was little used outside a small area around the city of Rome. We shall find reason to suspect that the latter may have been the case.

Ancient writers, in giving us the names of sieves and occasionally their material, do not provide any precise information about the size of their mesh or about the flour produced by them. Nor does the appearance of sieves on the tomb of Eurysaces and on the Zethus sarcophagus help much: the sieves on the former are indistinct and shown from the side in such a way that only the rim can be seen; that on the Zethus relief is shown clearly, but it resembles one of the sieves mentioned earlier, with holes punched into an otherwise solid surface. This is probably due to the sculptor's inability to show in any other way that a sieve is intended: whether made of reeds, linen, or wool, a sieve contemporary with a Pompeian mill must surely have been woven—and yet a flour-sieve made of hide appears to be mentioned in Diocletian's *Edict*.[2] The process of sifting is depicted also on the Bologna relief, where, as far as can be seen, a workman is employed in emptying the overtails from the sieve.[3]

The most interesting fact that emerges from these monuments is that, from the time of the 'Homeric' bowl onwards, the sieve is an invariable adjunct of the mill wherever a more or less complete bakery is shown; and where, as on the tomb of Eurysaces, the order of operations can be made out, sifting follows after grinding and must therefore be concerned with meal and not with unground grain. This only confirms what was clear already from literary evidence: it tells us nothing about the fineness of the sieves or about the quality of the flour. Fortunately, however, there are two further sources of information open to us, to which we must now turn.

[1] See especially *Corp. Gl.* iii. 197. 48, and cf. Schol. Ar. *Plut.* 1037 (κοσκινόγυρος).
[2] xv. 57: κόσκινον ἀπὸ δέρματος σιμιδάλια. The word σιμιδάλια suggests that a *farinarium*-grade sieve is meant; cf. below, p. 173.
[3] Blümner (p. 51) compares a similar sieve on Trajan's column, for which see, e.g., Cichorius, *Reliefs der Trajanssäule* (Berlin, 1896–1900), plate x, no. 25. Cf. also the sieves in Overbeck–Mau, *Pompeii*[4], pp. 444–5.

V

GRADES OF MEAL AND FLOUR

FOR almost all the questions of the present study we have more information about Italy in the first century A.D. than about any other area or period of classical antiquity. This is due both to the accident which has preserved Pompeii for our inspection in a condition unique among ancient sites, and to the limitless curiosity of the elder Pliny, which was to cost him his life in the very disaster that preserved Pompeii for us, and which impelled him to collect a vast number of facts and to set them down in a work which again is unique in ancient literature. Pompeii, however, was at the time of its destruction one of the more advanced towns of the Roman Empire, and Pliny, when reporting technical processes, was clearly more interested in the novel and unusual than in the old-established: hence we must be on our guard against taking the comparatively plentiful and easily accessible evidence for first-century Italy as necessarily relating also to other districts and to other centuries. In discussing ancient mills we saw that this can lead to serious errors, and for flour and floursieves the danger of similar errors is even greater. Here again firstcentury Italy has left behind it more evidence than all the rest of classical antiquity; and in view of the perishable nature of both the product and the implements used for its production, the evidence is even scarcer for other periods than it was in the case of mills.

The information regarding mills came from the material remains of the period: this time it comes from the literary evidence of Pliny. The limitations of this evidence, and the limited relevance of conclusions based upon it, must be recognized at the outset: yet the information contained in the eighteenth book of Pliny's *Natural History* is by far the most explicit evidence at our disposal, and the opportunity presented by it, however limited, must not be neglected. In the relevant passages of this book Pliny provides some statements enabling us to relate given quantities of ground products to the quantity of grain used in their production, and this in turn makes it possible to know something about the quality of the various products.

This evidence, however, is not easy to use, and we may not even be justified in always accepting it at its face value. Pliny was no original investigator in this field; we shall find reason to suspect that his information is derived from more than one source; and we cannot be sure that he understood and copied his sources correctly. Nor can we always be sure exactly what Pliny wrote: the manuscript tradition of his text is in general not very good, but it is particularly liable to error where numerals are concerned[1]—and most of the information that is of value in the present context is expressed in numerals.

And there is one further difficulty. Pliny's measurements are not always given in the same terms—at some points he states the volume of ground products, at others the weight of the bread produced from them—and none of his measurements are expressed in terms of the weight of ground products, as parallel modern measurements invariably are, since meal and flour are nowadays always sold by weight. Owing to considerable differences in the weight per volume unit, both between wheat and the ground products made from it and between various grades of the latter, it is much easier to calculate the percentage of the grain utilized for flour (the 'extraction rate') if it is expressed in terms of weight than if it is expressed in terms of volume; and it is necessary, therefore, to convert Pliny's volume figures into weights before any calculations can be based upon them. This conversion is no easy matter, and Jasny, whose analysis of Pliny's evidence will in some respects be criticized in this and the following chapters, has rendered a great service in attempting it and in drawing attention to the need for it.

It may not be possible to overcome all these difficulties; but in dealing with them we have, in addition to the ordinary methods of textual criticism,[2] another source of information in what modern experience shows to be practicable and probable. It was in order to exploit this source that the grinding experiments on a Romano-British quern at Lewes, mentioned previously, were carried out.[3] The results of these experiments cannot perhaps be

---

[1] e.g. 'p. xvii' in no. 3b of the passages cited below appears as 'p. xvi' in some manuscripts, and as 'cxvii' in others.

[2] In the instance just given these enable us to rule out 'cxvii', without allowing a decision between the other two readings.

[3] The results are reported in full in *Milling* of 24 June 1950. In the absence of a wheat of the emmer group we tried to discover something about the probable

regarded as fully reflecting those that would have been obtained on a Pompeian mill (with which Pliny is presumably concerned); but it has not proved possible to make similar experiments on a Pompeian mill,[1] and the information gained from the Lewes experiments is, as will appear, in most respects sufficient for what is needed here.

The relevant Pliny passages, numbered here for easier reference, run as follows (the text being based on that of Mayhoff in the Teubner series) :[2]

(1) *N.H.* xviii. 86–87 : 'Iustum est e grano Campanae (*sc.* siliginis), quam vocant castratam, e modio redire sextarios iv siliginis vel e gregali sine castratura sextarios v, praeterea floris semodium et cibarii, quod secundarium vocant, sextarios iv, furfuris sextarios totidem, e Pisana autem siliginis sextarios v, cetera paria sunt. Clusina Arretinaque etiamnum sextarios siliginis adiciunt, in reliquis pares.'

It is right that the grain of Campanian *siligo*, which is called *castrata*,[3] should yield 4 *sextarii* of *siligo* from each *modius* (or the common kind, which is not *castrata*, 5 *sextarii*) ; also half a *modius* of *flos*, 4 sextarii of *cibarium*—which is the name given to *secundarium*[4]—and an equal number of *sextarii* of *furfur*. The Pisan kind should yield 5 *sextarii* of *siligo*, the rest being equal; that from Clusium and that from Arretium add a further *sextarius* of *siligo*, but are equal otherwise.

(2) Ibid. 87, following immediately after (1): 'Si vero pollinem facere libeat, xvi pondo panis redeunt et cibarii iii furfurumque semodius. molae discrimine hoc constat. nam quae sicca moluntur, plus farinae reddunt, quae salsa aqua sparsa, candidiorem medullam, verum plus retinent in furfure.'

If, however, it is desired to make *pollen*, 16 (Roman) pounds of bread result, together with 3 pounds of *cibarius* bread[5] and

---

differences between *triticum* and *siligo* by using both a hard and a soft type of *vulgare* wheat.

[1] Since the reconstruction of the mills at Naples is itself uncertain, information obtained from them would in any case not have been conclusive.

[2] For the measurements mentioned by Pliny see below, *Note S*, p. 221.

[3] The meaning of this epithet is uncertain : it is usually taken to mean 'sifted' or 'bolted' (of the flour) ; but it is more probable that it refers to something that was done to the plant, and that *siligo castrata* was a particularly good wheat.

[4] i.e. 'which is the name given to what otherwise—in the case of *triticum* in list (3a)—is called *secundarium*' : this gives better sense than 'which is called *secundarium*', though grammatically the latter is also possible.

[5] It is just possible that this should be '3 *sextarii* of *cibarium*'; but fortunately the difference is not important. Cf. below, p. 193, n. 2.

half a *modius* of *furfur*. This depends on a difference in the mill. For that which is ground dry yields more flour; that which is first moistened with salt water yields a whiter 'marrow'[1] but retains more among the *furfur*.

(3) (*a*) Ibid. 89: 'Similago e tritico fit, laudatissima ex Africo. iustum est e modiis redire semodios et pollinis sextarios v— ita appellant in tritico quod florem in siligine; hoc aerariae officinae chartariaeque utuntur—, praeterea secundarii sextarios iv furfurumque tantundem,'
(*b*), following straight after (*a*) : 'panis vero e modio similaginis p. xxii, e floris modio p. xvii (*v.l.* xvi). pretium huic annona media in modios farinae xl asses, similagini octonis assibus amplius, siligini castratae duplum.'
(*a*) *Similago* is made from *triticum*, the best from African *triticum*. It is right that a *modius* (of grain) should yield half a *modius* and 5 *sextarii* of *pollen*—this is the name given in the case of *triticum* to what is called *flos* in the case of *siligo*; it is used by coppersmiths' and papermakers' workshops—; also 4 *sextarii* of *secundarium* and the same amount of *furfur*.
(*b*) The bread yield of a *modius* of *similago* is 22 (Roman) pounds, that of *flos* is 17 (or 16)[2] pounds. At average prices a modius of *farina* costs 40 *asses*, of *similago* 8 *asses* more, of *siligo castrata* double.[3]

(4) Ibid. 90:[4] 'Est et alia distinctio semel ⟨tenuiore cribro⟩ pollinatam xvii p. panis reddere, bis xviii, ter xix cum triente et secundarii panis quinas selibras, [totidem cibarii] et furfurum sextarios vi.'
There is also another distinction: meal from which *pollen* has (by means of a finer sieve) been extracted once yields 17 pounds of bread; if twice, 18 pounds; if three times, 19⅓, and 2½ pounds of *secundarius* bread, [the same amount of *cibarius*,[5]] and 6 *sextarii* of *furfur*.

---

[1] i.e., presumably, 'endosperm'.
[2] The manuscripts vary between the two figures, and no certain decision is possible, though 17 is rather more probable.
[3] These prices cannot here be discussed, but it must be pointed out that Pliny's text as it stands states a price of 80 or, less probably, 96 *asses* for *siligo castrata* (*pace* Jasny, following T. Frank, *Econ. Survey* v. 144): if other evidence makes 56 *asses*—i.e. 40 plus twice 8—necessary, *duplum* must be changed to *duplo*.
[4] The text is corrupt (for details see Mayhoff's critical note), and the version here given is no more than probable. The verb *pollinare* does not occur elsewhere, which may help to account for the corruption. The words *tenuiore cribro*, in particular, must be regarded as tentative.
[5] These words should probably be omitted; cf. below, p. 178, n. 1.

This is the evidence from which we must try to infer, if we can, how many grades of ground product were produced in Pliny's day; how the various grades were produced; what percentage of the wheat weight was used for each; and how their quality compared with modern products. But before a detailed discussion of this evidence is entered upon, something must be said about the various types of product which figure in it, so that terminological questions may not embarrass a discussion which will be intricate enough without them.

In (1) Pliny divides the yield of a *modius* of *siligo* into varying quantities of *siligo*, *flos*, *cibarium*, and *furfures*; and in (3a) he names *similago*, *pollen*, *secundarium*, and *furfures*, as the ground products of *triticum*. The difference between *triticum* and *siligo* itself was briefly discussed in the Introduction: *furfures* in both lists undoubtedly means bran,[1] while *pollen* in the case of *triticum*, and *flos* in that of *siligo*, must denote the finest product possible, which must have been the product closest to that denoted by our 'flour'.[2] The two terms are expressly equated in (3a), though Pliny does not always observe what he says there;[3] and our word 'flour' is itself cognate with *flos* and with the French *fleur de farine*.

Secundarium and *cibarium* again usually represent the same grade of product in Pliny's text,[4] and both names imply that this product was second-rate[5] and much more like bran than any of the other products mentioned—except, of course, *furfures*. In Pliny's lists *furfures* and *secundarium* (*cibarium*) always appear next to each other; and the physician Celsus in his list of grades of flour and bread, ranked according to their nutrient value,[6] puts *cibarius*

---

[1] See Plin. *N.H.* xviii. 304, xxii. 145; Col. viii. 4. 1; Voigt, p. 118; and below, p. 177.

[2] *Flos* often means 'the best part of anything'; cf. *LSh.* For *pollen* see above, p. 165, n. 9. Cf. also Voigt, pp. 116–17.

[3] Cf. below, p. 175, n. 5 and p. 176, n. 1. For similar confusions see 'Chiro', *Mulomed.* (ed. Oder; Leipzig, 1901), 674, 846, 912, on which cf. below, p. 213, n. 3. Cf. also Jasny, p. 155.

[4] Cf. above, p. 170, n. 4 and below, p. 178, n. 1. But in a list of oils in *Ed. Diocl.* iii. 1–3 ('olei floris, olei sequentis, olei cibarii') *sequens* and *cibarium* are different grades.

[5] For *secundarius* cf. Col. xii. 11. 1, 39. 2, Plin. *N.H.* xiv. 82, Hor. *Ep.* ii. 1. 123, Suet. *Aug.* 76; for *cibarius* Col. xii. 52. 18, Varr. *ap.* Non. p. 93. 10 M., Plin. *N.H.* xiv. 35 and 37, and especially Cic. *Tusc.* v. 97, Isid. *Or.* xx. 2. 15. Blümner's distinction (p. 77, n. 7) between *panis secundus* and *panis cibarius* is almost certainly wrong.

[6] ii. 18. The list, in descending order, is as follows: (1) *siligo*; (2) *simila*; (3) αὐτόπυρον; (4) *pollen*; (5) *cibarium*. But Celsus' views on nutrient value were somewhat peculiar; cf. also below, p. 175.

panis lowest. (He does not mention bran, presumably because no bread was made from it and because it was not used for human food.)

We are left with *siligo* and *similago*, which, if the other products have been correctly paired, were also parallel grades. *Siligo* as a ground product bore the name of the wheat from which it was made, which suggests that it was the main product from this wheat. This is not borne out by the figures which Pliny gives for it, but these figures must be left for later discussion, as must the possibility that they have become corrupted in the textual tradition. *Similago*, according to Pliny's figures, was the main product from *triticum*, although the yield of it amounts to only half the volume of the grain and therefore (since ground products are always lighter than the original grain) to less than half of the grain weight.

The word *similago*, with a variant *simila*, is familiar also from other sources,[1] and it is cognate with a number of words in other languages, among them the Greek σεμίδαλις:[2] this σεμίδαλις, and the σεμιδαλίτης bread made from it, is the regular equivalent in our Greek sources of the Latin *similago*.[3] *Siligo*, on the other hand, had no Greek equivalent, and Galen[4] is compelled to transliterate the Latin (as σίλιγνις) because of this. Similarly γῦρις appears as the Greek equivalent of *pollen* (from *triticum*),[5] but there is no equivalent for *flos* (from *siligo*).[6] The Greek name for *furfures* is πίτυρον, and, although there is no special name for *secundarium* or *cibarium*, the bread which was known as 'branny' (πιτυρίας)[7] was probably identical with the *panis secundus* made from *secundarium*: it is, as we shall see, unlikely that any bread was made from bran alone.

[1] e.g. Cat. *Agr.* 75; Cels. ii. 18 and 30; Martial, xiii. 10 *in lemm.*; Vulg. *Num.* vii. 13.

[2] Also the Doric ἱμαλίς; cf. *LS*.

[3] Cf. the medieval glossaries and Diosc. *M.M.* ii. 85. 1 W.; Dieuch. *ap.* Orib. *Coll.* iv. 7. 37; Gal. xi. 120 K.; Hipp. *Vict. Rat. II,* i. 676 Kühn; Voigt, p. 115.

[4] vi. 483, xiii. 11 K. Cf. also Voigt, p. 116, n. 25.

[5] Cf. above, p. 116 and n. 9.

[6] The reason may be that, while in Italy the soft wheats denoted by *siligo* could be either autumn- or spring-sown, the prevailing distinction in the Greek-speaking part of the ancient world continued to be between the hard wheats of the main autumn-sown crop on the one hand, and the comparatively unimportant soft wheats of the spring crop—denoted by σητάνιος and its variants—on the other; cf. above, pp. xix–xx.

[7] Poll. vi. 72, Gal. vi. 481 K. On *panis furfureus* see below, p. 177.

It was mentioned earlier in this chapter that Pliny's terminology is not consistent and that his figures are not always parallel, probably because he relied on at least two different sources: these difficulties are particularly apparent in connexion with *siligo*. Having divided the yield of *siligo* after grinding into *flos*, *siligo*, *cibarium*, and *furfures*, Pliny goes on to say—in (2)—that 'if it is desired to make *pollen*, 16 pounds of bread can be produced, together with three pounds of second-rate bread and half a *modius* of bran'. He says explicitly that this further statement represents a method of milling different from (1);[1] and it is probable that (2) is derived from a source different from that of (1): this is suggested both by the change from *flos* to *pollen*—in spite of what is said about these names in (3*a*)—and by the fact that, whereas in (1) flour volumes are given, in (2) he gives yields of bread for *pollen* and *cibarium*, and the volume for *furfures* alone, from which probably no bread was made. The moistening of the wheat, which preceded grinding when method (2) was employed, had the effect, according to Pliny, of producing whiter flour while retaining more of the endosperm among the bran; but apparently it also meant that only three products—*pollen*, *cibarium*, and *furfures*—resulted, instead of four. The difficulties of reconciling the amounts given in (2) with those of (1) will be discussed later: the point that is relevant here is the absence in (2) of *siligo*, which in (1) is one of the products.

Pollen (γῦρις) from *triticum* was used less for bread than for other purposes, medicinal and industrial, and especially for glue:[2] although bread was made from it,[3] this bread had a poor reputation for both flavour and nourishment.[4] But since *triticum* was probably 'macaroni' or 'rivet' wheat, which even in modern times is more often ground into semolina than into fine flour,[5] the low ranking of bread from *pollen tritici* is more understandable than a similar ranking would be for bread made from *flos siliginis*, which, as we shall see, was rated very highly: the name *flos*, moreover, implies good quality, which *pollen* does not.

---

[1] The difference is explained by the moistening, and is not connected by Pliny with any adjustment of the mill itself.
[2] Cf. (3*a*) and Plin. *N.H.* xiii. 82, xxii. 127; i *Index* xxii. 60; Diosc. *M.M.* ii. 85. 2 W.; Blümner, p. 324 and notes. Pliny gives neither a bread yield nor a price for *pollen tritici*.   [3] Cf. Diosc., loc. cit.; *Geopon.* xx. 41.
[4] Philist. *ap.* Ath. iii. 115d; Cels. ii. 18 (cf. above, p. 172, n. 6).
[5] Cf. above, p. xxi.

In Juvenal[1] and Martial,[2] however, it is not *flos siliginis* but *siligo*—absent from Pliny's list (2)—that is contrasted with 'black' or 'solid'[3] meal as being the material of which good and expensive bread was made: this probably implies not only that the 'soft' *siligo* wheat was preferred to the 'hard' *triticum*, but also that the flour which bore the name of the superior wheat was considered the best flour from which bread could be made. Similarly Celsus[4] ranks *siligo* flour highest for nutrient value, without mentioning *flos siliginis*. Now it is, of course, not to be expected that Juvenal and Martial should be technically precise in their language (though precision might be expected of Celsus), and it is quite possible that what they meant by *siligo* is that which Pliny calls *flos*: what is remarkable is not that Pliny should refer to the best flour possible as *flos*, while the satirists and even Celsus call it simply *siligo*, but that he should mention a second-grade flour bearing the name that is borne by the best in Juvenal, Martial, and Celsus.

Two possible explanations suggest themselves. One is that it was in fact unusual to draw off the finest grade of flour, in which case Pliny's *siligo* would have been the best flour actually in use, being distinguished from inferior grades both by its better raw material and by the fact that both bran and *cibarium* had been sifted out of it. This explanation is supported not only by the name *siligo*, which is identical with the name of the grain, but also by the absence of both *flos* and *pollen* from the list of flours for which prices are given in (3*b*); and if *pollen* in (2) is in fact the same as *flos* in (1), the wording of (2)—'if it is desired to make *pollen*'— itself shows that the finest grade was not always drawn off.

Now *pollen tritici* was, as we have seen, not considered very desirable for breadmaking, and if it was mainly used for glue it can hardly have been drawn off from all the *triticum* that was ground. This, however, does not apply to *flos siliginis*: the very name *flos* suggests the exceptionally good quality which modern experience with parallel grades would lead us to expect, and in (3*b*), where *pollen* is not mentioned, a bread yield is given for *flos*.[5] But if *flos siliginis* was of such high quality, it is unlikely that

---

[1] 5. 70.   [2] ix. 2. 3.
[3] i.e., presumably, badly leavened bread; cf. also Pers. 3. 112 and below, p. 181.
[4] ii. 18; cf. above, p. 172, n. 6.
[5] Unless indeed Pliny here uses the term *flos* for *pollen tritici*: but, although he does the converse in (2), this seems unlikely.

the sections of the population alluded to by Juvenal and Martial should have been satisfied with anything less desirable—or, at least, that they should be described as being satisfied with anything less desirable. For this reason alone it is hard to believe that, although it was possible to produce an extra-fine *siligo* flour, it was not in fact usual to do so; and the *siligo* mentioned by Juvenal and Martial cannot be explained by the assumption that it was identical with the *siligo* in (1), except that no *flos* had been sifted out of it.

There remains the second possibility. In (2) three ground products from *siligo* wheat are mentioned, in place of the four of (1), and only one of the three—*pollen*—can be considered real flour. The characteristic of this flour, which takes the place of both *siligo* and *flos* in (1), was, according to Pliny, its greater whiteness combined with a lower total extraction rate; and in view of this it seems probable that method (2) was employed to produce the most favoured flour: the strictly correct name of this flour may have been *flos* (or, less probably, *pollen*); but since it was the only flour produced, it would be natural to call it *siligo*.

If this is right, the inference must be that there were two different methods of milling *siligo* wheat: the flour resulting from both was known as *siligo*, just as the normal flour from *triticum* was known as *similago*; and if milling was preceded by moistening this was the only flour. If there was no moistening the flour was inferior, but this could be made good to some extent by sifting the finer part out of it, which was then called *flos*: if Pliny used the term *pollen* in (2), it must have been because he wanted to distinguish the superior from the inferior *siligo* flour.[1] Although his language is both inexplicit and confused (so that certainty on this as on many other points is impossible), Pliny himself helps to confirm this interpretation when, in a less technical passage, he tells us that *siligo* flour was highly thought of because of its quality *and because of the fine mesh of the sieve employed in its production*.[2]

---

[1] The change from *flos* in (1) to *pollen* in (2) is, however, so harsh that the text must remain suspect; but even this does not affect the main argument, since two different milling methods are in any case clearly involved.

[2] *N.H.* xviii. 105: 'summa laus siliginis bonitate et cribri tenuitate constat.'

VI

THREE-GRADE AND FOUR-GRADE MILLING

THE preceding discussion of the terms in Pliny's lists suggests that only one grade of real flour was normally produced in Pliny's day, but that it was possible to separate from this a finer grade. *Pollen* was almost certainly not always extracted when *similago* was prepared from *triticum*, and although *flos* from *siligo* was more desirable as a bread flour than *pollen* from *triticum*, the evidence makes it appear probable that *flos*, too, was not always drawn off when *siligo* was ground.

But even where there was only one grade of real flour there were still three products in all. Among these, however, *furfures* were probably not used for human food; and this is hardly surprising: since the human body cannot digest the fibrous material of which the coat of the wheat grain consists, it would be impossible to support life on a diet consisting predominantly of this. Bran appears frequently as food for animals,[1] and it was used also for medicinal purposes;[2] but it is always absent where cereal products eaten by human beings are listed. And even the Roman satirists, who liked to contrast the bread of the rich with that of the poor, do not speak of *panis furfureus*:[3] this can only mean that the poor, too, had something better than bread made from mere bran.

Where a name is given by Latin writers to the bread of the poor, it is called *panis secundus, secundarius,* or *cibarius*;[4] and from

[1] Cf. Plaut. *Capt.* 807; Varr. *R.R.* ii. 2. 19, 7. 12; iii. 14. 3; Phaedr. iv. 18. 4; Col. vii. 3. 19; Plin. *N.H.* xi. 78; Apul. *Met.* vii. 15; &c.—and a medieval rhyme (*Gloss. cod. Vat.* 5141): 'fur simplex latro, fur duplex fit cibus apro', '*fur* once for "robber" stood; *fur* twice for swinish food'.

[2] Cf. Cels. ii. 33. 2; iv. 16. 4; Plin. *N.H.* xxviii. 188; Diosc. *M.M.* ii. 85. 2 W.; Hipp. *Acut.* 21; &c.

[3] Yet the word would fit well into their verse. *Panis furfureus* does occur in Gell. *N.A.* xi. 7. 3, but almost certainly as the 'bread rich in bran' to be discussed in a moment: Gellius is commenting on the use of obsolete words by a man who uses the old *apluda* for *furfur*. His point could not be made if *secundus* or *cibarius* were used instead of *furfureus*.

[4] See, e.g., Hor. *Ep.* ii. 1. 123; Suet. *Aug.* 76; Varr. *ap.* Non. 88. 14; Fronto *ad Anton.* i. 3, p. 101 Naber; Isid. *Orig.* xx. 2. 15. It is also (e.g. Sen. *Ep.* 119. 3) called *panis plebeius*.

these names it is reasonable to infer that this bread was made
from the product which in all Pliny's lists appears between the
flour and the bran. This product, variously called *secundarium* or
cibarium,[1] must have been intermediate in quality between flour
and bran; and the question arises whether it was produced by
merely sifting the meal that resulted from a single grinding
operation through several sieves of different grades, or whether
more than one grinding was needed before *secundarium* could be
separated from *furfures*. When this problem was touched on
earlier[2] it had to be left open; but it was shown that the Lewes
experiments suggested that a second grinding was at least highly
desirable: had the grain been fed through the mill but once, a
large amount of endosperm would have remained attached to the
bran, and sifting could not have separated the two. Similarly it
was shown earlier that, if the grain were ground more than once,
it would be desirable to sift the meal from the first grinding
through a coarse sieve[3] and to regrind only that part of it which
did not pass the sieve. The second grinding at Lewes reduced the
'overtails' to approximately one-quarter of the original grist, and
some of the bran was by then well freed from endosperm.[4] By
using an even coarser sieve the amount of the overtails could have
been reduced somewhat further.

The greater weight of the upper stone of a Pompeian mill would
probably have meant fewer overtails, both after the first and after
the second grinding, than were produced by the Lewes quern;
but the difference could hardly have been sufficient to make a
second grinding entirely unnecessary. We shall see that Pliny's
figures suggest that the percentage of the grain which emerged
as bran from Roman milling was much smaller than the percentage of overtails with which we were left at Lewes after the second
grinding. To reduce these overtails to the amount that Pliny's
figures make probable, a third, and perhaps even a fourth grinding

---

[1] In (4) the two are separate products; but in view of the other passages—
especially (1)—it may well be that *cibarii* here was originally an alternative to
secundarii, and that there is some textual corruption in this part also of a sentence
whose earlier part is corrupt almost beyond recognition. Elsewhere the two terms
are interchangeable, and even in (1) Pliny may only be pointing out that they are
synonymous.   [2] See above, p. 157.

[3] At Lewes a no. 24 grit gauze (aperture 0·86 mm. = 0·034 in.) was used.

[4] Some allowance must be made throughout for our lack of experience and for
the defects in the reconstruction and mounting of the quern, on which cf. above,
pp. 85–86 and p. 117, n. 3.

would have been required on the quern; and it seems likely that two grindings on a Pompeian mill would have had a similar effect.

The literary evidence for more than one grinding is very scant, and Jasny, in his discussion of the present problem, felt compelled by the silence of our authorities[1] to assume that grain was not ground more than once in ancient Rome, since 'repeated grinding is too important not to have been mentioned by many if it were practised'. Yet there is a little more to go on than Jasny, who only cites one of the pseudo-Aristotelian *Problems*,[2] implies: we have seen already that the passage in Seneca's *Epistles* in which the action of the mill is compared to that of the teeth[3] suggests strongly that repeated grinding was usual, and the Lewes experiments have shown clearly that it must have been practised at least with querns. After one grinding on a quern the whole of the meal might have been used, but this would have been very coarse indeed; or else a comparatively fine meal could have been sifted out: but if so, the overtails would have contained far too much of the grain to be rejected in their entirety, and sifting could not after one grinding have separated the usable from the unusable part.

Grinding on a rotary quern is the only operation connected with flour production of which, in the pseudo-Virgilian *Moretum*, a literary description has survived from antiquity.[4] Now in this we are clearly told that the sieve was employed 'when the task of turning had reached its appointed end',[5] *and* that it was employed to separate, not the coarse part of the meal from the fine, but the refuse from the flour: the Lewes experiments have shown that on a quern this could not have been done after a single grinding, and we must infer, therefore, that the grain in question was ground more than once, although the text does not explicitly

---

[1] And by the silence of the Talmudic sources; *Wheat Prices*, p. 151.

[2] xxi. 7; cf. ibid. 3 (date uncertain). The problem is to find the reason for the fact (?) that of wheat flour (ἄλευρα) it is 'the first part' that is whitest, while of barley meal (ἄλφιτα) it is 'the last part': Jasny's belief, that this refers to repeated grinding, is probably correct; but if so, repeated grinding can hardly have been unusual, or it could not have been referred to in this indirect way.

[3] Cf. above, p. 157.

[4] Jasny (p. 151, n. 20) takes the *Moretum* to refer to barley meal; but the text nowhere says so, and it is intrinsically unlikely for Italy about the time of Christ.

[5] 39 ff.: 'postquam implevit opus iustum versatile finem,
transfert inde manu fusas (*or* tusas) in cribra farinas
et quatit, ac remanent summo purgamina dorso.
subsidit sincera foraminibusque liquatur
emundata Ceres.'

say so. The very fact, moreover, that in the one case where the
preparation of flour is fully described there is no mention of repeated grinding, though we can be certain on other grounds that
it was practised, must make us reluctant to accept Jasny's argument from silence: in spite of what Jasny says, it is not easy to see
where else in ancient literature repeated grinding, if practised,
ought to have been mentioned.

We must now return to the Lewes experiments. The first
grinding had produced meal to the extent of about half the
weight of the grist, while the other half consisted of unground and
partly ground grains with a little clean bran. These two halves
were separated by means of a coarse sieve, and a finer sieve[1] was
then used to divide what passed the coarse sieve into flour and
'middlings'. It seems likely that a flour produced in this way is
denoted by Pliny's *pollen tritici* and *flos siliginis* in (1) and (3):[2]
the amount of this flour could be increased by regrinding the
middlings and sifting again after each grinding, a process which
may, as we shall see later, be alluded to in (4).

A little earlier we saw that two main types of sieve, the
farinarium or *excussorium* and the *pollinarium*, were in use in the
Roman world. If only one grade of each of these was used—and
there is little reason to think otherwise[3]—it would not have been
possible to produce the four products mentioned in (1) and (3a)
by sifting after one grinding; but this would have been possible
after two grindings. The *farinarium*, used after the first grinding
(which would, of course, yield more meal with the Pompeian mill
than with the quern) could have produced the main flour, *similago*
or *siligo*; and the *pollinarium*, whose name would thus be exactly
right, could then have been used to draw off the finest grade—
pollen or *flos*—from this main flour. During the second grinding
a meal would be produced containing an admixture of powdered
bran much higher than the first meal; and sifting through the
farinarium could have divided this into *secundarium* (*cibarium*)

[1] Without previous experience to go on, we used a no. 7 silk sieve of aperture
0·21 mm. = 0·0083 in.
[2] Though probably not by *pollen* in (2); cf. above, p. 176.
[3] The only evidence for more than two sieves is Plin. *N.H.* xviii. 115, on which
see above, p. 166 and n. 4; but even the finest of the three sieves there mentioned
must have been coarser than the *pollinarium*. (In this passage, incidentally, *alica
secundaria* is distinguished from *alica cribraria*: perhaps there was some confusion
between *cribrarius* and *cibarius*, but if so, it is impossible now to discover what
it was.)

and *furfures*. The Lewes experiments have shown that this procedure would have been practicable, and since two grindings
must in all probability be assumed in any case, it seems likely,
though it cannot be certain, that this procedure was in fact employed in the four-grade milling alluded to by Pliny. Although
the name *secundarium* can be explained simply as 'second-rate', it
would be particularly appropriate if it described the inferior
flour produced by a second grinding; and when Persius, a contemporary of Pliny, describes such a flour as 'thrown off the
sieve',[1] his words give an easy and attractive sense if this flour
consisted of the overtails that came from the top of the sieve after
the first grinding. The only other way to produce four products
would have been to mix together the meal produced by the two
grindings (or to use the meal resulting from a regrinding of the
entire stock) and to sift this through three sieves of differing mesh
aperture: for the reasons given earlier this would have been both
uneconomical and undesirable.

It remains to ask how fine the sieves used are likely to have
been, and what was the quality of the various products. The finer
of the two sieves used at Lewes had a mesh aperture of 0·21 mm.
or 0·0083 in., and through this a flour of 24 per cent. extraction
was produced after two grindings, which we have assumed to be
the equivalent of one grinding on the Pompeian mill. It will be
shown presently that the quantity of this flour corresponds fairly
closely with the quantities probably implied in the figures given
by Pliny for *flos* and *pollen* in (1) and (3*a*); and it is probable,
therefore, if these figures can be trusted, that the sieve employed
for the production of these grades was of a similar mesh aperture
to that used at Lewes, though it was almost certainly of a less
regular weave than its modern counterpart.[2] The flour, too, must,
subject to the quality of the wheat, have been similar to that
produced at Lewes.[3] This flour, in spite of its low extraction rate,
was darker and higher in fibre content (though only by a small
margin) than a modern roller-milled flour of an extraction as

---

[1] 3. 112: 'populi cribro decussa farina.' (*Populi farina* probably = *farina plebeia*,
i.e. *secundarium*; cf. above, p. 177, n. 4.)

[2] The ancient sieve, moreover, was made of linen or wool, instead of silk; cf.
above, pp. 166 ff.

[3] The flour obtained at Lewes was analysed by Dr. C. R. Jones of the Research
Association of British Flour Millers, whose results are here being quoted. For
details see *Milling*, 24 June 1950.

high as 85 per cent. Its mineral content was considerably higher than that of the modern 85 per cent. flour, but this was due not, as is often believed, to contamination with stone dust,[1] but to pulverization of the detached inner (aleurone) layer of the bran, which contains much mineral matter. It was found, moreover, that the popular belief that stone-milled flour is richer in vitamins (esp. vitamin B1) than roller-milled flour is true only of hard wheat: with soft wheat the action of the stones leaves much of the 'scutellum',[2] which is the most prolific source of vitamin B1 in the wheat grain, in the form of coarser particles among the bran and middlings.

To this 24 per cent. flour was added in the experiments—again after two grindings—that part of the middlings which passed through a rather coarser sieve[3] of 0·53 mm. [= 0·021 in.] mesh aperture. This sieve was chosen because it was found that it gave the best division between the branny fractions and those relatively rich in endosperm; and the result was a meal of 71 per cent. extraction from the harder and of 54 per cent. extraction from the softer of the two wheats used.[4] This meal, which, if our explanation of Pliny's terms is right, corresponds closely to *siligo* (*similago*) flour from which no *flos* (*pollen*) has been extracted, contained considerably more fibre than the original flour; but although it was thus more branny and specky, it was otherwise remarkably similar to the latter: the mineral content remained almost constant; the content of vitamin B1 was a little higher; and the maltose content (indicating the extent of mechanically damaged starch particles) was somewhat lower. With the softer wheat the speckiness was approximately that of an 85 per cent. roller-milled flour from which 50 per cent. of white flour has been extracted by sifting; but the meal from the harder wheat was considerably more specky and darker in background colour.[5]

The middlings which were added to the original flour in order to produce this meal were not themselves analysed; but since the chemical analyses for flour and meal were similar, that of the middlings could not have been very different. (Such differences

---

[1] The amount of this (0·06 per cent.) was negligible.
[2] i.e. that part of the germ which in the young plant absorbs the nourishment provided by the endosperm. [3] No. 36 grit gauze.
[4] The difference between the two amounts was largely due to the fact that it proved impossible to regrind the middlings (between no. 7 silk and no. 24 grit gauze) of the softer wheat, because the stone surfaces quickly became clogged.
[5] There was a similar difference also between the two flours.

as did appear would, of course, be larger between the flour and the middlings than between the flour and the meal: this applies especially to the amount of speckiness, which was much higher for the middlings than for the meal.[1]) These middlings would, on the theory here advanced, have corresponded to *siligo* and *similago* from which *flos* or *pollen* had been extracted, as in (1) and (3a).

Throughout this discussion it has been assumed that the effect of two grindings on the quern was substantially identical with that of one grinding on the heavier Pompeian mill. On the same assumption, the overtails obtained at Lewes after two grindings would correspond to the material which was reground to yield *cibarium* (*secundarium*) and *furfures*.[2] The amount of these overtails varied considerably between the harder (*c*. 29 per cent., less waste) and the softer (*c*. 46 per cent., less waste) of the two wheats used, and this difference may well be analogous to the distinction made by Pliny between moistened and unmoistened *siligo*. They consisted partly of coarse middlings, partly (especially with the harder wheat) of well-cleaned bran coats, and partly (especially with the softer wheat) of bran which remained heavily coated with endosperm. Further grinding would have pulverized more of the endosperm and reduced the middlings in size. Its main purpose would have been to 'clean' the rest of the bran, and it would have achieved this to some extent, particularly with the harder wheat; but much of the bran would inevitably have been pulverized in the process.

The total bran content of the grain amounts to about 15 per cent.: some of this was, as we have seen, contained in the meal and in the flour—and some of the endosperm would remain with the bran even after all profitable grinding has been done. If, therefore, the amount of bran which finally emerged from Roman milling was as small as Pliny's figures will be shown to suggest, the *secundarium*—i.e. the meal obtained in the second grinding on a Pompeian mill—must have been very rich in bran; but it would still have contained enough endosperm to make it wasteful to discard it altogether so far as human food is concerned. In the kind of society that existed at Rome there was an obvious use for a meal of this type, and this is exactly the use to which our evidence suggests it was put.

[1] The particle size of the middlings is, of course, determined by the sieves between which they lie.   [2] See *Note R*, p. 221.

VII

PLINY'S EXTRACTION RATES[1]

WE have now reached the point at which some attempt must be made to interpret the figures given by Pliny in terms of extraction rate, and to infer what percentage of the wheat weight is represented by the various products in his lists. In spite of all the difficulties which this must involve, it is the only method by which we can hope to assess the quality of the various ground products mentioned by Pliny, and to discover to what extent they correspond to the products obtained at Lewes. The discussion of this and the next chapter is of necessity intricate, and since its results are summed up in Chapter IX, these two chapters may be omitted without loss of continuity.

Let us start with lists (1) and (3a), since these two lists appear to be the most straightforward and therefore the most promising: the information contained in these two lists is tabulated in Table III, from which it will be noticed immediately that the volume of

TABLE III

The Information contained in Pliny's Lists (1) and (3a)

		sextarii		sextarii
Raw material:	siligo	16	triticum	16
Yield:	siligo	4–6	similago	8
	flos	8	pollen	5
	cibarium	4	secundarium	4
	furfures	4	furfures	4
Total yield from 1 modius:	siligo	20–22	triticum	21

the yield considerably exceeds that of the raw material. However surprising this may seem, it is easily explained, since a given volume of ground products always weighs less than the same volume of raw grain: to convert Pliny's volume figures into weights will be our main problem.

[1] See *Note S*, p. 221.

The products, final and intermediate, of modern milling vary considerably in their weight for a given volume, and the variation between them unfortunately depends not only upon the difference in specific weight between bran and endosperm, but also upon the particle size of the product, since even the tightest packing possible is less tight than that by which nature packs the endosperm in the grain. Both fine grinding and high bran content make a product light in weight,[1] with the result that after the unground grain the heaviest stocks are those intermediate between bran and fine flour. The modern weight ranges for wheat and various ground products are set out in Table IV.[2] Now the weights of the

TABLE IV

Weight Ranges of Modern Mill Stocks

	lb./cu. ft.
Wheat	47–50
Flour	30–35
Semolina	35–40
Bran: fine	12–15
coarse	9–14

products obtained at Lewes turned out to be remarkably close to those of similar products from a modern roller-mill: if anything, the Lewes weights were a little lower than those given in Table IV, only the bran being somewhat heavier (*c.* 20 lb./cu. ft.), since it contained more endosperm than its modern counterpart. This discovery, that the weight of ancient ground products is likely to have been similar to that of the modern (subject, of course, to the weight of the wheat), is of paramount importance for the conversion of Pliny's figures, since it provides a basis other than mere guesswork for this conversion. All these weights are, incidentally, applicable to 'natural packing', and if products are packed at all tightly, a greater weight is needed to fill the same volume. But since we know—from, for instance, (3*b*)—that in Rome ground products were sold by volume, it is highly improbable that this

[1] Except that coarse bran tends to be lighter than fine bran.
[2] Based on J. F. Lockwood, *Flour Milling*[2] (Liverpool, 1948). Jasny (p. 154) gives the impression that the weight is greatest for the finest flour and smallest for bran, but this can be disproved by the simple experiment of comparing the weights of a cupful of flour and a cupful of semolina.

need be taken into account: a Roman flour-seller would hardly have 'tamped down' his flour if this meant giving the customer more than his due.[1]

Pliny himself does not mention any weights for ground products, but he does provide us with some weights for unground wheat:

(5) *N.H.* xviii. 66: 'Nunc ex his generibus (*sc.* frumenti), quae Romam invehuntur, levissimum est Gallicum atque Chersonneso advectum, quippe non excedunt modii vicenas libras, si quis granum ipsum ponderet. Sardum adicit selibram, Alexandrinum et trientem—hoc et Siculi pondus—, Baeticum totam libram addit, Africum et dodrantem.'

Nowadays the lightest of those kinds (of wheat) which are imported into Rome is that which comes from Gaul and the Chersonnese, since these do not exceed twenty pounds to the *modius*, if the grain alone be weighed. That from Sardinia adds half a pound, that from Alexandria a further third—this being also the weight of the Sicilian; that from Baetica [in Spain] adds a whole pound, and the African a further three-quarters.[2]

The information contained in this passage, together with its English equivalents, is set out in Table V, from the last column of which it will be seen that a range of 46¾–51 lb./cu. ft. covers

TABLE V
Pliny's Wheat Weights

Origin of wheat	Roman pounds per modius	lb./modius	lb./cu. ft.
Gaul Chersonnese	20	14·44	46·82
Sardinia	20½	14·80	47·99
Alexandria Sicily	20⅚	15·04	48·77
Baetica	21	15·16	49·16
Africa	21¾	15·70	50·92

[1] When flour is sold by weight, on the other hand, tight packing saves both packing material and space.
[2] It is not clear whether the pound 'added' by the Baetic wheat is added to the weight of the Gallic or to that of the Alexandrian. T. Frank (*Econ. Survey*, v. 144) adopts the latter interpretation, which would extend the upper limit of the range by five-sixths of a Roman pound to 52·87 lb./cu. ft.; but Pliny's language seems to argue against this view.

Pliny's figures. Since this compares with a modern range of 47–50 lb./cu. ft. (see Table IV), it can be said that Pliny's wheat weights are as much in agreement with modern experience as are the weights for ground products revealed by the Lewes experiments. For the calculations that follow a figure of 48 lb./cu. ft. has been selected from within the range because it is mathematically convenient: though probably a little too low, it is sufficiently accurate for the purposes for which it will be used.

Once the difference in weight between the various mill stocks is recognized, the difficulty with Pliny's figures is no longer that the volume of the ground products should exceed that of the raw grain, but rather that it should exceed it by so little. A given volume of flour nowadays weighs approximately two-thirds of the weight of the same volume of wheat, and fine bran as little as one-third: if, therefore, a given weight of wheat is milled into 75 per cent. of flour and 25 per cent. of (fine) bran, the volume of the ground products will exceed that of the grain by approximately seven-eighths,[1] and at 85 per cent. extraction the difference will still be little less than three-quarters.[2] If comparable products resulted from milling in antiquity, we should, therefore, expect a figure of between 28 and 30 *sextarii* for the total yield, instead of the 20–22 given by Pliny. *This discrepancy is the main difficulty with which any attempt to make sense of Pliny's figures must contend.*

Jasny[3] bases upon the information in (1) and (3a) a table of extraction rates in terms of weight which is here reproduced as Table VI. This table includes some allowance for the differences in weight per volume unit between the various stocks, and it is one of Jasny's greatest services to have drawn attention to the need for this—especially since it thus becomes clear that the amount of bran rejected from the flour was much smaller than would appear at first sight. The table, moreover, is attractive in its simplicity and precision.

The calculations themselves, and the premises upon which they are based, are not given by Jasny; but they can be inferred by 'working backwards': if, for instance, 8 *sextarii* of *similago*

---

[1] If 100 lb. of wheat fill 1 volume unit (v.u.), 75 lb. of flour at 66⅔ lb. to the same v.u. will fill 1⅛ v.u., and 25 lb. of bran at 33⅓ lb./v.u. will fill ¾ v.u.

[2] 1 v.u. of grain will yield 1·275 v.u. of flour plus 0·45 v.u. of bran, i.e. 1·725 v.u. of ground products.

[3] *Wheat Prices*, p. 154. (Jasny's figure for waste appears reasonable and is accepted throughout the present calculations.)

Table VI

Jasny's Extraction Rates

	From *triticum*			From Pisan* *siligo*	
Ground product	Sextarii per modius of wheat	Percentage in terms of the weight of the wheat	Ground product	Sextarii per modius of wheat	Percentage in terms of the weight of the wheat
pollen . .	5	27	flos . .	8	44
similago . .	8	44	siligo . .	5	27
secundarium or *cibarium* .	4	15	cibarium or . secundarium .	4	15
Bran . .	4	11	Bran . .	4	11
Waste . .	not given by Pliny	3	Waste . .	not given by Pliny	3
Total . .	21	100	Total . .	21	100

* Or 'common' *siligo* without *castratura*.

represent 44 per cent. of the wheat weight, 1 *modius* represents 88
per cent. of the wheat weight. On the assumption that wheat
weighs 48 lb./cu. ft., the weight of *similago* will then be 42·2
lb./cu. ft. The results of working backwards in this way are given
in Table VII, and this shows that Jasny's extraction rates involve
some assumptions regarding the weight of some of the ground

Table VII

Weights of Ground Products implied in Jasny's Calculations

	Triticum			Pisan siligo	
Product	Weight/ volume as percentage of weight/ volume of wheat	lb./ cu. ft. on basis of wheat @ 48 lb./ cu. ft.	Product	Weight/ volume as percentage of weight/ volume of wheat	lb./ cu. ft. on basis of wheat @ 48 lb./ cu. ft.
Wheat . .	100	48	Wheat .	100	48
pollen . .	86·4	41·5	flos . .	88	42·2
similago . .	88	42·2	siligo .	86·4	41·5
secundarium .	60	28·8	cibarium .	60	28·8
furfures . .	44	21·1	furfures .	44	21·1

products which are made very doubtful by modern experience and by the results of the Lewes tests: it is unlikely that Jasny is justified in assuming for *flos* (*pollen*) and *siligo* (*similago*) the high volume weights which underlie his calculations, and by means of which he overcomes the embarrassingly low volume totals of Pliny's lists.

Numerals, as was pointed out earlier, are always peculiarly liable to corruption in the textual tradition of an ancient author, and the discrepancy between Pliny's totals and those suggested by modern experience may after all be due to some such corruption. Hence we must ask (as Jasny failed to do) whether all the figures given by Pliny can be accepted as trustworthy, and if not, whether it is possible to decide which of them are trustworthy and which are not. To ask this question is, of course, greatly to complicate the inquiry: not to ask it, and to rest content with figures that are suspect, may provide a specious answer but not one that is satisfactory.

The numerals in the lists used by Jasny—(1) and (3*a*)—are even more liable to corruption than numerals usually are: in both these lists a measure, the *modius*, is said to yield a number of its own fractions in ground products, and the temptation must have been great for a copyist (or, for that matter, for Pliny himself when he copied his source) to try to make the sum of the fractions equal to the original measure. The figures for *flos*, *cibarium*, and *furfures* in (1), and those for *similago*, *secundarium*, and *furfures* in (3*a*) each add up to 1 *modius*, and in (3*a*) the 'reconciliation' would be complete if the copyist (or Pliny) assumed that the 5 *sextarii* of *pollen* came out of the *similago* by further sifting.[1] It may be said that this is mere speculation; but in view of the inadequate totals of both (1) and (3*a*) the possibility of this kind of textual corruption can certainly not be ruled out.

Lists (2) and (4), not used by Jasny, are not subject to the same danger. Here the yield of all products except bran is expressed in terms of the weight of the bread which could be made from them, and this would effectively prevent most copyists from engaging in mathematical calculations at the expense of the text they had before them. Unfortunately the text of (4) is almost hopelessly corrupt in other ways;[2] but it may well be worth while

[1] i.e. if *semodios* is taken to denote 5 *sextarii* of *pollen* plus 3 of 'overtail' *similago*.
[2] On it see above, p. 178, n. 1, and below, *Note W*, p. 222.

to ask whether a table of extraction rates can be based upon (2), where, it will be remembered, Pliny gives the yield of *siligo* wheat, ground into three grades of product, as 16 Roman pounds of bread, 3 pounds of *cibarius* bread, and ½ *modius* of bran.

A little earlier[1] we found reason to think that the flour from which the 16 pounds of bread in this list were made could be described as *flos*: but for *flos* Pliny—in (3*b*)—quotes a bread yield of 17 Roman pounds per *modius*,[2] so that 16 Roman pounds of bread would represent ¹⁶⁄₁₇ *modius*, or 15·06 *sextarii*, of flour. For the bread yield of *cibarium* Pliny provides no similar help; but modern experience (and, as will be shown later, Pliny's own evidence) suggests a range of between 130 and 140 lb. of bread from 100 lb. of meal. On the basis of this range 3 Roman pounds (982·5 grammes) of *cibarius* bread represent between 701·8 and 755·8 grammes of *cibarium* meal.[3]

The quantity of *cibarium* meal implied in (2) can thus be reconstructed in terms of weight, without any assumption about the weight needed to fill a given volume. For the other two products, however, and for the wheat itself a volume weight must be assumed in calculating the extraction rates represented by Pliny's list. For the wheat this weight may here, as throughout these calculations, be taken as 48 lb./cu. ft.; and for the main flour and for the bran a range of weights may be used within which comparable products from the softer of the two wheats used at Lewes were found to lie, since the behaviour of this wheat in the mill appears to have resembled that of *siligo* moistened before grinding.[4] In this way the extraction rates listed in Table VIII can be based on Pliny's list (2), which, it will be remembered, relates to *siligo* moistened with salt water before milling.[5]

It was mentioned earlier that, because of its higher endosperm

---

[1] Above, pp. 174 ff.

[2] The textual variant xvi (on which cf. above, p. 171, n. 2) is discussed separately, below, n. 5.

[3] Even if the range is trebled to 120–50 lb., the quantity of meal is still between 655 and 818·8 grammes: the corresponding extraction rate (last column of Table VIII) is then between 9·75 and 12·19 per cent., which would widen the range by less than 1 per cent. either way.

[4] Cf. above, p. 183 and below, p. 210.

[5] If the variant reading xvi in (3*b*) be accepted, the relevant line in Table VIII will read, '1 *modius* of main flour at 28–32 lb./cu. ft. represents an extraction of 58·33–66·67 per cent.'; and the totals will be increased to 92·61–103·85 per cent. This would, if anything, strengthen the argument.

TABLE VIII

Extraction Rates probably represented by Pliny's List (2)

Product	Quantity	Weight in lb./cu. ft. Range	Extraction rate as percentage of weight of wheat Range
Wheat . . .	1 *modius*	48	100
Main flour . .	$\frac{16}{17}$ *modius* =		
	15·06 *sextarii*	28–32	54·90–62·75
cibarium . .	701·8–755·8 grammes		10·45–11·26
Bran . . .	$\frac{1}{2}$ *modius*	20–22	20·83–22·92
Waste . . .	estimated		3·00– 3·00
	Total . .		89·18–99·93

Comparable figure for the meal obtained from the softer wheat at Lewes:

Meal through no. 36 grit gauze		*c.* 30	54

content, the bran obtained at Lewes weighed more than roller-milled bran; and consequently the bran weight assumed for Table VIII is higher than the modern figure in Table IV. (The endosperm content of the bran was particularly high with the softer wheat at Lewes—and Pliny explicitly says that it was high with the milling method described in (2).) The bran weight in Table VIII is very similar to that assumed by Jasny (Table VII); but it will be seen that the weight of the main flour, for which Jasny's figures were called in question, is in Table VIII very much lower: it will be shown later that this flour probably weighed 30 lb./cu. ft. or a little less.[1]

The list given in Table VIII at the top of its range completely accounts for a *modius* of wheat in terms of its ground products at reasonable weights, and even at the lower end of the range the discrepancy is little more than 10 per cent. In Table IX similar weights are applied to lists (1) and (3a), and it will be seen that the totals are far less satisfactory: the discrepancy is considerable even if the upper weight limits are put as high as they possibly can be, and the true weights were probably considerably less than the upper limits in the table. The same applies to the volume of the

[1] Cf. below, p. 204 and Table XVI.

TABLE IX

Extraction Rates based on Pliny's Lists (1) and (3a), with probable Volume Weights for the Ground Products

(i) *Triticum*

Quantity (sextarii)	Product	Weight in lb./cu. ft. Range	Extraction rate as percentage of wheat weight Range
16	Wheat	48	100
5	*pollen*	28–32	18·23–20·83
8	*similago*	30–40	31·25–41·67
4	*secundarium*	28–30	14·58–15·63
4	*furfures*	18–22	9·38–11·46
	Waste		3·00– 3·00
21	Total		76·44–92·59

(ii) *Siligo*

Quantity	Product	Weight	Extraction rate
16	Wheat	48	100
8	*flos*	28–32	29·17–33·33
5	*siligo* (Pisan)	30–40	19·53–26·04
4	*cibarium*	28–30	14·58–15·63
4	*furfures*	18–22	9·38–11·46
	Waste		3·00– 3·00
21	Total		75·66–89·46

With *siligo Clusina* the quantity would be slightly larger:

6	*siligo*	30–40	23·44–31·25
22	Total		79·57–94·67

With *siligo castrata* it would be even smaller:

4	*siligo*	30–40	15·63–20·83
20	Total		71·76–84·25

ground products, which is so embarrassingly low in (1) and (3a):
the volume of *cibarium* in (2) is likely to have been between 2·01[1]
and 3·46[2] *sextarii*, and the total volume of ground products,
therefore, between 25·07[3] and 27·46[4] *sextarii*—as against the 20–
22 of (1) and (3a).

The only way in which to make lists (1) and (3a) account for
anything like the whole of the wheat milled is to assume higher
volume weights than those in Table IX for some or all of the
ground products—in opposition to both modern experience and
the results obtained at Lewes. This is what Jasny did, and it is
even possible to see how he arrived at the improbable weights
that underlie his calculations: he appears to have taken probable
figures for bran, waste, and *secundarium* (*cibarium*)—which are
similar to those adopted here—and then to have allowed the
other figures to determine themselves mathematically (working
to the nearest whole number), thus:

$$48 \text{ lb.} - \left(\frac{4}{16} \times 29\right)\text{lb.} - \left(\frac{4}{16} \times 21\right)\text{lb.} - \left(\frac{3}{100} \times 48\right)\text{lb.} = 34 \text{ lb.};$$

wheat   secundarium   bran   waste

$$34 \text{ lb. fill } \frac{8+5}{16} = \frac{13}{16} \text{ volume unit;}$$

hence 1 volume unit is filled by 42 lb., and 42 lb./vol. unit is
the weight of the other products.[5] (The difference between the
weights for *pollen* and *siligo* on the one hand and *flos* and *similago*
on the other is apparently due merely to working to the nearest
whole number.) It is one of the main contentions of the present
argument that in the light of the Lewes experiments these weights
are far too high: since, moreover, Pliny himself gives us another
list which agrees well with modern experience, and since, as will
be shown in the next chapter, corroboration can be found elsewhere in Pliny for the evidence of this list, it seems likely that the
numerals in the lists used by Jasny are corrupt and contain mistakes made either by Pliny himself or during the handing-down

---

[1] At a weight of 40 lb./cu. ft. and a bread yield of 140 per cent.
[2] At 25 lb./cu. ft. and 130 per cent. (At 28 lb./cu. ft. and 140 per cent. 1 Roman
pound of bread represents just under 1 *sextarius* of meal.)
[3] i.e. 15·06+2·01+8.   [4] i.e. 16 (see p. 190, n. 5) +3·46+8.
[5] The 'volume unit' here is the cubic foot, but the calculation does not depend
on this. If it is assumed that bran weighs 44 per cent., and *secundarium* 60 per cent.
of the wheat weight for *any* given volume, the weight of the other products determines itself as 87·38 per cent. of the wheat weight.

of his text. Restoration of the correct figures is hardly possible now; but it does appear possible to say something about which of the figures in (1) and (3a) are likely to be affected.

The milling method of (2) is distinguished by Pliny from that of (1) as yielding a whiter flour but 'retaining more among the bran',[1] while the method of (1) is said to produce more meal. Hence the figure for bran in Table VIII must represent an upper limit, and the figure for 'main flour' a lower limit, so far as list (1) is concerned; and the figure for *furfures* in Table IX (ii) may well be right, while that for *cibarium* (which is close to the parallel figure in Table VIII) is at least possible. The figures for *flos* and *siligo*, on the other hand, are too low, and the error must be sought in either one or both of these. Since three different figures are given by Pliny for *siligo*-grade flour—and three different corrections must be made if this is the figure to be altered—there is some likelihood that of the two it is the figure for *flos* that is wrong: Table IX (ii) would suggest that *semodium* should be altered to *sextarios xii*, but this is mere conjecture, and the details of the correction must remain uncertain.

In the case of *triticum*—list (3a) and Table IX (i)—it is even less certain how the correction should be made; but here again the error probably lies among the figures for *similago* and *pollen*. Since *pollen* was not the main product which it was desired to produce, it is perhaps more probable that the error is in the figure for *similago* than that it is in the figure for *pollen* or distributed over both figures. Two manuscripts, moreover, have *sexmodios* for *similago*, instead of *semodios*, and this may (though it certainly need not) reflect an original figure expressed in *sextarii*.[2]

The result of these calculations must be that the extraction rates arrived at by Jasny (Table VI) are in themselves not improbable, though it is doubtful how much of the 71 per cent. comprised by the first two items in each list is to be ascribed to the first item and how much to the second. But even if Jasny's results may not be far from the truth, these results cannot be based on Pliny's text as it stands.

[1] That it is (2), rather than (1), which 'retains more among the bran' is shown by the relative quantities of bran—one-half as against one-quarter *modius*.

[2] On the other hand it may be argued that, since the *semodius* (both here and for *flos* in (1)) is the only quantity *not* denoted by a fallible numeral, the yield for *flos* and *similago* is more likely to be correct than that for *pollen* and *siligo*.

VIII

BREAD YIELD FROM WHEAT AND FLOUR

In addition to the statements discussed in the last chapter Pliny provides some further information relevant to this inquiry, most of which is contained in the following passage:

(6) *N.H.* xviii. 67: 'Lex certa naturae, ut in quocumque genere (*sc.* frumenti) pani militari tertia portio ad grani pondus accedat, sicut optumum frumentum esse, quod in subactum congium aquae capiat. quibusdam generibus per se pondus, sicut Baliarico: modio tritici panis p̄. xxxv (*v.l.* xxx) redit; quibusdam binis mixtis, ut Cyprio et Alexandrino xx prope libras non excedentibus. Cyprium fuscum est panemque nigrum facit, itaque miscetur Alexandrinum candidum, redeuntque xxv pondo. Thebaicum libram adicit.'

It is a sure law of nature that with all kinds (of wheat) army bread is heavier by one-third than the grain, just as (it is a law of nature that) the best wheat is that which for purposes of kneading absorbs one *congius* of water. Certain kinds have weight by themselves, like the Balearic, for which the bread yield from a *modius* of wheat is 35 (or 30) pounds. Certain kinds (have weight) when two are mixed, like the Cyprian and Alexandrian which do not exceed about 20 pounds. The Cyprian is red and makes the bread black: consequently the white Alexandrian is mixed with it, and the yield is then 25 pounds. The Theban adds a pound.

This passage must next be discussed, and the need for its discussion is the greater since we had to question the accuracy of the two lists which had looked the most promising and on which alone Jasny relies. For this discussion some data regarding the yield of bread from a given quantity of flour and wheat are relevant and must briefly be stated:[1]

(*a*) Bread yield from flour is determined largely by the water

---

[1] These data are based on E. R. Bennion, *A Primer on Breadmaking* (Oxford, 1951). Additional information (especially about the water absorption of meals of different rates of extraction) was supplied by Dr. P. Halton and Dr. C. R. Jones of the Research Association of British Flour-Millers.

absorption power of the flour, and can be calculated with reasonable accuracy by adding to the weight of the flour the weight of the water absorbed, and subtracting one-eighth from the total as an allowance for loss by evaporation during baking and cooling. (This allowance is approximate, and perhaps a little generous; but it is accurate enough for our purposes.) The weight of the other ingredients, salt and yeast, is normally offset by evaporation during the preparation of the dough.

(*b*) Water absorption in modern English experience normally varies between 14 and 17 gallons per sack of 280 lb.[1] It depends on the quality of the wheat, on the extraction of the flour, on the moisture content of the flour,[2] and on the kind of bread which it is desired to make. 'Strong' wheats absorb more water than 'weak' wheats, and wholemeal more than white flour; and for bread baked in tins the dough can be less stiff than for bread baked without tins.[3] If the allowance of one-eighth mentioned in (*a*) is taken into account, it will be seen that an absorption of 13·6 gallons per sack represents a bread yield of 130 lb. from 100 lb. of flour, and an absorption of 16·8 gallons a yield of 140 lb. This can be considered the normal modern range, for details of which see Table X.

(*c*) If 100 per cent. wholemeal is used, the bread yield from a sack of flour will also be the bread yield from 280 lb. of wheat; but if flour of a lower extraction is used, the bread yield from wheat will be correspondingly lower, since 400 lb. of wheat, for instance, will be needed to produce 280 lb. of a flour of 70 per cent. extraction. Figures for flours of various extractions, calculated on this basis, are given in Table XI; and the effective range for a given wheat is even greater than this table might suggest, for if wholemeal from it absorbs, for example, 16·8 gallons per sack, a 70 per cent. flour will absorb little more than 14 gallons.[4]

---

[1] This is a normal range: some white flours from very 'weak' wheats absorb only about 12 gallons per sack, and wholemeal from a very strong wheat may absorb over 18 gallons.

[2] The normal English range just given assumes a moisture content of *c.* 14½ per cent.: a decrease of 1 per cent. in moisture raises the water absorption by about ½ gallon/sack.

[3] For the former 15½–16 gallons per sack is now the rule, for the latter 15 gallons.

[4] See *Note T*, p. 222.

TABLE X

Water Absorption and corresponding Bread Yield

	Water absorption		Bread yield $= \frac{7}{8}$ (flour+water)	
Gallons per sack of 280 lb.	lb. per sack of 280 lb.	per cent. of flour weight	lb. per sack of flour	per cent. of flour weight
13·6	136	48·57	364·0	130·00
14	140	50·00	367·5	131·25
14·5	145	51·79	371·9	132·81
15	150	53·57	376·3	134·37
15·5	155	55·36	380·6	135·94
16	160	57·14	385·0	137·50
16·8	168	60·00	392·0	140·00

TABLE XI

Bread Yield from Flour as percentage of Original Wheat Weight

Water absorption in gallons per sack of flour	Bread yield in lb. per sack of flour	Bread yield as percentage of wheat weight if flour represents an extraction rate of						
from Table X		100%	95%	90%	85%	80%	75%	70%
13·6	364·0	130·0	123·5	117·0	110·5	104·0	97·5	91·0
14	367·5	131·3	124·7	118·1	111·6	105·0	98·4	91·9
14·5	371·9	132·8	126·2	119·6	112·9	106·3	99·6	93·0
15	376·3	134·4	127·7	121·0	114·2	107·5	100·8	94·1
15·5	380·6	135·9	129·1	122·3	115·5	108·7	101·9	95·1
16	385·0	137·5	130·6	123·8	116·9	110·0	103·1	96·2
16·8	392·0	140·0	133·0	126·0	119·0	112·0	105·0	98·0

We can now go on to discuss the passage quoted on p. 195, and it will be best to do so section by section:

(i) 'Lex certa naturae, ut in quocumque genere pani militari tertia portio ad grani pondus accedat.'
It is a sure law of nature that with all kinds (of wheat) army bread is heavier by one-third than the grain.

Table XI will show that a bread yield of 133⅓ per cent. of the *grain* weight is, if modern experience can be relied on, likely to be obtained only from wholemeal or from a meal of a least 95 per cent. extraction. And even if Pliny's 'one-third' is to be read as an approximation one-quarter would be more accurate for modern flours of 90 per cent. extraction or less. Taking into account that there must have been some waste (estimated at 3 per cent. in the last chapter) in ancient milling, we must infer that, on the basis of modern figures, *panis militaris* can only have been wholemeal bread: if it was wholemeal bread, Pliny's statement can be strictly accurate, and the yield range for wholemeal bread is narrow enough to make his use of the phrase 'a law of nature' understandable. But this is not yet proved: the statement shows only that if a meal other than wholemeal was used for *panis militaris*, the water absorption of this meal must have considerably exceeded that of modern meals,[1] and that in that case modern experience cannot be relied on; but we shall see that this would be difficult to reconcile with the statements that follow in Pliny's text.[2]

> (ii) 'sicut optumum frumentum esse, quod in subactum congium aquae capiat.'
> just as (it is a law of nature that) the best wheat is that which for purposes of kneading absorbs one *congius* of water.

One *congius* of water weighs 10 Roman pounds; and the absorption of this amount by 1 *modius* of a wheat weighing 20 Roman pounds per *modius*, ground into 100 per cent. wholemeal, would thus represent a water absorption of 50 per cent., or 14 gallons per sack: this is equal to the lowest quoted for normal modern flours,[3] and well below the lowest for modern wholemeal. But 20 Roman pounds per *modius* is the smallest of the wheat weights given by Pliny (see Table V), and for heavier wheats the percentage of water absorption will be even smaller. If, on the other hand, Pliny means that bran can be taken away from the wheat after grinding, and that the resulting flour still absorbs 1 *congius* of water, the water absorption power of this flour would be correspondingly higher, as is shown by Table XII. The corre-

---

[1] This is true even of the very strong wheat of which details are given in *Note T*, p. 222.

[2] See *Note U*, p. 222.

[3] White flour from some very weak wheats absorbs only *c.* 12 gallons/sack; but this does not affect the argument—and, in any case, wholemeal from the same wheats absorbs at least 14½ gallons.

sponding bread yields, calculated as before, are listed in Table XIII.

TABLE XII

Percentage Water Absorption represented by the Absorption of 1 congius by Meals of varying Extraction from Wheats of varying Weights

(*Weights in Roman pounds*)

Weight of wheat = wheat of 100% meal (as in Table V)	per cent. absorption if meal was of 100% extraction	90% meal		85% meal	
		Weight of meal from 1 modius of wheat	per cent. absorption	Weight of meal from 1 modius of wheat	per cent. absorption
20	50·00	18·00	55·56	17·00	58·82
20½	48·78	18·45	54·20	17·43	57·39
21	47·62	18·90	52·91	17·85	56·02
21¾	45·97	19·58	51·08	18·49	54·10

TABLE XIII

Bread Yields corresponding to Meals of varying Extraction from 1 modius of Wheats of varying Weights, assuming Water Absorption of 1 congius per modius of Wheat

(*a*) in Roman pounds; (*b*) as percentage of wheat weight; (*c*) as percentage of meal weight

	Weight of wheat (Roman pounds per modius)			
	20	20·5	21	21·75
100% meal (a) Roman pounds	26·25	26·69	27·13	27·78
(b) % of wheat	131·3	130·2	129·2	127·7
(c) % of meal	131·3	130·2	129·2	127·7
90% meal (a) Roman pounds	24·50	24·89	25·29	25·88
(b) % of wheat	122·5	121·4	120·4	119·0
(c) % of meal	136·1	134·9	133·8	132·2
85% meal (a) Roman pounds	23·63	24·00	24·37	24·93
(b) % of wheat	118·1	117·1	116·0	114·6
(c) % of meal	139·0	137·7	136·5	134·8

Now Pliny says that 1 *congius* is the quantity of water absorbed by the *best* wheat: if, therefore, he is here referring to wholemeal, the absorption power of ancient wheats in general must have been considerably lower than that of modern wheats; for less good wheats clearly absorbed less than 1 *congius*. The difference would be particularly marked in the case of the heavier wheats, since 1 *congius* represents a smaller proportion of a heavy than of a light wheat:[1] but weight is one of the two main characteristics by which the quality of a wheat was judged in antiquity,[2] and it is therefore unlikely that the 'best' wheat where water absorption is concerned was that judged worst by the criterion of weight (although there is not *in fact* any necessary connexion between wheat weight and water-absorption power). If, then, it was the heavier wheats that absorbed 1 *congius* of water—and if the figure relates to 100 per cent. meal—the absorption of Roman wheats must have been about 4 per cent. lower than the modern low limit: with 85 per cent. meal, on the other hand, it would be near the mean point of the modern range.

In interpreting (ii) we must, therefore, assume either that the absorption of ancient wheat was substantially *lower* than its modern counterpart, or else that the quantity of 1 *congius* relates to a meal from which some of the bran had been removed: but from (i) we had to infer that either Pliny was referring to wholemeal bread or the absorption of Roman wheat was considerably *higher* than modern experience suggests (for details see Table XIV). By comparing (i) with (ii) we can rule out one alternative

TABLE XIV

Water Absorbed by one modius *of Grain if Bread Yield exceeds Grain Weight by one-third, for Meals of varying Extraction Rates*

(*Expressed in Roman pounds and per cent. of grain weight*)

Weight of 1 modius of wheat in Roman pounds	100% meal Water absorbed in		95% meal Water absorbed in		90% meal Water absorbed in		85% meal Water absorbed in	
	Roman pds.	% of grain weight	Roman pds.	% of grain weight	Roman pds.	% of grain weight	Roman pds.	% of grain weight
20	10·48	52·38	11·48	57·38	12·48	62·38	13·48	67·38
20½	10·74	,,	11·76	,,	12·79	,,	13·81	,,
21	11·00	,,	12·05	,,	13·10	,,	14·15	,,
21¾	11·39	,,	12·48	,,	13·57	,,	14·66	,,

[1] Even if '1 *congius*' is to be read as a reasonable approximation, a wheat weighing 21¾ Roman pounds per *modius*—i.e. the 'best' wheat in (5)—would with an absorption of 16 gallons/sack absorb 12·43 Roman pounds, or nearly 1¼ *congius*, of water.
[2] Cf. Plin. *N.H.* xviii. 63 *init.*, on which see *CR*, N.S., v. 246.

in each case, and conclude that (i) relates to wholemeal, while (ii) must relate to a flour from which some of the bran had been extracted.

(iii) 'quibusdam generibus per se pondus, sicut Baliarico: modio tritici panis p̄. xxxv (*v.l.* xxx) redit.'
Certain kinds have weight[1] by themselves, like the Balearic, for which the bread yield from a *modius* of wheat is 35 (or 30) pounds.

The text of this sentence is corrupt at the vital point, and unfortunately (5) does not give a weight for Balearic wheat. But even if this wheat weighed as much as 22 Roman pounds per *modius*, a bread yield of 35 Roman pounds, or 159 per cent. of the wheat weight, is impossibly high (see Table XI and *Note T*, p. 222). The manuscript alternative of 30 pounds would represent a bread yield of 136·4 per cent. of a wheat weighing 22 Roman pounds per *modius*, which is possible, but only if wholemeal bread is meant.

The figure xxxv, then, must certainly be rejected, and if xxx is accepted we must assume that Pliny here meant wholemeal bread. We shall see, however, that this is difficult to reconcile with what follows, and it is possible on textual grounds that xxx is also a wrong reading and that the correct figure is xxv. A copyist may have failed to realize that the only difference between Balearic wheat and the wheats mentioned in the next three sentences was that the former required no blending for satisfactory results while the latter did: if he thought that the statement before him graded wheats according to the quantity of their bread yield, he may well have wished to increase the xxv he found, either by changing the v to an x or else by adding a third x. (The impossible xxxv, by preserving the original v, may show a trace of such a corruption.)[2] But this is hypothetical, and it is perhaps best not to base any inference on clause (iii).

(iv) 'quibusdam binis mixtis (*sc.* pondus est), ut Cyprio et Alexandrino xx prope libras non excedentibus.'
Certain kinds (have weight) when two are mixed, like the

---

[1] This phrase suggests that Pliny may have thought that his source was describing grain weight; but the context shows clearly that the figures refer to bread yield.
[2] The mistake may, of course, also have been made by Pliny himself in copying his source.

Cyprian and Alexandrian which do not exceed about 20 pounds (i.e., presumably, unless they are so mixed).

Alexandrian wheat is the only wheat in (6) for which a weight is given in (5), where it is said to weigh 20⅝ Roman pounds per *modius*. Here we are told that it produces approximately[1] 20 Roman pounds of bread, which is 96 per cent. of the wheat weight. Table XI shows that unless this represents the yield of a flour of little more than 70 per cent. extraction, both the bread yield and the water absorption implied by it are very much below modern experience: for long-extraction flour the discrepancy is considerable, and wholemeal (or anything approaching wholemeal) can be ruled out entirely.[2] But although Pliny's other figures make an extraction rate of 70–75 per cent. unlikely, it may be well to remember that Alexandrian wheat is here being singled out as exceptionally weak. The Cyprian wheat will be discussed in connexion with the next sentence.

(v) 'Cyprium fuscum est panemque nigrum facit, itaque miscetur Alexandrinum candidum, redeuntque xxv pondo. Thebaicum libram adicit.'
The Cyprian is red and makes the bread black: consequently the white Alexandrian is mixed with it, and the yield is then 25 pounds. The Theban adds a pound.

Both the Cyprian and the Alexandrian wheat were described as weak in (iv), but now we are told that the bread yield increases if these two wheats are mixed. Since this is clearly impossible, one of the two names must be wrong in one of the two places in which it occurs: this may be a copyist's mistake, but the run of the passage suggests that Pliny himself was under the illusion that a mixture of two weak wheats could produce a strong blend. Of the two names it is probably 'Cyprian' that is wrong, either in (v) or in (iv): normally white wheats are associated with desirable colour and red wheats with strength;[3] and the white Alexandrian

---

[1] *prope* may mean 'little more than'.
[2] For 100 per cent. meal the water absorption would be at the rate of 2·72 gallons per sack, or 9·71 per cent. Corresponding figures for lower extractions are: 90 per cent. extraction—6·13 gallons/sack, or 21·90 per cent.; 80 per cent. extraction—10·40 gallons/sack, or 37·14 per cent.; 70 per cent. extraction—15·89 gallons/sack, or 56·73 per cent. The discrepancy for wholemeal or long-extraction meal is made all the greater by the facts mentioned in *Note T*, p. 222.
[3] Cf. Bennion, op. cit., p. 12.

was presumably added to the strong red wheat (whatever the correct name of the latter) to produce a bread that was lower in yield than if the red wheat had been used by itself, but better in colour.

The relation of bread yields of 25 and 26 Roman pounds to some of the wheat weights given in (5) is shown in Table XV. If

TABLE XV

Percentage of Wheat Weight represented by Bread Yields of 25 and 26 Roman pounds per modius

Bread yield (Roman pounds per modius)	Weight of wheat (Roman pounds per modius)			
	20	20·5	21	21·75
25	125·0%	122·0%	119·0%	114·9%
26	130·0%	126·8%	123·8%	119·5%

this table is compared with Table XI, it will be seen that yields of 25–26 Roman pounds of bread from a *modius* of wheat are well within the modern range of bread yields from long-extraction flour: Table XI shows a variation from 110·5 per cent. of the wheat weight, for 85 per cent. flour with low water absorption, to 133·0 per cent., for 95 per cent. flour with high water absorption, while the variation in Table XV is from 114·9 per cent., for 25 Roman pounds of bread from heavy wheat, to 130·0 per cent., for 26 pounds of bread from light wheat. For a 100 per cent. meal the figures given in (v) would, by modern experience, be rather too low, and for short-extraction flour they would be too high.[1] Here again we must then assume either that the water absorption power of ancient wheat was considerably lower than that of modern wheat, or else that the bread yields given by Pliny relate to a long-extraction flour of between 85 and 95 per cent., rather than to a 100 per cent. meal. If these yields are compared, however, with that of 133⅓ per cent. given for 'army bread' in (i), which is a normal yield by modern standards for wholemeal bread from an average wheat with average absorption, the second of these possibilities is seen to be the more likely.

At this point it must be emphasized that, although frequent

---

[1] Similarly Table XIII, on the basis of an absorption of 1 *congius* of water by 1 *modius* of wheat, shows a range of bread yields of between 23·6 and 27·8 Roman pounds: this again suggests that 25–26 Roman pounds was a fair average yield.

reference was made in interpreting passage (6) to modern figures,
the conclusion, that the bread referred to in the later parts of the
passage—especially (ii) and (v)—was made from a meal of long,
but not 100 per cent., extraction, does not depend upon modern
figures. It is based essentially upon a comparison between the
yield of 'army bread' and other bread yields as given in Pliny's
text. The yield of 'army bread' is normal by modern standards if
wholemeal bread is meant, but otherwise it is too *high*: the other
absorption rates and bread yields are normal for a meal of long,
but not 100 per cent., extraction, but otherwise they are too *low*.
Since the bread yield cannot have been both too high and too low
by modern standards, the alternative—that ancient bread yields
were within the modern range—would seem to be established.

So much for passage (6); but the information gathered from it
will enable us to take a step farther the argument of the last
chapter, where, it will be remembered, the volume weights used
by Jasny for the better grades of flour were questioned, and some
extraction rates based on Pliny's list (2), which had not been used
by Jasny, were given in Table VIII. In this table a provisional
figure was given for the volume weight of the 'main flour' on the
basis of the Lewes experiments, but for the volume of this flour
Pliny himself had provided the evidence by his statement, in
(3b), that a *modius* of *flos* yields 17 Roman pounds of bread.[1] (This
statement differs from those in (6) in that it gives the bread yield,
not from a *modius* of wheat, but from a *modius* of flour.) We can
now take it that this bread yield falls within the modern range of
130–40 lb. of bread from 100 lb. of flour, and 17 Roman pounds
of bread must therefore represent between $12\frac{1}{7}$ and $13\frac{1}{13}$ Roman
pounds of flour: but since this quantity of flour fills 1 *modius*, the
weight of this flour must, whatever the weight of the wheat, lie
between 28·43 and 30·61 lb./cu. ft.[2] It can now be said, therefore,
that a weight range very similar to that accepted in the last chapter on modern evidence can be inferred, without modern evidence,
from the testimony of antiquity.[3]

[1] The variant xvi is here again relegated to the footnotes; but it will be seen that
here again it does no more than slightly enlarge the range.
[2] If xvi be read, the figures are $11\frac{3}{7}$–$12\frac{4}{13}$ Rom. pds. of flour at 26·75–28·81 lb./
cu. ft. (1 Rom. pd./*modius* = 2·341 lb./cu. ft.)
[3] On this basis the figures for 'main flour' in Table VIII will be 55·74–60·02
per cent., and the totals 90·02–97·20 per cent. (The variant xvi does not affect
these figures.)

In the same sentence in (3*b*) Pliny also states that a *modius* of *similago* yields 22 Roman pounds of bread: if the calculations that have just been applied to *flos* are used again, the volume weight of *similago*, too, can be determined on Pliny's evidence. The resulting range of 36·79–39·62 lb./cu. ft., which closely resembles the modern range for semolina (see Table IV), is again well below the figure used by Jasny, although the difference is less here than it was in the case of *flos*, where Jasny's error is in the region of 40–50 per cent. The relevant figures are set out in Table XVI,

TABLE XVI

Volume Weight of Flour as inferred from Bread Yield from a modius *of Flour*

(*Figures are given for the upper and lower limits—140 and 130 lb. of bread from 100 lb. of flour—of the normal modern range*)

Bread yield per modius of flour in Roman pounds	Volume weight of flour assuming bread yield from 100 lb. of flour of			
	140 lb.		130 lb.	
	Roman pounds per modius	lb./cu. ft.	Roman pounds per modius	lb./cu. ft.
16	11·43	26·75	12·31	28·81
17	12·14	28·43	13·08	30·61
20	14·29	33·44	15·38	36·01
22	15·71	36·79	16·92	39·62

which shows also that the volume weights thus inferred can be regarded as fairly reliable: in all cases the whole modern range of bread yield is covered by a variation in weight of less than 3 lb./cu. ft., and the assumption of weights substantially different from those here inferred would therefore make it necessary to assume bread yields differing far more widely from the modern range. On the basis of Jasny's figure of 42 lb./cu. ft. the yield of 17 Roman pounds of bread from 1 *modius* of *flos*, which is given by Pliny, would be the equivalent of 94·8 lb. of bread from 100 lb. of flour.[1] But if, as now appears certain, the weight of *flos* was between 28 and 31 lb./cu. ft. and that of *similago* between 36 and

[1] And if xvi be read, the bread yield would be equivalent to a mere 89·2 per cent. of the wheat weight. (Conversely, on the basis of 130–40 lb. of bread from 100 lb. of flour, the yield from a meal weighing 42 lb./cu. ft. would be between 23·32 and 25·12 Roman pounds of bread per *modius*.)

40 lb./cu. ft., the conclusion reached in the last chapter is confirmed: some of the figures in (1) and (3a) must be wrong, and Jasny's tables, though in themselves by no means improbable, cannot be based on those of Pliny's statements on which Jasny bases them.

To conclude this chapter we must now turn to yet another passage in Pliny's text which poses a slightly different problem:[1]

(7) *N.H.* xviii. 88: 'Siligineae farinae modius Gallicae xxii libras panis reddit, Italicae duabus tribusve amplius in artopticio pane. nam furnaceis binas adiciunt in quocumque genere.'
A *modius* of *farina* from Gallic *siligo* yields 22 (Roman) pounds of bread. From Italian *siligo* it yields two or three pounds more when *artopticius* bread is made from it, since the yield of the latter in all cases exceeds that of oven-baked bread by two pounds.

It will be noticed that the bread yield (and consequently the weight) here given for *siliginea farina* is the same as that for *similago* just discussed: the question that arises is what *siliginea farina* —and *artopticius* bread—was. *Farina* does not appear in statements (1) to (3);[2] and the reason for this is clearly that when *farina* was produced it was the only grade of meal produced, whereas Pliny's other statements relate to milling methods that yielded either two or three grades of meal and flour in addition to bran. At an earlier point[3] we found reason to doubt the common belief that this *farina* was 100 per cent. wholemeal, and we must now ask whether anything can be inferred from the present statement about its rate of extraction.

In (6) it is not clear which milling method was used to produce the various bread yields enumerated; but the fact that only one bread yield is given for each wheat suggests that it was the method that produced *farina*, rather than the three-grade grinding of (1) to (3). Now we have seen that the 'army bread', whose weight exceeded the weight of the grain by one-third, was almost certainly made from wholemeal; but that the 'normal' bread yield of 25–26 Roman pounds of bread from a *modius* of wheat

---

[1] The text here given is that of practically all manuscripts and editions. Mayhoff, however, adopts a variant xx, which is discussed below, *Note V*, p. 222.
[2] Except that a price is stated for it in (3*b*); but though this price shows that *farina* was less refined than *similago*, it does not show whether it was a 100 per cent. meal.
[3] Cf. above, pp. 164–5.

probably relates to a flour of long, but not 100 per cent., extraction. The yield of 'army bread' should, depending on the weight of the wheat (see Table V), have been between 26⅔ and 29 Roman pounds per *modius* of wheat; and if we assume that with the 'normal' bread yield, too, the weight of the bread exceeded the weight of the *meal* used in it by one-third, we can calculate the extraction represented by this meal; this is done in Table XVII. The figures in this table would, at the upper extreme of 97·5 per cent., agree with the assumption that all the wheat, except for a small amount of waste, was used in the bread; but this extreme relates to a wheat which, according to (5), was exceptionally light, and to a bread yield which appears to have been exceptionally high.[1] The general range in Table XVII suggests that an

TABLE XVII

Extraction Rates for farina *for Wheats of varying Weights if 1 modius of Grain yields 25 or 26 Roman pounds of Bread and Bread Yield exceeds Weight of Flour by one-third*

Bread yield per modius of grain in Roman pounds	Weight of one modius of grain in Roman pounds			
	20	20·5	21	21·75
25	93·75%	91·46%	89·29%	86·21%
26	97·50%	95·12%	92·86%	89·66%

amount of approximately 10 per cent. of the grain weight was rejected from the flour as bran in the milling processes that produced the *farina* for the 'normal' bread yield.

The same question may be approached in another way. If 1 *modius* of wheat yields 25 (26) Roman pounds of bread, and 1 *modius* of *farina* yields 22 Roman pounds of bread, 1 *modius* of wheat should, if *farina* was 100 per cent. wholemeal, have yielded 1·136 (1·182) *modii* of *farina*, and this *farina* should have weighed 42·24 (40·62) lb./cu. ft. if the wheat weighed 48 lb./cu. ft. But these weights are higher than those which we inferred from the fact that ancient bread yields apparently came within the modern range of 130–40 per cent. of the flour weight: on this basis *farina*

---

[1] 26 pounds is the yield for Theban wheat, which 'adds a pound'.

should have weighed between 36·79 and 39·62 lb./cu. ft. (see Table XVI), and if the bread yield exceeded the flour weight by one-third it should have weighed a little more than 38⅝ lb./cu. ft. If this was the weight of the flour, and if 1 *modius* of flour produced 22 Roman pounds of bread, 1 *modius* of wheat (at 48 lb./cu. ft.) would at 100 per cent. extraction have yielded 27⅓ Roman pounds of bread, which is considerably more than Pliny's figure of 25 (or at the most 26) Roman pounds. At 90 per cent. extraction, on the other hand, the bread yield would have been slightly under 25 (24·6) Roman pounds.

The indications in this case are slight, but such as they are they suggest that an amount of approximately 10 per cent. was rejected from the meal as bran when *farina* was prepared;[1] and even when more than one grade of flour was produced the amount ultimately rejected as *furfures* was probably similar: the figure here given, which agrees well with the conclusions arrived at earlier in this chapter, is very close to the figure for bran inferred by Jasny from (1) and (3a), which we were able to accept as substantially correct; and if more bran was sifted out in the milling method described in (2)—see Table VIII—this is only what Pliny's text leads us to expect. We saw earlier that even in the small-scale household milling described in the *Moretum* some bran was sifted out of the meal after grinding, presumably through the *cribrum farinarium*; and if this was normal even in a small household, Pliny's 'normal' bread yields must surely refer to a flour of this type. His figures then tell us that the extraction of this *farina* must have been about 90 per cent., and therefore very high indeed by modern standards: yet stone-milled flours of 90 per cent. extraction are still being produced.

We are left, finally, with *panis artopticius*, the weight of which from a *modius* of meal 'in all cases exceeds that of oven-baked bread by two pounds'. The tautologous[2] name of this bread is well established; and we know also that it was so called because it was cooked in a vessel known as *artopta*, which is mentioned by Plautus[3] and whose Greek name suggests that it had come into use before Plautus' day. But were it not for the present passage[4]—

[1] See *Note V*, p. 222.
[2] The word *artopticius* is clearly compounded from ἄρτος, 'bread', and ὀπτᾶν, 'to roast or bake'; cf. Blümner, p. 83 and notes.
[3] *Aulul.* 400 (cf. Plin. *N.H.* xviii. 107); see also Poll. x. 112.
[4] Cf. also section 105.

and for a very similar passage in Athenaeus[1]—we should know nothing of this bread; and from these passages we can infer only that it was not baked in any kind of oven.[2] The *artopta* was probably a kind of pan in which bread was occasionally baked, or rather roasted, on top of the fire: if so, it cannot have produced anything like bread in our sense, and there is little point in comparing the yield figures which Pliny gives for this 'bread' with other figures for bread yield. But it is not surprising that Pliny's figure for *artopticius* bread should be higher than his figures for oven-baked bread, since the dough for bread cooked in a pan can be much softer, and the water absorption correspondingly higher. A similar difference still exists between tin bread and bread baked without tins, and in the case of *panis artopticius* the difference is likely to have been considerably larger.[3]

[1] iii. 113a, quoting Chrysippus of Tyana.
[2] i.e. neither in a *furnus* nor in a *clibanus*: the *panis artopticius* is probably to be identified with the 'bread baked on top of the hearth' (ἐπὶ τῆς ἐσχάρας) of Gal. vi. 489 K.
[3] See *Note W*, p. 222.

P

IX

ROMAN FLOUR IN THE FIRST
CENTURY A.D.

IN the preceding two chapters we found that the information contained in Pliny's eighteenth book which is relevant to an assessment of the quality of the various grades of Roman flour is scattered over a number of separate statements. All these statements have to be taken into account, but those relating to *triticum* and unmoistened *siligo*—(1) and (3a)—at first sight looked the most promising, because they alone give the yield of a *modius* of wheat in terms of the volume of its ground products, and it might be expected that a simple conversion of these volume figures into weights would yield a table of extraction rates. Such a table was produced by Jasny, but his results (see Table VI) are difficult to reconcile both with modern experience and with the rest of Pliny's evidence, since the weights which Jasny found himself forced to assume for a given volume of the two better grades of product are too high. This suggests that some of the figures in (1) and (3a) are unreliable, either because Pliny misunderstood or wrongly copied his source, or because of some corruption in the later history of his text.

Textual corruption has also made valueless statement (4), but statement (2), which relates to *siligo* moistened before milling, agrees well, when analysed, with the results obtained during the Lewes experiments. The difference between moistened and un-moistened *siligo*, according to Pliny, was that the former yielded a whiter flour but retained more of the endosperm among the bran; and the difference between the two wheats used at Lewes was analogous to this. The flour from the soft wheat was much whiter; but the highest extraction of this flour that could be obtained was 17 per cent. lower than from the harder wheat. If *siligo* was distinguished from *triticum* by its softer and whiter grain, moistening (employed apparently in spite of the obvious disadvantage of a lower flour yield) must have increased the distinction and made the more desirable of the two wheats even more desirable. We saw earlier that this was probably the milling technique employed to obtain the best possible flour, and the experience gained at Lewes confirms this. List (2), when analysed (see Table VIII), suggests that by this technique a flour of about 60 per cent. extraction could be produced. 'Second-rate' bread appears to have accounted for rather more than 10 per cent. of the wheat weight, and bran for between 20 and 23 per cent. The volume weights involved in this analysis agree closely with those obtained at Lewes, but not with those assumed by Jasny; and it is impossible, therefore, to reconcile (2) with (1) and (3a).

That it is (2), rather than (1) and (3a), that is correct, can be demonstrated on the basis of some other statements in Pliny's text, which relate to the yield of bread from given quantities of wheat and flour, and which show that the bread yield in Roman times was similar to that obtained nowadays. Since Pliny expresses the bread yield in terms of weight, while he gives the quantity of wheat or flour in terms of volume, it is possible, once the 'normality' of the bread yield is established, to calculate the weight of flour needed to fill a given volume: the weights thus calculated do not agree with (1) or (3a), but they agree both with (2) and with the ground products obtained at Lewes.

The flour to which (2) relates was almost certainly the whitest flour obtainable in antiquity; but although its extraction rate was lower by 10 per cent. or so than that of a modern white flour of 70 per cent. extraction, it was probably speckier than even an 85 per cent. roller-milled flour.[1] The amount of bran produced by method (2) was, however, also smaller than when white flour is produced nowadays, and this was due to the fact that a considerable amount of bran was contained in an inferior meal, known as *cibarium* or *secundarium*. Since even this small amount of bran was considered by Pliny to be exceptionally high, the proportion of the wheat normally rejected as 'miller's offal' in ancient Rome must have been very much lower than is normal in modern times, and lower even in all probability than when an 85 per cent. flour is produced by the roller-mill. Jasny's figure of 11 per cent. for *triticum* and unmoistened *siligo* is probably near the mark, though the precise amount must remain uncertain: the bran from moistened *siligo* was probably between 21 and 23 per cent., and the difference between the bran yields of the two milling methods

[1] Cf. above, p. 182.

must have been considerable, or Pliny would not have commented on it.

When *siligo* was moistened before grinding, three products (*siligo, cibarium*, and bran) resulted, while *triticum* and unmoistened *siligo*, milled by methods (1) and (3a), yielded four products. *Farina*, which has no place in any of these lists, was probably a meal of 85–90 per cent. extraction,[1] resulting from a milling technique that produced only meal and bran. (Here, too, the amount of bran must have been in the region of 10 per cent.) But although the extraction rate of *farina* was roughly equal to that of a modern long-extraction flour, its quality must have been much worse. We saw earlier that, although such a meal would contain some fine flour, much of it would be coarse, and that it would be specky and have a high fibre content. But its vitamin content would also be high, at least in the case of hard wheat, though with soft wheat it might be lower than with a modern 85 per cent. flour. This *farina* was almost certainly the normal meal for non-commercial baking: how prominent it was in the commercial bakery it is impossible to assess, but here too it must have been used since Pliny gives prices and bread yields for it. Wholemeal, too, must have been used for bread at times, but the absence of a Latin name for it shows that it was probably rare, and there is no positive evidence for its use in commercial breadmaking: where it was used its quality must have been very similar to that of modern stone-milled wholemeal.

Both the milling method described in (2) and that described in (1) and (3a) yielded, in addition to flour and bran, the intermediate product that was known as *secundarium* or *cibarium*: we saw earlier that this was probably the meal of the second grinding after the removal of *furfures*. Although this *secundarium* probably contained at least as much endosperm as bran,[2] it undoubtedly contained enough bran to make it considerably darker than wholemeal; for even if its bran content was as low as one-third, this would still be twice the proportion contained in the grain and in wholemeal. The amount of *secundarium* normally produced is likely to have been in the region of 15–20 per cent. of the grain weight. With the milling method that produced only *farina* and bran this part of the grist formed part of the *farina*.

The extraction rates of *similago* and *siligo*, which were the main

---

[1] See pp. 206 ff.　　　　　　　　　[2] See *Note X*, p. 223.

products from the milling methods that also produced *secundarium* (*cibarium*), were of course lower than that of *farina*. These products are likely to have been similar in quality to the meals obtained at Lewes which were described earlier :[1] when produced from unmoistened grain they probably resembled the meal from the harder of the wheats used at Lewes, and *siligo* from moistened grain that from the softer. Flour of this grade was probably that most commonly produced in the commercial bakeries of the Roman Empire. The mere fact that *secundarius* bread was common among the poorer sections of the population points to a large-scale production of the meal required for this bread, and hence to the frequent employment of milling methods in which *secundarium* was one of the products. But these methods also produced approximately three times as much *similago* or *siligo* as *secundarium*.

In the grinding of *triticum* and unmoistened *siligo* it was possible to sift out of this main flour a quantity of fine flour, probably amounting to something like one-quarter of the original wheat weight, the characteristics of which must have been very similar to those of a modern long-extraction flour :[2] when such a flour was drawn off, the quality of the remaining *similago* (*siligo*) must have suffered accordingly.[3] In the case of *triticum* the fine flour drawn off in this way was, as we have seen, not considered a good bread flour : in the case of *siligo* it probably was considered desirable, but even here the best bread is commonly described as made from *siligo* rather than *flos siliginis*, and the Greeks did not even have a name for the latter.[4] The flour for this bread was in all probability normally produced by method (2), which involved preliminary moistening, since this enhanced the whiteness of the flour, which was the chief characteristic of *siligo* bread. This makes plausible a suggestion by Jasny[5] that the practice of drawing off a fine flour was by no means common; for there would be little

[1] Above, p. 182.
[2] Cf. above, p. 181.
[3] It was probably like that part of the Lewes meal which passed a no. 36 grit gauze sieve, but not a no. 7 silk; cf. above, p. 182. It may be mentioned incidentally that 'Chiro' (*Mulomed.* 674, 846, 912) speaks of *pollen* or *flos similaginis* (*similae*), rather than *pollen tritici*, &c.: he thus confirms that *pollen* (*flos*) was something that could be sifted out of flour of the *similago* (*siligo*) grade.
[4] *Siligo* as the name of the wheat may—in spite of Galen's statement to the contrary—often have coincided with σητάνιος; cf. above, p. 173, n. 6.
[5] p. 156: his argument to this end rests largely on the rare occurrence of the names for this grade of flour.

point in producing this grade for purposes of breadmaking either from *triticum* or from *siligo*.

Pliny's evidence, then, provides at least a general picture of the results usually achieved by flour-milling in the first century A.D.: a meal of 55–70 per cent. extraction, accompanied by a second-grade meal of about 20 per cent. extraction, was probably the most common product of the commercial mill, while the meal used in non-commercial breadmaking is likely to have been of a considerably higher, but not 100 per cent., extraction; and in either case the amount rejected as bran was extremely low by modern standards. It is obviously dangerous to apply these conclusions to other periods, or to parts of the Roman Empire far removed from the capital: but the use of sifted flour even in small-scale private milling suggests strongly that the normal meal produced and used for breadmaking in Roman times generally was of a grade similar—or at least not inferior—to that of the *farina* discussed a little earlier. Whether the more advanced methods of milling and sifting were at all widespread we cannot know; but the advanced grain-mills found in outlying parts of the Empire within a century of Pliny's death make it tempting to believe that advanced sifting methods, too, may have spread all over the Empire in the second and third centuries. In Pliny's day they may well have been a recent innovation even in the neighbourhood of Rome.

We have seen that the extraction rates of *similago* (*siligo*) and *farina* were probably very similar to those of modern white and long-extraction flours respectively, but that their quality is likely to have differed considerably from that of the modern products. This difference is due less to advances in sifting than to progress in milling itself: it reflects the greater success achieved by the modern roller-mill in keeping the bran intact while it is freed from endosperm. Some progress in this direction was probably made when stone-mills were improved—perhaps by 'setting' the stones, and almost certainly by more efficient grooving; but the real advance could not take place until the roller-mill with its cutting action came to replace the crushing action of the old millstones, and the white flour to which we are accustomed is essentially a modern product.

Whether or no this development should be considered progress has been a matter of some debate. Some valuable constituents are no doubt lost when a very white flour is produced, but the loss is probably less than has often been thought, and in modern practice it is largely made good by other means. Again, the process of refinement relieves the digestive system of some of the work that it would otherwise have to do, and this, too, is considered by some—both experts and laymen—to be not altogether desirable. But if it is right to say that civilization, where food is concerned, involves the development of technical processes to take over some of the work which the human body would otherwise have to do, the sifting of meal marks an advance, and the modern refinements further advances, along the road of civilization.

EPILOGUE

IN the England of the first Elizabeth the bread was, as a contemporary writer tells us,[1] 'made of such grain as the soil
yieldeth'. 'The gentility', he continues, 'commonly provide
themselves sufficiently of wheat for their own tables, whilst their
household and poor neighbours in some shires are forced to content themselves with rye or barley, yea, and in time of dearth,
many of bread made either of beans, peas, or oats, or of all
together and some acorns among.' The flour for this bread was
ground on rotary stone-mills, driven by wind or water, or on the
hand-quern; and it was sifted, if at all, through a single sieve
which could eliminate only the coarsest of the bran.

If we ask how this bread compared with that which was eaten
at the end of classical antiquity, the answer must be that all the
processes of manufacture had remained essentially unchanged,
and were to remain unchanged for another two centuries—and
this applies to the kneading, leavening, and baking of the dough
no less than to the preparation of the flour. The main difference
is that at the end of the classical period more wheaten bread was
eaten in the Mediterranean area than was eaten in Elizabethan
England, and this was due largely, if not entirely, to climatic
causes. In this respect the people who lived under the Roman
Empire had reached a higher standard of living, or a higher
degree of civilization in the sense in which the word was defined
at the beginning of this study; for they could eat the grain which
they preferred, rather than that which nature forced upon them.
In other respects Elizabethan England had added little or nothing
to the progress made during the classical period, though the
stage that had been reached under the Roman Empire had, on
the whole, been either maintained or reached again. It may be
that the kneading-machines and advanced sifting methods of
imperial Rome had been forgotten; but in general no more and
no less of the work of the human body was being done by artificial
means, and the technical processes by which this work was being
done still required the same amount of human effort. Between the

---

[1] Harrison, *Elizabethan England*, ed. Withington (Newcastle-on-Tyne, 1890),
p. 133.

beginning and the end of classical antiquity, on the other hand, immense progress had been made in both these spheres, as well as in making generally available the grain preferred by the ordinary consumer. And if the social differences of Elizabethan England had their parallel in imperial Rome, even the Roman poor had some form of wheaten bread.

On the day in A.D. 79 on which Pompeii was destroyed by a sudden eruption of Vesuvius, bread was, as on every other day, being baked in its bakeries, and some of the loaves that had been placed in its ovens remained there until the site was rediscovered and excavated during the last two centuries, when they were found completely carbonized but otherwise as the ancient baker had left them. Some of these loaves are shown in Plate 16, Fig. b:[1] they are much the most vivid of the extant remains of antiquity relevant to this study, which has been concerned with some of the processes involved in the preparation of bread. These loaves show us the final product in the most accomplished form reached in antiquity; and their long sojourn in the oven is symbolic of the fact that, after the techniques of milling and breadmaking had during the period of classical antiquity been brought from the very primitive to a high degree of perfection, little further progress was made until the time which coincided with the rediscovery of Pompeii and its loaves.

[1] Their round shape with indentations (for which cf. *Moret.* 47 ff.) is like that of the loaves shown on Pompeian wall paintings and elsewhere. They were known as ἄρτοι βλωμιαῖοι in Greek and *panes quadrati* in Latin.

NOTES

Note A, p. 1. Among books the most important is still the *History of Corn Milling* by R. Bennett and J. Elton (London & Liverpool, 1898), though a rather less detailed work (*Flour for Man's Bread* by J. Storck and W. D. Teague, Univ. of Minnesota, 1952) has in some respects superseded it. Among articles L. Lindet's epoch-making study ('Les Origines du moulin à grains', *Rev. Arch.* 1899, pt. 2, pp. 413 ff.; 1900, pt. 1, pp. 17 ff.) still deserves special mention, though much important work has been done since; cf., e.g., Jacobi, *Saalburg Jahrbuch*, iii. 75 ff.; Bloch, *Ann. d'hist. écon. et sociale*, vii. 538 ff.; Curwen, *Antiquity*, xi. 133 ff., xv. 15 ff.; and especially Childe, ibid. xvii. 19 ff. Among excavation reports special mention is due to Deonna, *Exploration archéologique de Délos*, xviii (Paris, 1938), 115 ff., and Robinson and Graham, *Excavations at Olynthus*, viii (Baltimore & London, 1938), 326 ff.

Note B, p. 6. This 'elimination' of Homer would lend special interest to any relevant passage in Hesiod's *Works and Days*, both because this is another very early Greek poem, and because its subjects are much closer to everyday life than those of Homer. Unfortunately, however, the *Works and Days* cannot help us: Lindet (1900, p. 17) quotes the word εὔτρόχαλος from l. 599, taking it to mean 'well-rounded' and to refer to a (lower) millstone; but the passage clearly refers to the threshing-floor, and the word probably means 'well-rolled'. Nor can either the use of μύλη in the meaning of 'lower millstone' (cf. above, p. 3, n. 4) or that of ὄνος for the upper millstone (below, pp. 10–12) be traced back to Hesiod, as Lindet implies.

Note C, p. 10. Apparently first by Xenophon (*An.* i. 5. 5). That the ὄνος was the upper, and not the lower, stone (or the mill as a whole, as might be inferred from Herod. 6. 83), is amply proved—in spite of a statement by Photius (*Bibl.* 533ᵇ8)—by Pollux (vii. 19, x. 112), Hesychius (s.vv. μύλη and ὄνος), Photius' own *Lexicon* (279. 22; 336. 20), &c.; cf. Blümner, p. 30, n. 1. Whether the Latin *asinus* was ever used in this sense is very doubtful, though *CIL*, i². 1665 (= Warmington, *Remains of Old Latin*, iv. 288–9, q.v.) must be added as a possible example to Catull. 97. 10, quoted by Blümner.

Note D, p. 26. Some incidental points may perhaps here be added: (*a*) Ἄλφιτα, the coarse ground product which in classical Greece was firmly associated with barley and the 'kneaded thing' made from it, may by the fifth century or so have been prepared in mortars; cf. below, p. 151, and *CQ*, xliii. 113 ff. (*b*) An inscription of the third century B.C. (*OGI* 729. 4) mentions an 'emmer-baker or -miller' (ὀλυροκόπος), thus suggesting that the reduction of ὄλυρα—again a husked grain—was a process distinct from ordinary milling. (*c*) *Far* as a ground product (cf. below, *Note O*) may have been a coarse meal produced in a mortar, coarser than the *farina* which resulted from milling proper.

Note E, p. 62. *Asinus molarius* (10. 1 and 11. 1: in 10. 1 the word *molarius* is a certain restoration from Varr. *R.R.* i. 19). That in the case of the vineyard this donkey had to serve three mills is probably explained by the presence of two wagon-donkeys (*asini plostrarii*) who could, for the greater part of the time, be used to drive two of the mills. The *molilia* which accompany the mills in Cato's lists are usually thought to have been the harnesses by which the donkeys were attached to their mills; but it seems more probable—etymologically, and because in chap. 11 Cato prescribes fewer *molilia* than donkey-mills—that they were 'mill-rests' or tables, used in connexion with Cato's *non-rotary* mills and similar, perhaps, to the tables shown on the Megarian bowl. [It may be that the τράπεζαι mentioned above (p. 45, n. 1) were also these tables, rather than the lower stones of the actual mills.]

NOTE F, p. 63. If the figures in the text are not corrupt, Cato allowed one grain-mill for about every four persons employed (3 mills for 13 in chap. 10; 4 for 16 in chap. 11); but this seems an inordinately high ratio, since, on the basis of the 'rations' given in Cato's chap. 56, one mill would have had to grind less than 10 lb. of grain daily. (Cf. below, p. 186 and Table V: an average monthly ration of 4 *modii* per person at, say, 20½ Roman pounds to the *modius* is the equivalent of *c.* 2¾ Roman, or 2 English, pounds per person per day.)

NOTE G, p. 65. Cf. also below, p. 111. It may be relevant here that Diocletian's *Edict on Maximum Prices* (xv. 52–53) distinguishes between a horse-mill at 1,500 and a donkey-mill at 1,250 *denarii*, one presumably being larger than the other. [The prices are probably 3·6 and 3 times the cost of an imperial bushel of wheat respectively. Cf. Jasny, *Wheat Prices*, 157 ff., but Segrè (*Byzantion*, xv. 278, pointed out to me by Professor A. H. M. Jones) makes it appear likely that Diocletian's *castrensis modius* was half of what Jasny took it to be.]

NOTE H, p. 66. *N.H.* xxxvi. 135 (see above, p. 60, and below, p. 74, and cf. also the *opus versatile* of [Virg.] *Moret.* 39). The passage is introduced haphazard in the middle of some chapters dealing with kinds of stone, and it is even uncertain whether the word *inventas* is intended to mean 'invented' or 'found'. Pliny's obvious ignorance of his subject-matter may, however, be the best guarantee that he correctly copied his source, and it is the latter that concerns us here.

NOTE I, p. 70. For the 'Greek tone' cf. also the occurrence of *polenta* in this play (ll. 33 and 37) almost alone among Plautus' extant works. [It occurs again only in *frag.* 2 (Lindsay), and in *Curc.* 295 the noise produced by *polenta* (*crepitus polentarius*) is one of the offensive attributes of Greeks.] *Polenta* (cf. below, p. 149) was made from barley and was almost certainly despised by the Romans. (But this argument cannot be pressed, since in the *Asinaria*, too, *polenta* is treated with scant respect.)

NOTE J, p. 72. This raises the question what the recipients of cheap or free corn in the capital from the time of C. Gracchus onwards (123 B.C.; cf. *PW*, vii. 172 ff.) did with the corn they received, before the Emperor Aurelian (A.D. 270–5) replaced the monthly grain issues with daily issues of bread (cf. *PW*, v. 1397; Script. Hist. Aug. *Aurel.* 35. 1, and Magie, ad loc.). No answer has yet been found, but Aurelian's action (apart, perhaps, from an increase in quantity) may have meant only that the beneficiaries were to be saved the trouble of having to arrange for their corn to be baked into bread, and not that they had hitherto milled and baked it themselves. (If they had done so, one would have to ask further whether they ate only wholemeal bread, and, if not, what they did with the bran.)

NOTE K, p. 100. 'Ye gods, what a pack of runts the poor creatures were who looked after us! Their skins were seamed all over with the marks of old floggings. . . . They had letters branded on their foreheads, and half-shaved heads and irons on their legs. Their complexions were frightfully yellow, their eyelids caked with the smoke of the baking ovens, their eyes so bleary and inflamed that they could hardly see out of them, and they were powdered like athletes in the arena, but with dirty flour, not dust. As for my fellow animals, what a string of worn-out old mules and geldings, and how they drooped their heads over their piles of straw! . . . their hooves had lengthened into something like slippers from the everlasting march round and round the mill.' (*Met.* ix. 12–13, trans. R. Graves, Penguin Books, 1950.)

NOTE L, p. 101. Women certainly could not have worked a Pompeian mill: in the Gospels (Matt. xxiv. 41, Luke xvii. 35: 'two women shall be grinding together: the one shall be taken and the other left') the reference is either to a rotary quern or to a saddle-stone (cf. below, pp. 113–15), and it may be to a rotary quern worked by two women simultaneously: for a modern parallel see *BE*, i. 168. In *Anth. Pal.* ix. 418 (cf. above, p. 97) the mill-girls obviously offer a better contrast to the water-nymphs than a donkey would, and the epigram shows only that women still ground grain—presumably on a quern.

NOTE M, p. 114. The one hellenistic example which Macalister (loc. cit.) supposes to have been used for corn agrees with this hypothesis: its upper stone is not completely perforated, and it may well be parallel to the unsuccessful British 'Hunsbury' type. The medieval pot-quern (Curwen, 1937, p. 150), which resembles the Palestinian 'paint-grinder' in respect of the raised rim round the lower stone, still had a spindle and a rynd, and in any case lies outside the line of development of the quern in antiquity.

NOTE N, p. 122. x. 5. 2: 'eadem ratione etiam versantur hydraletae, in quibus eadem sunt omnia, praeterquam quod in uno capite axis tympanum dentatum est inclusum. id autem ad perpendiculum conlocatum in cultrum versatur cum rota pariter. secundum id tympanum maius item dentatum planum est conlocatum quo continetur. ita dentes tympani eius, quod est in axe inclusum, inpellendo dentes tympani plani cogunt fieri molarum circinationem. in qua machina inpendens infundibulum subministrat molis frumentum et eadem versatione subigitur farina.' The text and translation are based on Granger's Loeb edition, with a few divergences which are discussed in *CR*, N.S., vi. 193 ff. For discussions of the passage see Blümner, p. 48, notes 1–2, p. 64, n. 4; Jacobi, *Saalburg Jahrbuch*, iii. 91 ff.; Parsons, *Hesperia*, v. 76 ff.

NOTE O, p. 149. *Far subtile* in Cat. *Agr.* 143. 3 and Varr. *R.R.* iii. 5. 4 might mean merely 'emmer (i.e. the grain) made small'; but (a) *farina subtilis* in Plin. *N.H.* xviii. 74 suggests that *far subtile*, too, is a 'product name' —and in Cato *far subtile* appears next to *farina bona*; (b) in, e.g., Col. vi. 10. 2, viii. 5. 17, 11. 14; Pallad. *R.R.* i. 28. 5, 29. 2, where *far* is 'made from naked wheat' or 'made from barley', the name can hardly refer to a grain: *far subtile*—and then simply *far*—had become the name first for crushed emmer and later for a similar grade of product, coarser than *farina*, from other grains also. Cf. also Plin. *N.H.* xviii. 62.

NOTE P, p. 151. *N.H.* xviii. 97, where *evalli* must (*pace* Blümner, p. 9, n. 1) mean 'to be hulled', and *triticum* must—exceptionally—refer to a husked wheat (see *CQ*, N.S., v. 140, n. 7); cf. also ibid. 112 and Plaut. *Asin.* 33. [Pliny elsewhere (ibid. 72 ff.) uses the words *mola* and *molere* in connexion with *polenta*; but the phrase *molis frangunt* (72 *fin.*) suggests a 'breaking' less fine than that of the mill, and the 'mixing in the mill' (73 *fin.*) suggests a mortar which could also serve as a mixing-bowl; cf. Blümner, pp. 10–11, n. 7.]

NOTE Q, p. 154. These figures ignore the germ or embryo, which usually accounts for another 2·5 per cent. of the grain. The germ is an important source of vitamins, and modern milling pays much attention to it. Ancient millers probably never succeeded in consciously separating it from the endosperm, although the Lewes experiments have shown that it may at times have been flattened in the mill, to remain with the bran on top of the sieve. (The figures are based on Lockwood, *Flour Milling*[2], pp. 286 ff.)

NOTE R, p. 183. The discovery that no. 36 grit gauze gave the best separation between bran and endosperm was made only during the analysis after the actual experiments, during which a no. 24 grit gauze had been used for sifting off the material to be reground. The material lying between these two sieves (c. 5 per cent. from the harder, and c. 20 per cent. from the softer wheat) must therefore, for the purposes of this argument, be added to the overtails over no. 24 g.g. (c. 25 per cent. from both wheats) actually obtained at Lewes.

NOTE S, p. 184. The following conversion factors are used throughout the calculations that follow:
(i) VOLUME OF GRAIN AND GROUND PRODUCTS. 1 *modius* = 16 *sextarii* = 8·733 litres = 0·24 imperial bushel = 0·96 peck = 1·92 imperial gallons = 0·25 U.S. (Winchester) bushel. 1 cubic foot = 28·317 litres; hence 1 *modius* = 0·3084 cu. ft. (For the conversion of the *modius* cf. *PW*, xv. 2328. Jasny, p. 138, n. 2, gives an equivalent of 8·47 litres, for which I can find no authority: it looks like a copying mistake, but is used by Jasny throughout his calculations.)
(ii) WEIGHT OF GRAIN AND GROUND PRODUCTS. 1 Roman pound = 327·5 grammes = 0·722 lb. avoirdupois.
(iii) VOLUME WEIGHT OF WATER. 1 *congius* = 6 *sextarii* = 3·275 litres = 0·722 gallon = 10 Roman pounds = 3·275 kg. = 7·22 lb. (For simplicity's sake this is based on distilled water weighing 10 lb. per gallon or 1 kg. per litre: the difference between this and undistilled water is insignificant.)

Note T, p. 196. The water absorption is *c.* 2½–3 gallons per sack higher for wholemeal than for a 70 per cent. flour. The largest part of the increase falls between 90 and 100 per cent. extraction, as the following example, for a very strong wheat (supplied—without the last two columns—by Dr. P. Halton), will show:

	Water absorption in		Bread yield in	
% Extraction	gallons/sack	% of flour	% of flour	% of wheat
70	15·6	55·7	136·2	95·4
80	15·8	56·4	136·9	109·5
90	16·5	58·9	139·0	125·1
100	18·3	65·4	144·7	144·7

Between the first two lines the increase in water absorption is 0·7 per cent.; between the last two lines it is 6·5 per cent.

Note U, p. 198. It will be seen that the argument of the present chapter does not assume *a priori* that modern experience can be relied on. Such an assumption would largely invalidate the argument, since it is likely, for instance, that for climatic reasons Roman wheat contained less moisture than English wheat, with the effects mentioned above, p. 196, n. 2. But since the present argument relies essentially on a comparison of the parts of Pliny's statement with each other, this and similar points can be ignored: if Roman wheat was drier *and* modern figures are found to apply, Roman wheat must have been correspondingly stronger.

Note V, p. 208. The conclusion is made even less certain by a textual variant xx in one manuscript of (7). This variant does not affect the first of the two arguments in the text, but it would, if accepted, affect the second: at 100 per cent. extraction a *modius* of grain would then have yielded 1·250 (1·300) *modii* of *farina*, weighing 38·4 (36·9) lb./cu. ft. This weight would support the assumption that *farina* was 100 per cent. meal; but, even apart from textual probability (which favours xxii), we should still be left with the other arguments suggesting that a 90 per cent. meal was produced, and such a meal can only have been called *farina*. Cf. also Curwen, *Antiquity*, xv. 29.

Note W, p. 209. In the corrupt passage (4) Pliny seems to be saying that the bread yield from a *modius* of meal increases the more *pollen* is extracted from it (presumably by regrinding and resifting). This might well be true, both because finer grinding would up to a point increase the weight per *modius* of the meal, and because absorption is higher for a low-grade than for a high-grade meal. If, therefore, list (4) represented the yield of bread from a *modius* of *similago* of different grades, the text given on p. 171 would make reasonable sense: it looks, however, as if the list were intended to state the yield from a *modius* of wheat, and if so, it is impossible to make sense of it. Some words may have been lost, or the end of the sentence may have become displaced from elsewhere.

Note X, p. 212. Jasny (p. 154) concludes that *secundarium* must have been almost wholly bran, since the probable extraction for it and *furfures* together is similar to that for miller's offal when a white flour is produced nowadays. But bran only accounts for *c.* 15 per cent. of the grain weight, and the further 15 per cent. rejected from modern white flour merely reflect the margin by which the miller fails to effect a complete separation. A considerable amount of bran, moreover, is likely to have found its way into the main flour.

INDEX

Superior numerals and letters refer to notes.   *Mere references in footnotes are not indexed.*

adjustment of mills, *see* graded grinding.
ador, xxii.
Aegina, hopper-rubbers from, 51.
Aeschylus, 150.
Africa, querns from, 98; wheat from, 186.
Alexandria, wheat from, 186, 195, 201–2.
Alexis, 160.
Algeria, querns from, 109, 112.
alica, 26, 147–8, 151, 164, 166[4], 180[3].
Alishar (central Asia Minor), hopper-rubbers from, 51.
Amiens, animal-mill from, 95.
amylum, 147[1].
Andernach, millstones from, 92.
animal-mill and slave-mill, 64 ff., 97 ff.; and water-mill, 135 ff.; on reliefs, &c., 15; *see also* donkey-mill.
Antipater of Thessalonica, 131[2].
Antiphilus of Byzantium, 131[2].
apluda, 177[3].
Apuleius, 16[8], 89, 100, 220[K].
Arcadius, 137, 138[4].
Archimedes, 1, 104.
Aristophanes, 16, 34, 36, 38, 159, 160, 162–3.
Aristotle, 12, 179.
army bread, *see militaris panis*.
artopta, 208–9.
artopticius panis, 206, 208–9.
asellus, 16.
Asinaria, 67 ff.
asinus, 218–19[C, E].
ass, *see* donkey.
Astarte, priests of, 16.
Athenaeus, 160, 209.
Athens, bakeries at, 34–36; rotary mill (?) from, 56, 70; saddle-querns from, 38–39; terracotta group at, 33; water-mill at, 137.
Augustine, St., 26.
Aurelian, 219–20[J].
Ausonius, 100, 138.
autopyrus, 154[4].

Baetica, wheat from, 186.
baking, 145, 216.

baking qualities of flour, xviii ff., 157.
Balearic wheat, 195, 201.
barley, xviii, xx ff., xxiv, 26, 147 ff., 151, 160, 162, 216, 218[D], 221[O].
Bennett, R., and Elton, J., 29, 30, 32, 44[4], 61[1], 126–7, 137, 218[A].
Blegen, C. W., 19[2].
blinkers, 89, 95.
Bloch, M., 218[A].
Blümner, H., 2, 3[6], 31[3], 44[4], 146.
Bologna, relief at, 78, 86[2], 167.
Boscoreale, quern from, 112–13.
Boundazeza (S. Attica), 36, 40–41.
bran, xix, xxiv, xxvi, 145, 153 ff., 160, 162, 165–6, 170 ff., 177 ff., 184 ff., 201, 207–8, 211 ff., 216, 221[Q, R], 223[X].
bread, xviii ff., 71–72, 146, 148, 150, 152, 153–4, 170 ff., 190 ff.; yield from wheat and flour, 195 ff., 211 ff.
bread-sellers at Athens, 34, 36.
bridge-tree, 88[4], 118, 120.
Britain, animal-mill found in, 95; querns found in, 107 ff.

Cabira (Pontus), water-mill at, 131.
Caesar, C. Julius, 116, 153.
Caligula, 99, 135, 139.
Capito, Ateius, 69.
Careieus, M., tombstone of, 95.
castratura, 170–1, 188.
castrensis modius, 219[G].
catillus, 76 ff., 95, 106, 112.
Cato, 26, 52, 57, 62 ff., 67, 68, 74, 90, 104–5, 110, 148, 164–6, 219[E, F].
Caulonia, hopper-rubbers from, 51.
Celsus, 172–3, 175.
centuria, 116, 124.
Ceramon, 34.
cereals, xvii ff.
Ceres, 7.
Chersonnese, wheat from, 186.
Chew Park (N. Somerset), 139[2].
Childe, V. Gordon, 17[3], 18[1], 43[1, 4], 53[1], 55, 57, 61[1], 103 ff., 218[A].
'Chiro', 172[3], 213[3].
Chollerford Bridge, 136.
Chrysippus of Tyana, 209[1].

Q

ISBN 0-19-	Author	Title
8264011	ALEXANDER Paul J.	The Patriarch Nicephorus of Constantinople
8143567	ALFÖLDI A.	The Conversion of Constantine and Pagan Rome
9241775	ALLEN T.W	Homeri Ilias (3 volumes)
6286409	ANDERSON George K.	The Literature of the Anglo-Saxons
8219601	ARNOLD Benjamin	German Knighthood
8208618	ARNOLD T.W.	The Caliphate
8142579	ASTIN A.E.	Scipio Aemilianus
8144059	BAILEY Cyril	Lucretius: De Rerum Natura (3 volumes)
814167X	BARRETT W.S.	Euripides: Hippolytos
8228813	BARTLETT & MacKAY	Medieval Frontier Societies
8219733	BARTLETT Robert	Trial by Fire and Water
8118856	BENTLEY G.E.	William Blake's Writings (2 volumes)
8111010	BETHURUM Dorothy	Homilies of Wulfstan
8142765	BOLLING G. M.	External Evidence for Interpolation in Homer
814332X	BOLTON J.D.P.	Aristeas of Proconnesus
9240132	BOYLAN Patrick	Thoth, the Hermes of Egypt
8114222	BROOKS Kenneth R.	Andreas and the Fates of the Apostles
8214715	BUCKLER Georgina	Anna Comnena
8203543	BULL Marcus	Knightly Piety & Lay Response to the First Crusade
8216785	BUTLER Alfred J.	Arab Conquest of Egypt
8148046	CAMERON Alan	Circus Factions
8143516	CAMERON Alan	Claudian
8148054	CAMERON Alan	Porphyrius the Charioteer
8148348	CAMPBELL J.B.	The Emperor and the Roman Army 31 BC to 235
826643X	CHADWICK Henry	Priscillian of Avila
826447X	CHADWICK Henry	Boethius
8222025	COLGRAVE B. & MYNORS R.A.B.	Bede's Ecclesiastical History of the English People
8131658	COOK J.M.	The Troad
8219393	COWDREY H.E.J.	The Age of Abbot Desiderius
8241895	CROMBIE A.C.	Robert Grosseteste and the Origins of Experimental Science 1100–1700
8644043	CRUM W.E.	Coptic Dictionary
8148992	DAVIES M.	Sophocles: Trachiniae
814153X	DODDS E.R.	Plato: Gorgias
825301X	DOWNER L.	Leges Henrici Primi
814346X	DRONKE Peter	Medieval Latin and the Rise of European Love-Lyric
8142749	DUNBABIN T.J.	The Western Greeks
8154372	FAULKNER R.O.	The Ancient Egyptian Pyramid Texts
8221541	FLANAGAN Marie Therese	Irish Society, Anglo-Norman Settlers, Angevin Kingship
8143109	FRAENKEL Edward	Horace
8142781	FRASER P.M.	Ptolemaic Alexandria (3 volumes)
8201540	GOLDBERG P.J.P.	Women, Work and Life Cycle in a Medieval Economy
8140215	GOTTSCHALK H.B.	Heraclides of Pontus
8266162	HANSON R.P.C.	Saint Patrick
8581351	HARRIS C.R.S	The Heart and Vascular System in Ancient Greek Medicine
8224354	HARRISS G.L.	King, Parliament and Public Finance in Medieval England to 1369
8581114	HEATH Sir Thomas	Aristarchus of Samos
8140444	HOLLIS A.S.	Callimachus: Hecale
8212968	HOLLISTER C. Warren	Anglo-Saxon Military Institutions
9244944	HOPKIN-JAMES L.J.	The Celtic Gospels
8226470	HOULDING J.A.	Fit for Service
2115480	HENRY Blanche	British Botanical and Horticultural Literature before 1800
8219523	HOUSLEY Norman	The Italian Crusades
8223129	HURNARD Naomi	The King's Pardon for Homicide – before AD 1307
9241783	HURRY Jamieson B.	Imhotep
8140401	HUTCHINSON G.O.	Hellenistic Poetry
9240140	JOACHIM H.H.	Aristotle: On Coming-to-be and Passing-away
9240094	JONES A.H.M	Cities of the Eastern Roman Provinces
8142560	JONES A.H.M.	The Greek City
8218354	JONES Michael	Ducal Brittany 1364–1399
8271484	KNOX & PELCZYNSKI	Hegel's Political Writings
8212755	LAWRENCE C.H.	St Edmund of Abingdon
8225253	LE PATOUREL John	The Norman Empire
8212720	LENNARD Reginald	Rural England 1086–1135
8212321	LEVISON W.	England and the Continent in the 8th century
8148224	LIEBESCHUETZ J.H.W.G.	Continuity and Change in Roman Religion
8143486	LINDSAY W.M.	Early Latin Verse
8141378	LOBEL Edgar & PAGE Sir Denys	Poetarum Lesbiorum Fragmenta
9240159	LOEW E.A.	The Beneventan Script
8115881	LOOMIS Roger Sherman	Arthurian Literature in the Middle Ages
8241445	LUKASIEWICZ, Jan	Aristotle's Syllogistic
8152442	MAAS P. & TRYPANIS C.A .	Sancti Romani Melodi Cantica

8113692	MANDEVILLE Bernard	The Fable of the Bees (2 volumes)
8142684	MARSDEN E.W.	Greek and Roman Artillery—Historical
8142692	MARSDEN E.W.	Greek and Roman Artillery—Technical
8148178	MATTHEWS John	Western Aristocracies and Imperial Court AD 364–425
9240205	MAVROGORDATO John	Digenes Akrites
8223447	McFARLANE K.B.	Lancastrian Kings and Lollard Knights
8226578	McFARLANE K.B.	The Nobility of Later Medieval England
814296X	MEIGGS Russell	The Athenian Empire
8148100	MEIGGS Russell	Roman Ostia
8148402	MEIGGS Russell	Trees and Timber in the Ancient Mediterranean World
8141718	MERKELBACH R. & WEST M.L.	Fragmenta Hesiodea
8143362	MILLAR F.G.B.	Cassius Dio
8142641	MILLER J. Innes	The Spice Trade of the Roman Empire
8147813	MOORHEAD John	Theoderic in Italy
8264259	MOORMAN John	A History of the Franciscan Order
8181469	MORISON Stanley	Politics and Script
8142218	MORITZ L.A.	Grain-Mills and Flour in Classical Antiquity
8274017	MURRAY H.J.R.	History of Board Games
8274033	MURRAY H.J.R.	History of Chess
9240582	MUSURILLO H.	Acts of the Pagan Martyrs & Christian Martyrs (2 volumes)
9240213	MYRES J.L.	Herodotus The Father of History
9241791	NEWMAN W.L.	The Politics of Aristotle (4 volumes)
8219512	OBOLENSKY Dimitri	Six Byzantine Portraits
8270259	O'DONNELL J.J.	Augustine: Confessions (3 volumes)
8144385	OGILVIE R.M. & RICHMOND I.A.	Tacitus: Agricola
263268X	OSLER Sir William	Bibliotheca Osleriana
8116020	OWEN A.L.	The Famous Druids
8131445	PALMER, L.R.	The Interpretation of Mycenaean Greek Texts
8143427	PFEIFFER R.	History of Classical Scholarship (volume 1)
8143648	PFEIFFER Rudolf	History of Classical Scholarship 1300–1850
8111649	PHEIFER J.D.	Old English Glosses in the Epinal-Erfurt Glossary
8142277	PICKARD–CAMBRIDGE A.W.	Dithyramb Tragedy and Comedy
8269765	PLATER & WHITE	Grammar of the Vulgate
9256497	PLATNER S.B. & ASHBY T.	A Topographical Dictionary of Ancient Rome
8213891	PLUMMER Charles	Lives of Irish Saints (2 volumes)
820695X	POWICKE Michael	Military Obligation in Medieval England
8269684	POWICKE Sir Maurice	Stephen Langton
821460X	POWICKE Sir Maurice	The Christian Life in the Middle Ages
8225369	PRAWER Joshua	Crusader Institutions
8225571	PRAWER Joshua	The History of The Jews in the Latin Kingdom of Jerusalem
8143249	RABY F.J.E.	A History of Christian Latin Poetry
8143257	RABY F.J.E.	A History of Secular Latin Poetry in the Middle Ages (2 volumes)
8214316	RASHDALL & POWICKE	The Universities of Europe in the Middle Ages (3 volumes)
8154488	REYMOND E.A.E & BARNS J.W.B.	Four Martyrdoms from the Pierpont Morgan Coptic Codices
8148380	RICKMAN Geoffrey	The Corn Supply of Ancient Rome
8141556	ROSS Sir David	Aristotle: De Anima
8141076	ROSS Sir David	Aristotle: Metaphysics (2 volumes)
8141084	ROSS Sir David	Aristotle: Parva Naturalia
8141092	ROSS Sir David	Aristotle: Physics
9244952	ROSS Sir David	Aristotle: Prior and Posterior Analytics
8142307	ROSTOVTZEFF M.	Social and Economic History of the Hellenistic World (3 volumes)
8142315	ROSTOVTZEFF M.	Social and Economic History of the Roman Empire (2 volumes)
8264178	RUNCIMAN Sir Steven	The Eastern Schism
814833X	SALMON J.B.	Wealthy Corinth
8171587	SALZMAN L.F.	Building in England Down to 1540
8218362	SAYERS Jane E.	Papal Judges Delegate in the Province of Canterbury 1198–1254
8221657	SCHEIN Sylvia	Fideles Crucis
8148135	SHERWIN WHITE A.N.	The Roman Citizenship
825153X	SHERWIN WHITE A.N.	Roman Society and Roman Law in the New Testament
9240167	SINGER Charles	Galen: On Anatomical Procedures
8113927	SISAM, Kenneth	Studies in the History of Old English_Literature
8113668	SKEAT Walter	Langland: The Vision of William Concerning Piers the Plowman (2 volumes)
8642040	SOUTER Alexander	A Glossary of Later Latin to 600 AD
8270011	SOUTER Alexander	Earliest Latin Commentaries on the Epistles of St Paul
8222254	SOUTHERN R.W.	Eadmer: Life of St. Anselm
8251408	SQUIBB G.	The High Court of Chivalry
8212011	STEVENSON & WHITELOCK	Asser's Life of King Alfred
8212011	SWEET Henry	A Second Anglo-Saxon Reader—Archaic and Dialectical
8143443	SYME Sir Ronald	Ammianus and the Historia Augusta
8148259	SYME Sir Ronald	History in Ovid
8143273	SYME Sir Ronald	Tacitus (2 volumes)
8142714	THOMPSON E.A.	The Goths in Spain
9256500	THOMPSON Sir E.Maunde	Introduction to Greek and Latin Palaeography
8200951	THOMPSON Sally	Women Religious
924023X	WALBANK F.W.	Historical Commentary on Polybius (3 volumes)
8201745	WALKER Simon	The Lancastrian Affinity 1361–1399
8161115	WELLESZ Egon	A History of Byzantine Music and Hymnography
8140185	WEST M.L.	Greek Metre